THIRD PARTY PROTECTION IN SHIPPING

AF695561

# CONTEMPORARY COMMERCIAL LAW

**Causation in Insurance Law**
Meixian Song

**Insurance Law in China**
Johanna Hjalmarsson and Dingjing Huang

**Illegality in Marine Insurance Law**
Feng Wang

**Insurance Law Implications of Delay in Maritime Transport**
Ayşegül Buğra

**Online Arbitration**
Faye Fangfei Wang

**Double Insurance and Contribution**
Nisha Mohamed

**FIDIC Yellow Book**
*A Commentary*
Ben Beaumont

**The Law and Autonomous Vehicles**
Matthew Channon, Lucy McCormick and Kyriaki Noussia

**The Contract of Carriage**
*Multimodal Transport and Unimodal Regulation*
Paula Bäckdén

**FIDIC Red Book**
*A Commentary*
Ben Beaumont

**Blockchain Technology and the Law**
*Opportunities and Risks*
Muharem Kianieff

**Maritime Law in China**
*Emerging Issues and Future Developments*
Edited by Johanna Hjalmarsson and Jenny Jingbo Zhang

**Third Party Protection in Shipping**
Carlo Corcione

For more information about this series, please visit:
www.routledge.com/Contemporary-Commercial-Law/book-series/CCL

# THIRD PARTY PROTECTION IN SHIPPING

CARLO CORCIONE

informa law
from Routledge

First published 2020
by Informa Law from Routledge
2 Park Square, Milton Park, Abingdon, Oxon OX14 4RN

and by Informa Law from Routledge
605 Third Avenue, New York, NY 10017

First issued in paperback 2021

*Informa Law from Routledge is an imprint of the Taylor & Francis Group, an informa business*

Copyright © 2020 Carlo Corcione

The right of Carlo Corcione to be identified as author of this work has been asserted by him in accordance with sections 77 and 78 of the Copyright, Designs and Patents Act 1988.

All rights reserved. No part of this book may be reprinted or reproduced or utilised in any form or by any electronic, mechanical, or other means, now known or hereafter invented, including photocopying and recording, or in any information storage or retrieval system, without permission in writing from the publishers.

*Trademark notice*: Product or corporate names may be trademarks or registered trademarks, and are used only for identification and explanation without intent to infringe.

*British Library Cataloguing-in-Publication Data*
A catalogue record for this book is available from the British Library

*Library of Congress Cataloging-in-Publication Data*
Names: Corcione, Carlo, author.
Title: Third party protection in shipping / Carlo Corcione.
Description: Abingdon, Oxon [UK]; New York, NY: Routledge, 2019. |
Series: Contemporary commercial law |
Includes bibliographical references and index.
Identifiers: LCCN 2019018237| ISBN 9781138326828 (hardback) |
ISBN 9780429449635 (ebook)
Subjects: LCSH: Marine insurance—Law and legislation. |
Freight and freightage. | United Nations Convention on the
Carriage of Goods by Sea (1978) | Bills of lading. | Maritime law.
Classification: LCC K1226 .C67 2019 | DDC 346/.0862—dc23
LC record available at https://lccn.loc.gov/2019018237

ISBN 13: 978-0-367-77802-6 (pbk)
ISBN 13: 978-1-138-32682-8 (hbk)

Typeset in Times New Roman
by codeMantra

# CONTENTS

# DETAILED TABLE OF CONTENTS

# FOREWORD

It has been a privilege to work alongside Dr Corcione over the last decade. With him the manager of a prestigious shipping company and me a claims director at a P&I (Protect & Indemnity) club, we would regularly tackle together issues common to carriers in the shipping industry. In doing so, I personally have always viewed the carriage of goods by sea in the traditional sense: namely, a bilateral relationship between two parties, with third parties representing a risk to the venture. Little did I appreciate until I read this book that Dr Corcione was working on a new theoretical platform which would fundamentally alter the way in which I would look at the world of international commerce and trade. I do hope that he will forgive me for this shortcoming!

There is no doubt that shipping has changed dramatically over the last century, with advancements in technology challenging the traditional concepts of carriage, particularly in the container trade. However, the law has not always kept pace. All too often, I have seen our shipowner members be held accountable for liabilities that should properly be shouldered by third parties responsible for their part in the seaborne logistics chain. Whilst under a contract of carriage, carriers can generally rely upon protection clauses enshrined in conventions to reduce or limit their liability, but all too often they are left bearing a disproportionate amount of the risk. Although this risk is transferred from carrier to insurer, it comes at a cost.

Offshore construction contractors have adapted to the challenges specific to their industry by adopting an approach to the allocation of risk which is more equitable and proportionate to the risks borne by the participating parties. This, in turn, drives efficiency and reduces costs. What Dr Corcione is proposing is that the shipping industry should be looking to do the same. If carriers, shippers, third parties, and insurers were to acknowledge and embrace their role in the *multilateral common enterprise*, and this, in turn, was supported by legislative change, it would be the first step towards realising Dr Corcione's vision: a vision which in the long term would benefit everybody.

James Bean
Managing Director, The Standard Club UK Ltd

# ACKNOWLEDGEMENTS

This book began life in 2011 when Professor Jason Chuah, Head of the Academic Law Department at City, University of London gave me the opportunity to write a PhD in Commercial and Maritime Law under his supervision. I must say that this whole process would have not been achievable without his experience and guidance and the professionalism of the Editors team at Routledge Amy Jones, Caroline Church and Naomi Hill.

Eight years is a long period, and a lot of things have happened meanwhile. This is, of course, neither the right time nor the right place to tell about the backstage of this book, but I can assure that life has not remained calm watching me writing it. It has been a tough and painful journey, and I must say my parents have been here every day to support me. My wife Ramona was not here when this all started, but she is the main reason why I made it until the end.

This book is entirely dedicated to Mr Luigi D'Amato. Without his belief and constant investments in both the shipping industry and myself this book would be incomplete, and I would be much less.

Needless to say, errors or omissions, if any, are entirely mine.

**Dr Carlo Corcione** is the General Counsel and Managing Director at D'Amato Shipowners Group. He is also a Teaching Fellow at the University of Naples Parthenope, and a Visiting Lecturer at City, University of London.

# TABLE OF CASES

# TABLE OF LEGISLATION

CHAPTER 1

# Background of third party protection in shipping

## The key point

**1.1** This book revolves around the protection of third parties in shipping.[1] Frequently, the central issue in third party disputes is whether or not someone who is not party to the contract should be allowed to benefit from the protection of the contract. More specifically, should someone who is neither the carrier nor the shipper be entitled to benefit from a protection provision in a carriage of goods by sea contract?

**1.2** Consider the following scenario: Shipper (X) contracts with carrier (Y), a shipowner or a charterer. Y then carries X's goods from port A to port B. In the contract, there is a provision that Z (someone who is not X or Y but who could, for instance, work at port A or B) will not be liable and will benefit from a limitation of liability if sued. The problem is that, strictly speaking, Z has a contract only with Y and has nothing to do with X. Moreover, in the carriage of goods by sea, Z does not fall into only one category; there are usually different categories of parties that, although in the same commercial position as Z, might not be mentioned specifically in the contract. Ultimately, the aim is to determine the extent to which such parties are entitled to the same protection enjoyed by Z.

## The outcome thus far

**1.3** The complexity of third party protection has long been present in maritime law. Originally, the problem centred on certain categories of third party, such as the shipowner in the *Elder Dempster* case,[2] or the master and boatswain in the *Himalaya* case.[3] Over time, however, the issue has grown to include other categories of third party such as independent contractors.[4] Furthermore, the situation has recently become more complex: vessels are now being sued as third parties[5] and relying on protection clauses in a contract, and sometimes the third

1 The terms 'shipping', 'carriage of goods by sea' and 'transport of goods by sea' are used interchangeably as is the practice within the industry.

2 *Elder, Dempster & Co. Ltd. v Paterson, Zochonis & Co. Ltd. (Elder Demspter)* (1924) AC 522 (HL).

3 *Adler v Dickson (The Himalaya)* (1954) 2 Lloyd's Rep 267; (1955) 1 QB 158.

4 *Scruttons Ltd. v Midland Silicones Ltd. (Scruttons)* (1961) 2 Lloyd's Rep 365.

5 *Mazda Motors of America, Inc. v M//V Cougar Ace (Mazda Motors)* (2009) 565 E3d 573; 2009 AMC 1220 (9th Cir. 2009).

parties in question operate completely outside the maritime world (see the inland carrier in the *Kirby* case).[6] This usually happens because it is in the interest of one of the parties to the contract to avoid the limitation of liability that the other party has under the contract; the third party therefore becomes the target of a suit. Though it seems unfair, this is what actually happens in practice. The claimant cannot sue the carrier in tort to circumvent the contract, since the carrier will be able to rely on a contract and on its legal protection:

> When the act is done in the course of rendering the very services provided for in the bill of lading, the limitation on liability therein contained must attach, whatever the form of the action and whether owner or charterer be sued. It would be absurd that the owner of the goods could get rid of the protective clauses of the bill of lading, in respect of all stowage, by suing the owner of the ship in tort.[7]

**1.4** The target of the suit who, a century ago, might have been a shipowner or a master or boatswain, could today be literally anyone involved in the relevant supply chain. The real, factual context of the shipping industry has changed, effectively creating a multilateral common enterprise between the parties.

**1.5** A variety of solutions to the problem have been proposed, but to date there is great disparity and little uniformity. Shipping has changed dramatically over the last century; its status in the trade has been altered, and boundaries have been eroded. On occasions when third party protection has been granted, the logic guiding such decisions has invariably been different in each case. In some cases, for instance, vicarious liability has been used to justify the protection of certain categories of third party (such as employees). Yet, in others it has provided the basis for commercial or insurance advantages or merely the autonomy of parties. The latest convention on the carriage of goods by sea – the Rotterdam Rules[8] – offers a more international and coherent perspective. Although not yet ratified, the Rotterdam Rules take into consideration the fact that it is currently not only a carrier who performs the job but also several other parties, referred to as 'performing parties'. The convention defines a performing party as 'any person who performs or undertakes to perform any of the carrier's responsibilities under a contract of carriage and acts, either directly or indirectly, at the carrier's request or under the carrier's supervision or control'.[9] Although in principle the approach of the Rotterdam Rules is in line with the concept of multilateral common enterprise, the convention still considers a third party to be an appendix party to a contract.[10] Moreover, the Rotterdam Rules set geographic boundaries

6 *Norfolk Southern Ry. v James N. Kirby, Pty Ltd. (Kirby)* (2004) 543 US 14.

7 *Elder, Dempster* (n. 2).

8 United Nations Convention on Contracts for the International Carriage of Goods Wholly or Partly by Sea (2008).

9 Article 1(6). See also, more generally, Tomotaka Fujita, 'Performing Parties and Himalaya Protection' (2009) Colloquium on the Rotterdam Rules 21 September 2009.

10 The explanation of 'performing party' under the Rotterdam Rules, for instance, states that they perform any of the carrier's obligations under the contract of carriage.

for such protection; conversely, in deciding *Kirby*,[11] the United States Supreme Court defined and advanced commercial approach to the problem. This represents a strong foundation on which to construct a new understanding of the issue.

**1.6** The book argues that the carriage of goods by sea – especially the segment specifically related to the container sector – is currently part of a more expanded enterprise. In this enterprise, all parties perform their obligations not exclusively depending on one principal party, but rather in accordance with a more extensive factual framework, created by the integration of the carriage of goods by sea with the whole supply chain. In this context, the supply chain is considered not only a process but also – and more importantly – a network; a common enterprise between different participants.[12] This work evaluates the logic beyond this outlook and offers a new framework that does not rely merely on freedom of contract, autonomy of party and commercial convenience. In the carriage of goods by sea, the argument for protection should now move away from the willingness of the parties (X and Y) and towards the consideration that all other parties participating in the multilateral common enterprise should rely on the protection. They are part of the common enterprise, effectively contributing to the movement of the cargo, regardless of their relationship with the main formal parties to the contract, the nature of their business, or the geographic area where they perform the business.[13]

*Definition and role of third parties*

**1.7** It seems appropriate here to highlight the lack of uniform definitions regarding third parties, both in domestic law and in international conventions. The *Oxford English Dictionary* states that a third party is, 'a person or group besides the two primarily involved in a situation'.[14] For the purposes of this book, the definition provided by the Contract (Right of Third Parties) Act 1999 shall be used. The Act defines a third party as 'anyone outside the contract'.[15]

**1.8** In the carriage of goods by sea, third parties are currently still not considered part of the contract. Instead they are seen as an outsider, even though they perform most of the carrier's duties. When the industry makes significant technical or logistical progress – as in the development of electronic solutions – the law is often not able to keep up. The nature of the shipping industry itself is responsible for the discrepancy between the factual context of the carriage of goods by sea and the logic behind third party protection within it.

11 *Kirby* (n. 6).

12 Third party protection should, therefore, be considered from a supply chain perspective, not solely from a transport perspective.

13 Some of these categories of third party that could benefit from such protection are mentioned in the book. However, the list is not intended to be exhaustive; instead it serves to add practical instances to the default position.

14 *Oxford English Dictionary*, 'Third Party' (2015) <www.oxforddictionaries.com/definition/english/third-party>. Accessed 27 April 2015.

15 Precisely, Article 1(1) of the Act defines a 'third party' as a person who is not a party to a contract.

**1.9** Within the traditional frameworks that govern thinking about the carriage of goods by sea (i.e., tackle-to-tackle[16] and port-to-port[17]) it is easy to understand who is part of the process (carrier and shipper) and who lies outside its scope (third parties). With the more recent door-to-door framework, the circle of actors has become bigger, but defining it is still possible. Within the wider picture of the supply chain – broadened to fully embrace transport elements – third parties have shed their peripheral role and become bona fide stakeholders in the chain.

**1.10** That modes and processes of carriage are continuously evolving represents the first peculiarity in the issue of third parties in the carriage of goods by sea and provides a significant obstacle in resolving the tensions therein. National and international legal instruments can seldom be re-engineered quickly enough to deal with such evolutions before they begin to evolve once again. In recent decades, developments in containerisation and shipping technology have facilitated multimodal carriage, which requires uniformity and harmonisation in terms of legal framework in order to operate smoothly. Such carriage evolution from tackle-to-tackle to door-to-door has rendered many existing regulatory instruments inadequate, leaving the trade with many legal uncertainties.[18] The 'status' of third parties is a prime example; it has changed considerably since the time when carriage was considered in the context of tackle-to-tackle or port-to-port. Though insufficiently modern from a commercial perspective, tackle-to-tackle and port-to-port systems solve innumerable problems, covering detectable specifics of carriage and providing better-defined roles. However, with the lengthening of the transport chain and the increasing complexity of interests involved, the position of third parties in the carriage of goods by sea has become highly ambiguous and complicated in definition. The lack of uniformity and ensuing confusion raised by the many and substantially different conventions on the carriage of goods by different modes do little to encourage possible solutions.

**1.11** Although it matches the new transport requirements from a commercial point of view, the fact that the carriage of goods by sea is part of a broader supply chain creates problems, such as mandatory liability systems that must be applied to the various stages involved in the transport of goods, as well as expanded periods for which each carrier is responsible. These can clash with

16 J Bes and N Lopez, in *Bes' Chartering And Shipping Terms* (11th edn, Barker & Howard Ltd. 1992), state that the ambit of tackle-to-tackle begins 'when the loading commences, that is, when the vessel's cargo-handling equipment is attached to the goods, and ends when the goods have been discharged from the vessel or removed from its cargo-handling equipment'.

17 Port-to-port means from loading port to discharging port. Bes defines port-to-port transport as 'the traditional form of carriage of goods by sea where one carrier carried the goods from one port to another port' (ibid.) However, there are no official definitions of ports and interpretation of the meaning is left to national legislations, which often creates problems.

18 See generally, Renato Midoro and Francesco Parola, *Le Strategie delle Imprese di Linea nello Shipping ed Intermodalita: Dinamiche Competitive e Forme di Cooperazione* (Franco Angeli, 2013). Midoro and Parola explain that, in this regard, the world economy has changed dramatically. Globalisation and the open market have affected the transport sector, and containerisation has engendered a complete transformation through the introduction of multimodalism as a new concept. Ports have had to change from being locations of mere loading and discharging to becoming an integrated system within a network of transport.

other liability systems that might be applied to the carriage of goods by other means.[19] Today, because contracts rarely operate on a tackle-to-tackle basis, there are many more types of people for whom the carrier is responsible than in the middle of the last century. Furthermore, goods being traded internationally are usually handled by multiple carriers, using a variety of forms of transport.

## The carrier and the shipper

**1.12** The roles of 'carrier' and 'shipper' were once easily identified and defined. Today, the same cannot be said. The carrier used to be someone who entered into a contract of carriage with a shipper. Over time, this definition has gradually expanded to include (according to contract and international conventions) first the actual carrier, performing carrier and performing party. Nowadays, the job of carrier is often arranged by a freight forwarder or a non-vessel operating common carrier (NVOCC). The situation is the same for the concept of the shipper. In the past, the shipper was defined as 'an owner or person for whose account the ocean transportation is provided or the person to whom delivery is to be made'.[20] In recent years, a variety of entities have emerged as intermediaries between the shipper of the goods and the provider of the transport services – taken in this case to be the ocean carrier – including shippers' associations, NVOCCs, transportation brokers, freight forwarders and export trading companies. Identifying the shippers in modern-day supply chains is not always straightforward; many service providers and suppliers contribute to the process of transporting cargo across international borders. Historically, the distinction between shipper and consignee was more easily drawn. Buyers and sellers would handle shipments directly, with the assistance of, for example, a port terminal and the carrier.[21] Trade today is invariably far more complex, and the identities of the actual manufacturer, shipper, and final consignee are more nebulous.

**1.13** In the past, the carrier and the shipper were the most economically and legally powerful parties. Now, after much commercial and economic evolution, the circumstances are totally different. The industry is much more capital intensive rather than labour intensive. In particular, in the carriage of goods by sea, the carrier cannot perform all of the activities concerned with the carriage but it nonetheless assumes responsibility for the whole leg.[22] Moreover, with longer contracts, parties to the contract usually request higher and more specific levels

19 Tomotaka Fujita, 'The Comprehensive Coverage of the New Convention: Performing Parties and the Multimodal Implication' (2009) 44 Texas International Law Journal 3, 349.

20 For definitions of carrier and shipper see Bes and Lopez (n. 16).

21 For further explanation of the concept of shipper – specifically the distinction between shipper and consignee – see Frank Stevens, *The Bill of Lading: Holder Rights and Liabilities* (Routledge 2017).

22 See Jason Chuah, 'Impact of the Rotterdam Rules on the Himalaya clause: the Port Terminal Operators' Case' in D Rhidian Thomas (ed.), *The Carriage of Goods by Sea Under the Rotterdam Rules* (Informa 2010) referring to the Australian case of *Chapman Marine Pty Ltd. v Wilhemsen Lines* (1999) FCA 178 at para 67. Midoro and Parola (n. 18) argue that, in general, carriers moved away from using labour contractors such as stevedores. Instead, these carriers became highly capital-intensive parties who wielded serious sway in negotiations.

of protection.[23] The problem, therefore, hinges on the conflict between the commercial need for the main parties to contract with third parties in order to carry out their duties and the fact that, once involved, the third party will require a certain legal protection.

**1.14** The impact of electronic solutions, information technology, and the ensuing automisation of the shipping industry have also had their effects, primarily through an increase in the integration of the shipping sector in the supply chain.[24]

## The port community system

**1.15** The port community system must be taken into account. The various participants in the carriage of goods by sea look to ports as physical centres of integrated infrastructure, providing loading and unloading, land access, quays, facilities for storage, physical security, and so on. Ports continually invest in this infrastructure to improve efficiency and remain competitive and, as such, these factors have been key drivers in deciding where and how to inject such investments. Ports also function as centres of 'infostructure' integration; computer and information systems connecting players across the logistics community help to improve the monitoring of operational processes, from start to finish.[25] This does little, however, to help the protection of third parties in the carriage of goods by sea. Furthermore, it does not improve the law in general but rather contributes to a discrepancy between higher speed and integration on the one hand and lack of uniformity in terms of law on the other hand.[26]

23 Changes in payment methods and the various means of transportation have also expanded the liability and risk factors, as logistics services (particularly multimodal transportation) are central to effective supply chain management R Masakorala (2012) 'Who is a "Shipper" on a Bill of Lading?', *Daily FT*, <www.ft.lk/article/99753/Who-is-a-%E2%80%98shipper--on-a-bill-of-lading?>. Accessed 5 April 2016.

24 As Martin Christopher explains, 'the whole nature of logistics management has been dramatically changed by the information technology revolution'. M Martin Christopher, *Logistics and Supply Chain Management* (2nd edn, Prentice Hall 2011) 231.

25 On the topic see generally International Port Community Systems Association, 'Port Community Systems' (2014) <www.epcsa.eu/pcs>. Accessed 3 December 2015; Alan Long, 'Port Community Systems' (2009) 3 World Customs Journal; United Nations Economic Commission for Europe, 'How to Develop a Port Community System' (2011) <www.unece.org/fileadmin/DAM/trade/Trade_Facilitation_Forum/BkgrdDocs/HowToDevelopPortCommunitySystem-EPCSAGuide.pdf>. Accessed 3 December 2015, 63–67.

26 The higher speed which nowadays allows cargo to move more quickly from one port to another and consequently from one jurisdiction to the other has alarmed the Chamber of Shipping that has stated that the applicable law should be the same and that the international community needs certainty and uniformity in order to reduce confusion and avoid increasing insurance and legal costs. FIATA Position on the UN Convention on Contracts for the International Carriage of Goods Wholly or Partly by Sea (The 'Rotterdam Rules')' (UNCITRAL 11, Doc. MTI/507 Annex II August 2009) <www.uncitral.org/pdf/english/texts/transport/rotterdam_rules/FIATApaper.pdf>. Accessed 1 September 2011.

## The law

**1.16** The unusual and rather unstable concept of a 'third party' has evolved continuously and in tandem with developments in commerce and transport linked to logistics chain management.[27] The problem, however, has traditionally been viewed more from an economic perspective than a legal perspective. Furthermore, examination of the literature from the perspective of supply chain integration (with the shipping trade considered a substantial component of this) shows that this type of investigation has traditionally been focussed on the bilateral relationships between two players in this chain; the carrier and the port. This is particularly true where economic concerns are prioritised. Scant analysis has been undertaken that considers the system as a network.[28] From a purely legal standpoint, third party protection is a grey area, not currently well-defined or easily definable.

**1.17** Thus far, the matter has been examined according to exculpatory and limitation of liability clauses,[29] commenting on specific cases,[30] specific categories of third party,[31] international conventions,[32] and problems that different jurisdictions have in accepting third party protection.[33]

27 Yung-Yu Tseng, Wen Long Yue and Michael A P Taylor, 'The Role of Transportation in the Logistic Chain' (2005) 5 Proceedings of the Eastern Asia Society for Transportation Studies 1657.

28 Shang-Min Lin, Andrew Potter, Stephen Pettit and Rawindaran Nair, 'A Systems View of Supply Network Integration in Maritime Logistics' (2014) 19th Logistics Research Network Conference (Huddersfield, 3–5 September 2014). Marian Hoeks, *The Law Applicable to the Multimodal Contract for the Carriage of Goods* (Kluwer Law International 2010). Christine Besong, 'Towards a Modern Role for Liability in Multimodal Transport Law' (PhD thesis, University College London, 2007).

29 Among others: Chen Liang, 'Benefits and Burdens of Third Parties under Exception Clauses in Bills of Lading' (1999) 24 Tulane Maritime Law Journal 225; JC Sweeney, 'Crossing the Himalayas: Exculpatory Clauses in Global Transport – *Norfolk Southern Railway Co. v James N. Kirby*' (2005) 36 Journal of Maritime Law and Commerce, 155.

30 Among others: Haylin Low, 'Shipowners' Liabilities: *Elder Dempster* Revisited' (1998) 13 *Maritime Law Association of Australia and New Zealand Journal*, 42 (1998) 13 *MLAANZ Journal* – Part 1; William H Theis, 'Third-Party Beneficiaries in Multimodal Contracts of Carriage. *Norfolk Southern Railway Co. v James N. Kirby*, Pty Ltd., 125 S. Ct. 385, 2004 AMC 2705 (2004)' (2005) 36 Journal of *Maritime Law* and *Commerce* 201.

31 Per Zerman, 'Liability for Stevedore Damage Claims' (Skuld Copenhagen, 13 February 2012) <www.skuld.com/topics/legal/defence/liability-for-stevedore-damage-claims/>. Accessed 10 March 2014; D R Owen, R B Acomb Jr and J J Donovan, The MLA Report (The Maritime Law Association of the United States, 1984) Report Document 652 (The MLA Report); Edwin Anderson III, 'The Status and Associated Liability of Ocean Freight Forwarders' (2009) 36 Transportation Law Journal 121.

32 Francesco Berlingieri, 'A Comparative Analysis Of The Hague-Visby Rules, The Hamburg Rules And The Rotterdam Rules' (Paper delivered at the General Assembly of the AMD, Marrakesh, 5–6 November 2009); Fujita (n. 9); The CMI International Working Group on the Rotterdam Rules, 'Questions and Answers on The Rotterdam Rules' (Ver. 2009.10.10); Anomi Wanigasekera 'Comparison of Hague-Visby and Hamburg Rules' (Messrs Julius & Creasy, 1 November 1992) <www.juliusandcreasy.com/inpages/publications/pdf/comparison_of_hague_and_hamburg-AW.pdf>. Accessed 13 April 2014.

33 Tan Pei Meng, 'Circumventing the Privity Rule in Malaysia' (2009) 4 International *Journal* of Information *Technology* and Decision Making 262; Fernanda Ruiz, 'Legal Study of Sea Carrier Limitation of Liability According to Brazilian Law in Comparison to the Hague-Visby Regime' (2010) 1 Lawinter Review 1, 144.

Third party issues in the carriage of goods by sea have been a focus of general examination since the 1950s and 1960s. During this period, the two leading cases were *Adler v Dixon* (a British case from which the Himalaya clause takes its name) and the United States case of *Herd v Krawill*.[34]

**1.18** The concept of the carriage of goods by sea as an expanded network of interests – rather than as a bilateral relationship – has been explored according to the position of shipowner and charterer[35] by Tetley, who has been one of the major exponents in the theory of third party protection. In his work *Marine Cargo Claims*, Tetley explains that the carriage of goods by sea is a 'joint venture' between shipowner and charterer with regard to cargo interests.

> Carriage of goods by sea can be characterised as a joint venture between the shipowners and the charterers, because they share the responsibilities of a carrier under the HVR, which cannot be contracted out of in virtue of Article 3(8) HVR. As a result of the shared responsibilities, the carrier and the charterer should be held jointly and severally responsible as carriers.[36]

**1.19** It is often reaffirmed that Courts should consider both charterers and shipowners as the carrier.[37] This book accepts this concept and seeks to develop it through the assertion that, in the current state of carriage of goods by sea, the common enterprise exists amongst a variety of different players and not only between shipowner and charterer.

**1.20** In considering the protection of third parties in international conventions of the carriage of goods by sea, Fujita (amongst others) has outlined the substantial distinction between maritime and non-maritime performing parties and the legal consequences that flow from such a distinction.[38] Furthermore, Chuah advances the concept that third parties should be now seen in the context of a broader and integrated framework, examining the specific complex position of the Terminal Operators in the Rotterdam Rules.[39] Additionally, in support of the concept of multilateral common enterprise, Merkin explains that:

34 The Rotterdam Rules demonstrate the willingness of the international community to accept the carriage of goods by sea as a multilateral system (performing parties). The *Kirby* case (n. 6) was decided in 2004, opening the door to a commercial approach for identifying third party protection and outlining the carriage of goods by sea as a complex network of interests reaching beyond the sea's boundaries. In the 1999, the UK (which has historically always been involved in shipping law and is relatively the most reluctant to accept third party protection) enacted the Contract (Right of Third Parties) Act 1999.

35 The problems between shipowner and charterer have been the subject of long and protracted discussion in the carriage of goods by sea field. It is one of the first examples of third parties seeking protection (as stated in *Elder, Dempster* (n. 2). The issue is that, under the charterparty, only one of the two parties is a carrier. Therefore, the other (namely the shipowner) has to be treated as a third party in order to enjoy protection.

36 William Tetley, *Marine Cargo Claims* (Ch 10, 4th edn, Yvon Blais 2007). According to this book, the concept of joint venture as expressed by Tetley is expanding to include other participants.

37 William Tetley, 'Case Comment: The House of Lords Decision in *The Starsin*' (2004) 35 JMLC 121–139.

38 Fujita (n. 9).

39 Jason Chuah, 'Impact of the Rotterdam Rules on the Himalaya clause: The Port Terminal Operators' Case' in D Rhidian Thomas (ed.), *The Carriage of Goods by Sea under the Rotterdam Rules* (Informa 2010).

> The law of contract as perfected in the nineteenth century was based on a model of bilateral transactions. The reality is, and to some extent was at the time, that many commercial contracts form part of a wider set of arrangements or chain of relationships.[40]

**1.21** The same author asserts that contracting is about allocating risks between parties of the contract.[41] It follows, therefore, that once third parties are considered to perform part of the contract, then the allocation of risks must also consider third parties.

Third party protection therefore falls into a broader discussion of risk allocation between parties to the contract, and whether a third party is factually an outsider or actually part of such a contract. In this respect, the law is – in some way at least – moving towards sectoral regulation.

**1.22** The carriage of goods by sea (as per contracts) is still broadly regulated bilaterally. International conventions (specifically the Rotterdam Rules) acknowledge multilateralism, but the Rotterdam Rules have not been ratified, and their geographic approach is not necessarily appropriate. In contrast, the conventions currently in use, i.e., the Hague/Hague-Visby Rules[42] and the Hamburg Rules,[43] approach the issue mainly from a bilateral perspective.

**1.23** Domestic law from major shipping jurisdictions (both case and statutory law) shows a disparity of decisions and lack of uniformity. As Sweeney points out, the rationale for approval and limitation of Himalaya clauses in England now differs from the rationale in the United States provided by the *Kirby* decision, and this divergence demonstrates the need for an international solution to this major trade problem.[44] The *Kirby* decision in the United States appears to be a first step towards some harmonisation – for example, deciding to allow the train company the benefit of the bill of lading in question – and lends credence to a commercial approach. A third party should not, therefore, be considered as sitting outside the contract, but rather being a third party *to* the contract.

**1.24** As Heaver states, the global sourcing and outsourcing of logistics functions have required the transportation industry to provide integrated logistics services covering wider geographical bases.[45] These challenges have moved and integrated the transport industry into global supply chains.[46] In this context,

40 Robert Merkin, *Privity of Contract: The Impact of the Contracts (Right of Third Parties) Act 1999* (Oxford, Taylor & Francis 2013) 67.

41 Ibid.

42 International Convention for the Unification of Certain Rules of Law relating to Bills of Lading (1924); First Protocol (1968); Second Protocol (1979).

43 United Nations Convention on the Carriage of Goods by Sea (1978).

44 Sweeney (n. 29).

45 T Heaver, H Meersman and E Van de Voorde, 'Co-Operation and Competition in International Container Transport: Strategies for Ports' (2001) 28 Maritime Policy and Management 3, 293.

46 Su-Han Woo, 'Seaport Supply Chain Integration and Orientation, and their Impact on Performance' (PhD thesis, Cardiff University, 2010).

there have been vertical and horizontal processes of integration.[47] It is widely held that, in this commercial revolution, third parties have the most complicated position. Third party locus has shifted from the peripheries of the carriage of goods by sea to an integral part. The issue is to what extent third parties should be allowed the same protection as the traditional contract parties. Such allowances are bounded by several factors such as the fact that third parties have to be mentioned somewhere (e.g., contracts, international conventions, or statutory law), and, specifically from the perspective of the carriage of goods by sea, they have to perform one of the carrier's duties under the contract and often the duty has to be of 'maritime nature'.

**1.25** The issue with third parties emerges because the sphere of the carriage of goods by sea has expanded but the regulations have not. Accordingly, it is argued that third parties today need legal protection because they are a *de facto* part of the enterprise, even if formally they still reside outside it. The underlying problem of the existing legal system is that for too long it has been linked to the mode-by-mode basis. Shipping has been considered as a separate entity from the supply chain; something that is no longer the case.[48]

**1.26** As reported by Hevia, third party beneficiaries should be allowed to enforce a contract only if:

1. Allowing the beneficiary to enforce the contract is a necessary or important means of effectuating the contracting parties' performance objectives, as manifested in the contract read in the light of surrounding circumstances.
2. Allowing the beneficiary to enforce the contract is supported by reasons of policy or morality independent of contract law and would not conflict with the contracting parties' performance objectives.[49]

Permitting a third party to enforce a contract guarantees that contracting parties' objectives are prioritised, rather than simply affording them such benefit.[50] This concept needs to be extended from the benefit of the main parties to the benefit of all the parties in need.

**1.27** This book does not seek to understand 'who is my neighbour'[51] in the context of third party protection in the multilateral common enterprise. Instead, based more on substance than label, it aims to extend the protection to whoever is 'in need'. In this respect, a general causal connection between the claimant's

47 T Heaver, H Meersman and E Van de Voorde, 'Co-Operation and Competition in International Container Transport: Strategies for Ports' (2001) 28 Maritime Policy and Management 3, 293.

48 As stated by Paul Stephen Dempsey, 'The Law of Intermodal Transportation: What It Was, What It Is, What It Should Be' (2000) 27 Transportation Law Journal 367.

49 Martin Hevia, *Reasonableness and Responsibility: A Theory of Contract Law* (Springer Science & Business Media, 2012).

50 Ibid.

51 Ibid.

claim and the defendant/third party (sufficient for a claim to exist) will allow protection to be extended to the defendant/third party.

## Book structure

**1.28** Chapter 2 will deal with the concept of third party protection in the normal bilateral scheme of carriage of goods by sea between carrier and shipper. Specifically, an introduction will be provided to the limitation of liability and its importance in the carriage of goods by sea; how it has been extended to third parties and an outline of the contract framework.

**1.29** Chapter 3 outlines the current factual context and how the role of third parties has changed as a result of its development. Specifically, it focusses on how shipping has changed within the context of the supply chain as a result of integration, and how the role of third parties has changed accordingly.

**1.30** Chapters 4 and 5 will detail the bilateral approach of both the Hague/Hague-Visby Rules and the Hamburg Rules that favour a two-party approach with only a few references to third parties. Although the Hamburg rules have a bilateral approach, to some extent they anticipate the concept of performing parties.

**1.31** Chapter 6 explores the approach of the Rotterdam Rules, a never-ratified convention that deals with the issue in a more multilateral way. Criticism will be given, however, to the shortcomings of its geographical approach.

**1.32** Chapter 7 is about the English legal tradition surrounding the topic. The reader will be guided through the history of the issue under English law through the topics of agency, bailment, privity, and consideration, up to the Contract (Right of Third Parties) Act 1999.

**1.33** Chapter 8 will show that United States law has a different and more pragmatic approach to third party protection starting with the differences with bailment up to the case of *Kirby*.

**1.34** Chapter 9 draws together themes explored in the preceding chapters and provides final remarks as well as potential solutions. In particular, the concept of channelling liability and multilateral insurance will be advanced as possible solutions, and a case is made for using civil law protection of third parties to assist with common law understanding.

## Conclusion

**1.35** This chapter establishes the foundation for a profound and much needed evaluation of the third party protection framework. It further highlights the importance of perceiving third party protection through a modern, commercial lens, appropriate to the industry today. In turn, it is useful to understand how the shipping industry will be affected in years to come as the role of third parties continues to change significantly.

**1.36** Furthermore, this chapter contends that, in contrast to current approaches, the framework of third party protection should not be based on the central role of the carrier and shipper in the carriage of goods by sea. The role of third parties in the carriage of goods by sea today is very different from the past, but the protection afforded to third parties by the law has not changed commensurately. This lack of understanding creates inefficiency and calls for a replacement of the bilateral approach to protection with a multilateral approach befitting the complexity of the modern industry.

**1.37** As Lord Roskill suggested, for anyone hoping to be part of the trade, understanding the law is essential. Particularly, one must understand that while on the one hand the law must be certain, on the other hand, it must also be adaptable to the needs of the present situation.[52]

52 Lord Roskill, 'Half a Century of Commercial Law 1930–1980' (1982) 7 HLR 1.

CHAPTER 2

# Third party protection in shipping: risk allocation and management

## Limitation of liability in shipping

**2.1** Even though, in terms of the parties involved, carriage is very complex business, the 'official' perspective is that there are still only two main parties to a carriage contract. First, the carrier, who is the party that offers to transport goods in exchange for a price.[1] Second, the owner of the cargo being transported.

**2.2** Shipping goods from one country to another always involves the risk of damaging the goods in transit. Thus, the law governing the carriage of goods by sea has always sought a satisfactory allocation of risk between carriers and cargo interests.[2] Because the structure of these arrangements has evolved from a single category of participants performing the work (i.e., the carrier), to a multi-faceted group of participants, this bilateral scheme has now lost its clarity, especially as far as the carrier is concerned.[3]

**2.3** Protection clauses in international contracts are essential for the allocation of risk between parties, serving as tools for establishing how risk inherent in international operations (including specific legal risks) should be divided amongst the parties.[4]

**2.4** It is common knowledge that an international transaction typically involves different parties.[5] The carriage of goods by sea, however, has not always been seen as part of this enterprise. There was a time when the shipowner was

1 Under bills of lading is, 'freight'; under charter parties, 'hire'. See also J C Sweeney, 'Crossing the Himalayas: Exculpatory Clauses in Global Transport – *Norfolk Southern Railway Co. v James N. Kirby*' (2005) 36 Journal of Maritime Law and Commerce, 155.

2 This allocation has now changed.

3 According to Sweeney, 'slot charters' (a type of agreement covering vessel-sharing) prevent shippers from ever contracting with actual shipowners, let alone with the owner of the carrying vessel. Ocean carriage by sub-contract is now performed for non-vessel-owning common carriers as well as traditional ocean carriers. As an entity, a non-vessel-owning common carrier is likely to function as a shipper to shipowners or a carrier to cargo owners. By the same token, many (if not all) operations traditionally carried out as part of ocean carriage – weighing, measuring, documentation, pre-loading, loading, fumigation, stowage on board, unloading, examination, warehousing, storage – are likely to be carried out, even if not entirely, by the carrier's sub-contractors. As a result, the notion of 'carrier' on which modal frameworks have historically been based has 'lost most of its traditional meaning' (n. 1), 171–172).

4 Jerzy Rajski, 'Limitation of Liability and Exclusion Clauses in International Contracts' (2002) 3 International Business Law Journal 4, 321.

5 Buyers, sellers, forwarders, carriers, bankers, lenders, insurers, and various regulatory authorities amongst the others.

not only the carrier of the vessel[6] but also the cargo owner, the captain, and its own insurer. There were no banks, nor were there any lenders. In this sense, there was little impetus for the law to be elaborate, and regulatory regimes were non-existent.[7] Stevedores and port terminals were not worldwide organisations. The field was mainly labour-intensive, not capital-intensive. Nowadays, each transaction requires the involvement of many interests. Limitation and exculpatory clauses help these transactions to go smoothly.

**2.5** Understanding how the limitation of liability in the carriage of goods by sea started and evolved is essential in introducing the concept of third parties. As Wyatt notes:

> Under general maritime law, the ocean carrier was liable as an insurer of the goods; excused from cargo loss or damage only by an act of God, the shipper, public enemy, or by an exception in the contract of carriage.[8]

Additionally, it is important to understand the significance of the evolution of the relationship between the carrier and third parties.

**2.6** Liability protection is an essential part of the trade and, in the carriage of goods by sea, has a substantial impact on the carrier and the shipper. Besong highlights the questions that invariably come up in such carriage cases: How much am I liable for? What is my exposure and limit? Who pays for what damage?[9]

**2.7** Contractually, these clauses are referred to differently: limitation clauses, exculpatory clauses, exception clauses, and so on. For ease, this book refers to them as 'protection clauses'. Allocation of liability is essential for trade operations. Without limitation of liability, it is likely that such trade as it is known today would not exist. Brunner puts it bluntly: 'No trade, no goods, no shipping, no ships'.[10] It might be more accurate to extrapolate one step further: *no limitation of liability*, no trade, no goods, no shipping, no ships.

**2.8** Providing an essential framework, Rajsky acknowledges that there are a number of ways in which liability can be limited: first, the application of financial caps on liability regarding the maximum recoverable amount; second, the imposition of a limited time period; third, restrictions (procedural or otherwise)

6 This goes back to medieval times when merchants generally opted to sail with their goods. In the nineteenth century, specialisation changed everything. The all-purpose merchant disappeared and opposing interests of the corporate shipowner and the cargo owner emerged. Raphael Brunner, 'Electronic Transport Documents and Shipping Practice Not Yet a Married Couple' (PhD thesis, University of Cape Town, 2007); Sik Kwan Tai, Ownen Tang and Peter Wong, 'Note and Comments on the first decision based on the Chinese Regulations on International Maritime Transportation Concerning Terminal Handling Charges' (2007) 38 Journal of Maritime Law and Commerce 111.

7 The first regime in the field was the Harter Act 1893.

8 Marva Jo Wyatt, 'Contract Terms in Intermodal Transport: COGSA Comes Ashore' (1991–1992) 16 Tulane Maritime Law Journal 177.

9 Christine Besong, 'Towards a Modern Role for Liability in Multimodal Transport Law' (PhD thesis, University College London, 2007).

10 Brunner (n. 6).

on a party's grounds to a claim; and fourth, the exemption of various categories, including unforeseeable loss, indirect loss, or consequential loss.[11]

**2.9** When analysing this protection in relation to contracts regarding the carriage of goods by sea, there is one immediate doubt that should be clarified: the main convention on the carriage of goods by sea currently in operation is the Hague-Visby Rules. Article 3(8) of the Hague-Visby Rules invalidates any clause that 'purports to relieve or lessen the responsibilities of the carrier and the ship as they are set out in the Rules'.[12]

**2.10** According to Article 3(8), the Hague-Visby Rules have in themselves limitation provisions for the carrier and for the carrier's third parties. Therefore, the Hague-Visby Rules do not allow any other limitation provision other than what they expressly provide. In other words, they do not allow the carrier to limit their liability in a different way.

**2.11** Another immediate distinction that warrants attention here is the gap between limitation and exemption. The difference between these two provisions appears here to be fundamental; while exclusion clauses are often considered contrary to the policy of international trade and unusually employed,[13] limitation clauses are nonetheless a way to make contracts and relationships easy. The word 'crucial' has been used by The Ninth Circuit of the United States in *Tessler Bros. (B.C.) v Italpacific Line*, to define the difference between the two:

> The distinction between a limitation on liability and an exemption from liability is crucial because if on one hand is true that the carrier (and consequently third parties) cannot immunise himself from responsibility, he can on the other hand, limit his liability.[14]

**2.12** In *Bisso*, the Supreme Court offered the following explanation for its disapproval of exculpatory provisions:

> The two main reasons for the creation and application of the rule have been (1) to discourage negligence by making wrongdoers pay damages, and (2) to protect

11 Rajski (n. 4). On the topic see also Patson Wilbroad Arinatiwe, *Risk Allocation in Oil and Gas Service Contracts* (Lambert Academic Publishing 2014) 24.

12 William Tetley, 'Limitation, Non-Responsibility and Disclaimer Clauses' (1986) 11 Maritime Law 203. Specifically Article 3(8) states,

> Any clause, covenant, or agreement in a contract of carriage relieving the carrier or the ship from liability for loss or damage to, or in connection with, goods arising from negligence, fault, or failure in the duties and obligations provided in this Article or lessening such liability otherwise than as provided in this Convention, shall be null and void and of no effect. A benefit of insurance clause in favour of the carrier or similar clause shall be deemed to be a clause relieving the carrier from liability.

13 Rajski (n. 4).

14 *Tessler Brothers (BC) Ltd. v Italpacific Line and Matson Terminals, Inc.* 494 F 2d 438 para 18. For a similar analysis see Thomas R Denniston, Carter T Gunn and Alfred E Yudes, 'Liabilities of Multimodal Operators and Parties other than Carriers and Shippers' (1989–1990) 64 Tulane *Law Review* 517.

> those in need of goods or services from being overreached by others who have power to drive hard bargains.[15]

Limitation of liability and general protection clauses have been crucial for the functioning relationship between the two parties of the contract. However, the parties of the carriage have also felt the need to protect their contractors and auxiliaries as well.

## Third parties risk

**2.13** In business, risk is typically understood as 'a probability or threat of damage, injury, liability, loss, or any other negative occurrence that is caused by external or internal vulnerabilities, and that may be avoided through pre-emptive action'.[16] Megens defines a risk as a 'hazard, exposure to mischance or chances of bad consequences or the probability of an event occurring coupled with the consequences if it does occur'.[17] In the carriage of goods by sea, risk has always been negotiated and allocated between carrier and shipper. In the context of this book it is referred to as economic and liability risks.

**2.14** Hallebeek has defined the protection of third parties in the carriage of goods by sea as a natural way to give justice to the economic and risk allocation of a contract between cargo interests and carriers. The *ratio decidendi* can be summarised thus:

> It would have been unfair if the cargo, once agreed on terms and took into account economic and liability risks, could just ignore all of it suing someone who is commercially related to the carrier and for whom the carrier is (in one way or another) responsible.[18]

Third party protection has so far been viewed as part of a risk allocation and management between the two parties of the shipping operations.

**2.15** Risk is an essential part of shipping life; it cannot be avoided but instead has to be managed.[19] There is no business that is risk-free, but there also would not be any business without managing the risk. Risk management is the systematic process of understanding, evaluating, and addressing these risks in order to maximise the chances of achieving objectives.[20]

15 Sweeney (n. 1).

16 Anon, 'Risk' (Business Dictionary, 2014) <www.businessdictionary.com/definition/risk.html>. Accessed 8 January 2014.

17 Peter Megens, 'Different Perspectives of Construction Risk: How Should It be Allocated?' (1996) 15 Ampla Bulletin 179, 179–180.

18 Jan Hallebeek and Harry Dondorp, *Contracts for a Third-Party Beneficiary: A Historical and Comparative Account* (Martinus Nijhoff Publishers 2008) 121.

19 Anon, 'About Risk Management' (Institute of Risk Management, 2015) <www.theirm.org/about/risk-management/>. Accessed 4 May 2015.

20 Ibid., Accessed 8 January 2014.

**2.16** The major forms of risk management strategies are summarised as follows:

1. Risk avoidance
2. Risk control
3. Risk retention
4. Risk transfer[21]

Risk avoidance means the avoidance of risk by not engaging in any activity with risk. Risk retention, as the name suggests, is when risk is contained and borne by only one individual or company.[22]

**2.17** Naturally, risk avoidance and risk retention are not relevant to shipping in the way that they might be to any other business activity. Most pertinent to this discussion are the concepts of risk control and risk transfer. Billah argues convincingly that no amount of precautionary measures can entirely and consistently preclude serious and unpredictable losses. Risk control cannot be the sole risk management strategy.[23]

**2.18** In shipping, risk management is vital for shipping companies and participants and therefore very common across the industry. Risk control is the first step, but alone it is not enough. Therefore, risk transfer is essential. The primary instrument for transferring risk is insurance.[24] In essence, and again quoting Billah, anything we do now to avoid a future risk is a risk management strategy.[25] Focussing on the context of the carriage of goods by sea, risk allocation has been defined as a problem as old as maritime law itself.[26]

**2.19** According to Lowe, deep-seated economic changes of the latter part of the twentieth century prompted the development of risk management strategies. Lowe contends that whichever party is best able to control, manage, or insure against the economic consequences of a given risk should be the one to bear the cost of that risk[27] and by extension be responsible for managing the risk arising from interactions between related parties.[28]

21 Muhammad Masum Billah, *Effects of Insurance on Maritime Liability Law: A Legal and Economic Analysis* (Springer Science & Business Media 2014).

22 David Frederick Ross, *Distribution Planning and Control; Managing in the Era of Supply Chain Management* (3rd edn, Springer 2015).

23 Billah, Ch 2 (n. 21).

24 Ibid.

25 Ibid.

26 Jan Lopuski, 'Liability for Damage in Maritime Shipping under the Aspect of Risk Allocation' (1979–1980) 10 Polish Yearbook of International Law 177. The idea of spreading the risk of maritime adventure lies in the roots of ancient Greek and Roman concepts of Maritime Law, such as *foenus nauticum* or *lex Rhodia de iactu* and various forms of 'community of interests' in medieval shipping. It also lies in the roots of limitation of shipowners' liability deriving from the latter period. See also Lord Diplock, 'Conventions and Morals: Limitation Clauses in International Maritime Conventions' (1969–1970) 1 Journal of Maritime Law and Commerce 525).

27 David Lowe, *Commercial Management: Theory and Practice* (Wiley-Blackwell 2013).

28 Ibid.

**2.20** The parties to a carriage of goods by sea contract rely on limitation clauses in contracts to mitigate their respective risks.[29] This work argues that, in the carriage of goods by sea, third party protection has been seen as a tool to allocate the transportation of risk between the parties involved in the operation.[30]

**2.21** Taking the above into consideration, there are two main approaches to managing risk in shipping. The first is controlling it through the mechanism of contract; limitation of liability functions as a tool with which to allocate the risk.[31] The second approach relies on transferring the risk to an insurance provider. Regarding the first, third parties can affect the result of a contract because they are a risk for the contractual party responsible for them. According to Arinatiwe, contracts are still the primary means of forestalling negative outcomes, even though other risk allocation mechanisms (such as insurance) still exist. The lower the degree of precision offered by a contract, the greater the level of risk to which contracting parties are exposed.[32] Contractual risk allocation is actually considered part of risk management and one of its primary aims.[33]

**2.22** The contract is the foundation of risk control. Additionally, the allocation of risk from a contractual perspective has been considered as one of the most essential characteristics of a contract, together with the definition of the responsibilities of the parties, and the determination of the effective payment terms.[34]

**2.23** Shipping has been heavily dependent upon the contract mechanism to allocate risks, not only between the parties of it but also between parties not formally part of the contract. Downie provides an extensive list of the ways risk can be allocated in an agreement.

1. The obligation undertaken by the parties
2. The warranties given by the parties
3. The extent to which the parties exclude or limit the damage that would otherwise be recoverable for breaching the agreement
4. Indemnities given with respect to particular events
5. Requiring one or more parties to take out specified levels and types of insurance[35]

**2.24** Regarding the second component of managing risk (i.e., transferring to insurance), Buglass deems it 'unnecessary' to say that the principle of limitation

29 Rajski (n. 4).

30 José Vicente Guzmán, 'The Limitation of Liability of the Carrier from an Allocation of Risks Point of View' (Comité Maritime International 2012) <www.comitemaritime.org/Uploads/Rotterdam%20Rules/Paper%20 of%20Jose%20Vicente%20Guzman.pdf>. Accessed 24 March 2014.

31 Contract management is a way of monitoring the allocation and making sure nothing untoward happens.

32 Arinatiwe, *Risk Allocation in Oil and Gas Service Contracts*, 24.

33 Ibid., 19.

34 Lowe (n. 27).

35 See David Downie, *Contractual Risk Allocation* (Inter Alia Publishing, 2012). If an agreement is silent on liability then each party's liability under the agreement is considered to be subject to the law of the agreement.

of liability is important to marine insurance and that marine insurance industry relies on it. Underwriters stipulate insurance contracts with shipowners relying on the right that the shipowners have to limit their liability benefiting the underwriters.[36] The same author points out that liability insurance premiums might increase almost by one-third if shipowners – and, in turn, underwriters – were deprived of this protection.[37] The aforementioned right to limit affects the relationship between P&I Club and shipowners[38] as well as the shipowners' coverage and related costs under the Hull and Machinery market.[39] Essentially, limitation clauses help the assured to obtain a policy more easily and more cheaply.[40]

**2.25** In analysing the limitation of liability in relation to the insurance, the first consideration is the 'cost argument' that insurers usually attribute only to shipowners, rather than those who, through negligence or sheer bad luck, have caused an accident.[41]

**2.26** Billah highlights a negative aspect of limitation of liability, explaining that 'lower liability leads to lower precaution. Limitation of liability thus encourages negligent navigation'.[42] Billah also casts limitation of liability in opposition to the concept of full liability; the existence of one would reduce the effect of the other. If full liability is necessary to create optimal deterrence, such deterrence would be so effective that the extent of liability would be reduced due to a limitation of liability.[43] From a specific degree, limitation of liability is also seen as a cause of social loss because it does not induce to have the proper care.[44]

**2.27** Tetley's view on the matter is clear: 'It is a fundamental principle of good business practice and of efficient, fair and low-cost insurance that persons who are responsible for losses should be held accountable, in some way, for those losses'.[45] On the other hand the concept of limited liability may encourage settlements and save in litigation costs while without it, parties to a lawsuit may wait for the trial outcome.[46]

**2.28** De la Mare deftly explains the importance of limitation of liability for the insurers with an illustration of its commercial mechanism:

> Without limitation of liability, ocean carriers and insurers would face enormous claims for damages in cases where goods are damaged. In order to bear these risks, the carrier will increase the rate of the carriage. In other words, shippers

36 Leslie J Buglass, 'Limitation of Liability from a Marine Insurance Viewpoint' (1979) 53 Tulane Law Review 1364.

37 Ibid.

38 Ibid.

39 Ibid.

40 Rajski (n. 4).

41 Erik Roseg, 'The Impact of Insurance Practices on Liability Conventions', originally published in legislative approaches in maritime law (Proceedings from the European Colloquium on Maritime Law, Lysebu, Oslo, 7–8 December 2000). Marlus No. 283.

42 Billah, Ch 3 (n. 21).

43 Ibid.

44 Ibid.

45 William Tetley, *Marine Cargo Claims* (Ch 10, 4th edn, Yvon Blais 2007).

46 Billah, Ch 3 (n. 21).

> allow carriers to have limitation and in exchange receive more affordable shipping rates.[47]

The position of insurance in the role of limitation of liability in the carriage of goods by sea is crucial. An example is in a contract between the carrier and the shipper. The shipper carries cargo insurance for the event that cargo is damaged. Should the cargo be damaged, the shipper recovers from their insurer. The insurer is then subrogated to the rights of the shipper and would proceed to sue the carrier. The carrier has the protection and indemnity insurers (P&I) cover which (if the carrier is liable) will pay (under deductible) on behalf of the carrier.

**2.29** As Lord Diplock explains, the allocation of liability is 'eventually an allocation of liability between cargo insurers, P&I for a loss incurred through neither's fault'.[48] In other words, as Hellawell summarises: 'What superficially may be regarded as an allocation of risk between the Carrier and Shipper is in reality between the carrier's insurers and the shipper's insurers'.[49]

**2.30** However, and taking into account the above, the shipping industry has gradually taken into consideration the risk of parties 'outside' the bilateral relationship and therefore the necessity of extending them their legal protection.

## The extension of the protection to third parties

**2.31** As Sturley points out, anyone involved in the contract of carriage but not party to the contract can be sued. As anticipated bringing an action against them instead of suing the contractual parties can have an economic benefit.[50]

**2.32** Currently, third parties are protected by the main parties to a contract because third parties affect them. The justifications for this have been vicarious liability, commercial convenience, or simply autonomy of parties. According to Tetley:

> The basic problem is to find a way to permit third parties who are neither agents nor servants to limit their liability; specifically, to find a way to allow stevedores and terminal operators, whom the carrier declares are not his agents or servants but independent contractors, to nevertheless benefit under the contract of carriage.[51]

47 William T J de la Mare, 'Jurisprudential Problems of Attribution of Liability in the Area of Admiralty Contracts for Carriage Following *Norfolk Southern Railway v Kirby*' (2007) 22 Connecticut Journal of International Law 203.

48 Lord Diplock (n. 26).

49 Robert Hellawell, 'Allocation of Risk between Cargo Owner and Carrier' (1979) 27 American Journal of Comparative Law 357.

50 Michael F Sturley, 'An Overview of the Considerations Involved in Handling the Cargo Case' (1996–1997) 21 Tulane Maritime Law Journal 263.

51 Tetley (n. 45).

This clearly helps to define the issue of finding a way to make a third party benefit from a contract.[52] The purpose of third party protection clauses is to extend the carrier's legal defences to independent contractors such as stevedores.[53]

**2.33** With carriage expanding, the protection from the carriage of goods by sea has also been sought by third parties outside the carriage of goods by sea. This is a particularly pertinent issue, the best-known relatively recent example of which derives from *Kirby*.[54] In *Kirby*, the essential question was whether a contract to which the maritime shipper was not a party nevertheless limited the rights of the shipper against a land carrier, namely, a railroad. The Supreme Court, in a unanimous opinion, protected the railroad.[55]

**2.34** Sweeney gives further attention to the concept of expansion of the carrier's job. He argues that almost any transaction completed upon transfer of goods from a seller's premises to a buyer's premises will require the engagement of other land-based parties whose presence was – until now – either unnecessary or unobserved. Himalaya clauses seek to extend the ocean carrier's protection to these new non-maritime participants. Today, argues Sweeney, the transport of goods from one premise to the other by rail or road is a crucial part of international trade. Fierce competition is leading an increasing number of traditional ocean carriers to diversify into services beyond their usual sphere of operations: 'The sub-contracting of cargo-related services has developed to such an extent that the traditional ocean carrier is now sub-contracting even the ocean carriage itself'.[56]

**2.35** As explained, the carrier contracts with the shipper but then has to delegate all or part of this job to other parties (being an employer or independent contractor). As carriage evolves, more people become involved in the process and consequently the carrier shoulders responsibility for an increasing number of parties.[57] The reason often lies in the concept of vicarious liability, through which the carrier is responsible for any fault committed by its servants or agents during the performance of the contract,[58] or for commercial agreements between the carrier and third parties. Liang expands the concept of the carrier's interests in protecting third parties, suggesting that even if an exception clause

52 However, for the sake of clarity, it has to be said that the problem is not only one of finding a way for third parties to benefit from the contract but also understanding how this could be permitted within international conventions and, domestic law.

53 When the Himalaya clause was first drafted, employees of the carrier also had to be protected. With time, these categories of third parties have been automatically included in the international conventions regulating carriage of goods by sea leaving only the difference between employees and independent contractors.

54 *Norfolk Southern Ry. v James N. Kirby, Pty Ltd. (Kirby)* (2004) 543 US 14.

55 Sweeney (n. 1).

56 Ibid.

57 Chen Liang, 'Benefits and Burdens of Third Parties under Exception Clauses in Bills of Lading' (1999) 24 Tulane Maritime Law Journal 225.

58 Vicarious liability: legal responsibility and liability of an employer for the wrongful acts of its employees. Definition in Corbet Spurin, 'The Law of International Trade and Carriage of Goods' (Ch 1, Nationwide Mediation Academy for NADR UK Ltd. 2004), 10 <www.nadr.co.uk/articles/published/shipping/001CHAPTERONETRADE.pdf> Accessed 17 March 2013.

exists that excludes the carrier from vicarious liability, the carrier is likely to be in a similar position if the owner of the cargo brings against its agents or servants direct action in tort for fault in performance of the contract. If the owner wins the legal battle, the carrier may end up having to provide compensation for the loss to the agents or servants in order to demonstrate corporate integrity and/or to maintain good working relationships. The same is true, argues Liang, if direct action is brought against any of the carrier's independent contractors.[59]

**2.36** The concept of vicarious liability (specifically regarding a carrier and third parties) has been discussed by Viscount Cave in *Elder Dempster.*[60] His theory states that an agent is entitled, while performing the contract, to any immunity conferred on his principal. This is known more commonly as vicarious immunity. This theory was later much criticised because it was considered 'a departure' from a fundamental principle in English Law: namely, 'one who is not party to a contract cannot acquire rights under it'.[61]

**2.37** This protection has always found obstacles in a principle of English Law (that states a stranger to a contract cannot enjoy the benefit of an exception clause embodied in the contract) originated in *Tweddle v Atkinson*[62] and confirmed by the House of Lords in *Dunlop Pneumatic Tyre Co. v Selfridge and Co.*[63]

**2.38** As far as the contract of the carriage of goods by sea is concerned, a third party is not simply the crew (including, as Liang says, the master and the stevedores) but can include many other categories of participant.[64] The vicarious liability concept affects the difference between employees and independent contractors. According to Sweeney:

> Actual employees of carriers and agents of carriers create liability for carriers because of 'respondeat superior', without eliminating the personal liability of such employee or agent, although the recovery of money damages from uninsured crew members, including officers (as in The Himalaya, supra), may prove futile. Consequently, cargo plaintiffs usually disregard the crew members or agents despite their personal fault. The general maritime law, like the common law, assumed the liability of shipowner employers for the damage-causing faults of employees.[65]

**2.39** However, as far as the position of independent contractors is concerned, there does not seem to be a strong justification for why they must be protected from the parties of the contract. Mankabady's assessment is as follows:

> In their view a contractor who is independent of the carrier should not, by the mere fact that he performs duties which the carrier himself might have performed,

59 Liang (n. 57).

60 *Elder, Dempster & Co. Ltd. v Paterson, Zochonis & Co. Ltd. (Elder Dempster)* (1924) AC 522 (HL).

61 Samir Mankabady, *The Hamburg Rules on Carriage of Goods by Sea* (Brill Archive, London 1978) 66.

62 *Tweddle v Atkinson* (1861) EWHC QB J57.

63 *Dunlop Pneumatic Tyre Co. v Selfridge and Co. (Dunlop)* (1915) AC 847.

64 Liang (n. 57).

65 Sweeney (n. 1).

become entitled to the limitation and exceptions of the Rules. Therefore, a distinction should be drawn between, on the one hand, the carrier, his servants or agents and, on the other, the independent contractor.[66]

**2.40** Before entering into details of distinct categories, a further distinction should be drawn between servants and agents on the one hand and independent contractors on the other hand. The background of this is vital to understanding the evolution of the protection that was at first limited to master, servant, and agent but now extends to independent contractors.

**2.41** Mankabady refers us to the Hague Rules: 'The servants and agents should be protected for social reasons and should have the benefits of the Rules whereas these reasons do not apply to the independent contractor, who should thus not have this benefit'.[67] Burnett sees the distinction between an employee and an independent contractor arising from a difference of contract: on the one hand, a contract *of* service, made between employer and employee; on the other hand, a contract *for* services, made between principal and independent contractor. Traditionally, this contractual difference emerged from a difference in control; independent contractors were typically instructed to generate an end result but given a degree of self-determination when carrying out the work, whereas employees were usually told what to do and exactly how to do it.[68]

**2.42** In *The International Law of the Shipmaster*, Carter, Fiske, and Leiter elaborate upon the reasoning behind the division. They note that the Visby Protocol to the Hague Rules included the addition of a provision which entitled the carrier's servants or agents to 'the defences and limits of liability available to the carrier in respect of damage to goods covered by a contract of carriage whether the action be founded in contract or tort'.[69] These benefits are lost, however, if it is proven that damage arose from 'an act or omission of the servant or agent done with the intent to cause damage or recklessly and with knowledge that damage would probably result'.[70] Carter et al. note that these provisions were tacked on to the original convention following a host of problems created by suits 'based on negligence against the master and agents of the carrier to bypass the carrier's limitation of liability based on the privity of contract'. After the decision in *Adler v Dixon*, carriers began to include Himalaya clauses to extend the benefits to their servants, agents, and independent contractors (such as stevedores). Carter et al. point out that, although independent contractors lay outside the scope of the protection offered by the Hague-Visby Rules – and therefore relied on Himalaya clauses – any servants of the carrier are liable towards third parties 'within

66 Samir Mankabady, 'Rights and Immunities of the Carrier's Servants or Agents' (1973–1974) 5 Journal of Maritime Law and Commerce 111.

67 Ibid.

68 Jonathan Burnett, 'Avoiding Difficult Questions: Vicarious Liability and Independent Contractors in *Sweeney v Boylan Nominees*' (2007) 29 Sydney Law Review 163.

69 John Carter, Richard Fiske and Tara Leiter, The International Law of the Shipmaster (2009) Informa Law from Routledge, Part 2, 121–227.

70 Ibid.

the same limitations and with the same defences as their principals', and the Hamburg Rules have adopted a similar provision.[71]

**2.43** The topic has also been addressed from a case law perspective. Quoting Denning's judgement in the *Himalaya* case, Smeele reports that there is a distinction between a carrier's servants and agents (both categories in fact are protected by the mandatory liability regime of the Hague-Visby Rules) and independent contractors (left from the same protocol to their own devise).[72] Minichello defines a sub-contractor as:

1. one who takes a portion of a contract from the principal contractor or another sub-contractor
2. one who has entered into a contract, express or implied, for the performance of an act with the person who has already contracted for its performance
3. one who takes from the principal or prime contractor a specific part of the work undertaken by the principal contractor[73]

**2.44** The above analysis is essential in addressing the evolution of the protection of the categories of third parties. At the beginning of the last century, the parties to be protected were primarily the carrier's servants and the master. Some categories of third parties were not even well distinguished:

> In the first American case in which a terminal operator claimed the protection of a Himalaya clause, the court of appeals struggled with the differences between stevedores and terminal operators, but eventually came down in favour of protecting a stevedore who was acting as terminal operator at the time the goods were lost.[74]

**2.45** In summary, third parties have often received protection in the past for the commercial convenience of doing so. This has been supported by principles such as *respondeat superior* and vicarious immunity.[75]

**2.46** With an explanation of the orthodox reasons behind third party protection firmly secured, the next section provides an overview of the contractual framework necessary to extend carrier protection to third parties.

71 Carter, Richard Fiske and Tara Leiter, The International Law of the Shipmaster.

72 Frank Smeele, '*The Maritime Performing Party in the Rotterdam Rules 2009*' (2011) European Journal of Commercial Contract Law 1, 72–86.

73 Quoting Black Dictionary, Dennis Minichello, 'Who and What Are You Insuring? Cargo Transportation Liability Exposures are Changing' (2008–2009) 21 *University of San Francisco Maritime Law Journal* 2, 167.

74 Sweeney (n. 1).

75 See Carlo Corcione, 'The Evolution of Third Party Protection in Carriage of Goods by Sea: From the Himalaya Clause to the Himalaya Protection' (2014) 49 European Transport Law Journal 3, 271.

## Contractual framework to extend the carrier protection to third parties

**2.47** This contextual framework is achieved through clauses in contracts. It gives protection to third parties but it is also important for carriers because, as explained by the Maritime Law Association report:

> While carriers are free to decide whether or not to extend their defences limitation and immunities under COGSA to stevedore, terminal operators and other parties, the use of these particular clauses to accomplish that purpose should substantially reduce third party litigation between carriers and their independent contractors in cargo damage cases. Moreover the widespread use of these clauses will help to promote certainty and uniformity in the law of carriage of goods – a goal sought by shippers, carriers, stevedores and terminal operators alike.[76]

The carrier shall be entitled to sub-contract on any terms the whole or any part of the carriage, loading, unloading, storing, warehousing, handling, and any and all duties whatsoever undertaken by the carrier in relation to the goods.[77]

**2.48** The Himalaya clause is the most frequently used to dissuade cargo owners from imposing any liability upon a stevedore or terminal operator for damage to the goods greater than the liability which the carrier has under the terms of the bill of lading.[78]

**2.49** Literature on cases involving Himalaya clauses is vast, but the essential principles stated by Courts regarding Himalaya clauses can be summarised thus:

- The parties to a bill of lading may extend a contractual benefit to a third party only by clearly expressing their intent to do so.
- The benefits may be extended to agents and sub-contractors only with respect to their actions in the performance and fulfilment of the principal contract.

**2.50** The Himalaya clause for servants and agents of the carrier was accepted by the international community in the Hague-Visby Rules of 1968. The same result of Himalaya clauses, as explained by Hooper, relates to bailment law.[79] Generally, the intent of the parties, as expressed through the clarity of the

76 D R Owen, R B Acomb Jr and J J Donovan, *The MLA Report* (The Maritime Law Association of the United States, 1984) Report Document 652 (The MLA Report).

77 *Instel Corp. v M/V Antonia Johnson (Antonia Johnson)*, 1983 AMC 1153 (W D Wash 1982).

78 Tetley defines the Himalaya clause as, 'an ingenious, short-term solution to a difficult problem, but … a solution which raises infinitely more problems than it solves' William Tetley, 'The Himalaya Clause – Revisited' (2003) 9 Journal of International Maritime Law 40. The same concept is also expressed in William Tetley, 'The Himalaya Clause: Heresy or Genius?' (2003) 9 Journal of Maritime Law and Commerce 111, 113.

79 Chester D Hooper, 'Legal Relationships: Terminal Owners, Operators, and Users' (1989–1990) 64 Tulane Law Review 595.

language used in the provision, controls the determination of whether a third party is an intended beneficiary.[80]

**2.51** Additionally, the International Group of P&I Clubs (IGP&I)[81] and The Baltic and International Maritime Council (BIMCO)[82] recognise not only that Himalaya clauses are complicated, but also that it is extremely difficult to outline a clause that works on every situation and in every jurisdiction. Therefore the IGP&I and the BIMCO have been working to produce a clause which should be recognised and effective at least in most major shipping jurisdictions.[83]

**2.52** The Himalaya clauses are numerous and different in contents, but their fundamental purposes are as follows:

- Exempt the carrier and the identified third party from liability under a contract.
- Confer on such third party all the rights, limits, defences, and exemptions from liability enjoyed by the carrier under the contract.
- Impose on the other party to the contract, the obligation not to sue the third party in tort, bailment, or otherwise.
- Make the carrier an agent or trustee for the third party in relation to the contract, and that such third party is deemed to be a party to such contract.
- Provide protection in respect of operations related to the carriage of goods but which are not necessarily carried out on board the ship: for example operations which take place before loading or after discharge from the vessel.

**2.53** The Himalaya clauses, even if often similar to each other, show a degree of diversity. Listing them would neither be possible nor add anything to the argument here. It is worth mentioning, however, that the search for a good practice in Himalaya clauses pushed the Maritime Law Association of the United States in 1983 to create a sub-committee regarding Himalaya clauses. As a result, it provided a report in which experts tried to draft the 'perfect' Himalaya clause, which (according to the report) states:

1. The carrier shall be entitled to sub-contract on any terms the whole or any part of the carriage, loading, unloading, storing, warehousing, handling, and any and all duties whatsoever undertaken by the carrier in relation to the goods.

80 Minichello (n. 73). This mainly depends on different jurisdictions and on Courts approaches.

81 International Group of P&I Club (2015) <www.igpandi.org/>. Accessed 11 November 2014.

82 Baltic International Maritime Council (BIMCO) (2015) <www.bimco.org/>. Accessed 11 November 2014.

83 BIMCO, 'Revised Himalaya clause for Bills of Lading and Other Contracts' (Special Circular No. 6, 17 September 2010) <www.bimco.org/~/media/Chartering/Special_Circulars/SC2010_06.ashx>. Accessed 11 November 2015.

2. The terms of this bill of lading constitute the contract of carriage, which is between the shipper; consignee; holder of the bill of lading and authorised owner of the goods; and the carrier, shipowner, or demise charterer of the vessel designated to carry the shipment. It is understood and agreed that no claim or allegation shall be made by the shipper, consignee holder of the bill of lading, or authorised owner of the goods against any servant, agent, sub-contractor, or independent contractor (including but not limited to the master, officers and crew of the vessel, all employees and representatives, all terminal operators, warehousemen, stevedores, watchmen, and all other sub-contractors and independent contractors whatsoever) used or employed by the carrier from time to time in connection with the performance of any of the carrier's obligations under the bill of lading, which imposes or attempts to impose upon any of them any liability in connection with the goods greater than that of the carrier under this bill of lading, but if any such claim or allegation should nevertheless be made party making such claim or allegation agrees to indemnify the carrier against all consequences thereof.
3. Without prejudice to any other provision hereof, it is hereby expressly agreed that any and all servants, agents, and independent contractors (including but not limited to, the master, officers and crew of the vessel, all employees and representatives, all terminal operators, warehousemen, stevedores, watchmen, and all other sub-contractors and independent contractors whatsoever) used or employed by the carrier in connection with the performance of any of the Carrier's obligations under this Bill of Lading, in consideration of their agreement to be so used or employed, shall be express beneficiaries under this Bill of Lading or by Law, so that in no circumstances shall any servant, agent, or independent contractor of the Carrier be under any liability, in contract or tort, greater than that of the Carrier hereunder. It is further expressly agreed that for the purposes of this provision, the Carrier is or shall be deemed to be acting as agent or trustee on behalf of and for the benefit of all who are or may be its servants, agents, or independent contractors from time to time in connection with the performance of any of the Carrier's obligations under this Bill of Lading, and that all such persons shall to this extent be or be deemed to be parties to the contract contained in or evidenced by this Bill of Lading.
4. It is further agreed that the expression 'servant, agent or independent contractor' in this Bill of Lading shall include direct and indirect servants, agents, and independent contractors of the Carrier as well as their respective servants, sub-agents, or sub-contractors.[84]

84 The MLA Report (n. 76).

**2.54** There has been, as always, an evolution in the way the Himalaya clauses are drafted.[85] Although the Himalaya clause is the core of the third party protection clauses in the carriage of goods by sea, other clauses are necessary in order to apply full protection to third parties. The 'circular indemnity' clause, for instance, is often used together with the Himalaya clause. The indemnity clause requires the cargo owner to compensate the carrier for any claim, made by shipper interests outside the bill of lading. In other words, under an indemnity clause, the cargo owner cannot bring any claim against any carrier contractor or sub-contractor and in the case event that such a claim is brought, the cargo owner has to indemnify the carrier against any loss incurred by the latter.[86] However, it must be acknowledged that a circular indemnity clause has the same problem as a Himalaya clause concerning Article 3(8) of the Hague-Visby Rules.[87]

**2.55** The 'demise' clause is also relevant here.[88] As Tetley explains, the demise clause regulates the liability between shipowner and charterer in the charterparty. This is because the shipowner and the charterer share responsibilities in loading, carrying, caring for, and discharging cargo. In respect of third parties, they should both be the carrier. Tetley strongly comments that allowing them to stipulate that one of them is not the carrier is the most opprobrious of non-responsibility clauses.[89]

The liability and the apportionment of risks between shipowner and charterer in a charterparty has also been developed with the influence of the P&I clubs, under the Inter-Club New York Produce Exchange (NYPE) Agreement. It is an agreement between the shipowners and the charterers that exists to help with apportioning the liability for cargo claims, mainly for NYPE signatories, but also in conjunction with other charter parties.[90]

85 For instance, in United States law, the importance of the language in the Himalaya clause has been pointed out in *Herd & Co. v Krawill Machinery Corp.* 359 US 297, 1959 AMC 879 (1959). In being so specific, the Court provided a significant opportunity to broaden the categories of third parties. If the criterion for protecting or not protecting a third party is merely whether or not they are mentioned in the clause, also sub-categories such as sub-agents and sub-contractors of the carrier's agents, for instance, could be included in a Himalaya clause.

86 Freight Transport Association, 'Himalaya and Other Warranty and Indemnity Clauses' (Freight Transport Association 2015) <www.fta.co.uk/policy_and_compliance/sea/long_guide/himalaya.html>. Accessed 13 October 2015. See also *'Elbe Maru'* (1978) 1 Lloyd's Rep. 206.

87 Tetley (n. 45).

88 A demise clause usually states:

> If the ship is not owned or chartered by demise to the company or line by whom the bill of lading is issued the bill of lading shall take effect as a contract with the owner or demise charterer as the case may be as principal made through the agency of the said company or line who act as agent only and shall be under no personal liability whatsoever in respect thereof.

89 William Tetley, 'Case Note: *Homburg Houtimport B.Vv Agrosin Private Ltd. (The Starsin)* (2003) 1 Lloyd's 571, 2003 AMC 913 (HL) 121 (Bills of Lading)' (2004) 35 Journal of Maritime Law and Commerce 1.

90 Draft Charterparty Clause Promoting the Use of the Inter-Club New York Produce Exchange Agreement 1996 (As Amended September 2011) <www.shipownersclub.com/media/2016/05/Draft-Charterparty-Clause-promoting-Inter-Club-New-York-Produce-Exchange.pdf>. Accessed 21 June 2016; Stefan Bjarnelöf-Sovtic, 'The Inter-Club Agreement: Certain Aspects' (Master's thesis, University of Lund, 2006).

**2.56** Other relevant clauses necessary for an appropriate legal contractual framework for third parties are:

1. The opportunity to declare a higher value clause.[91]
2. One year suit limitation clause.[92]
3. The choice of law clause.[93]
4. The separability clause.[94]

On the one hand, the contractual scheme of third party protection can be considered pragmatic and essentially functional in practice. On the other hand, it leaves the protection of third parties subject to the willingness of the two main parties and to the interpretation of the clauses wording.

## Conclusion

**2.57** This chapter has introduced the concept and importance of legal protection between two parties of a commercial relationship as well as presenting the traditional view of the carriage of goods by sea as a bilateral relationship and allocation of risks between the two parties with third parties serving a risk. Furthermore, details have been provided about why and how this risk has been managed so far. It is believed that, generally speaking, the contractual framework for third party protection in the carriage of goods by sea is acceptable mainly because contracts are an easy and practical way to deal with protection. The intention of the parties is precisely stated in clauses such as a Himalaya clause, where the parties to the contract essentially list all the other parties to whom they wish to extend their limitation of liability.

**2.58** Contract is a very common mechanism for controlling risk throughout the shipping industry today.[95] The role of contract has changed dramatically, emerging as a purely legal necessity for protecting against possible mishaps,

91 The MLA Report (n. 76). This clause originated in *Tessler Brothers* (n. 14) where the Court held that in order to take advantage of the USD 500 package limitation, the carrier has to give the shipper notice of the limitation and a fair opportunity to declare a higher value for its good.

92 In any event, the carrier and the ship are discharged from all liability for loss or damage to the goods unless suit is brought within one year after delivery of the goods or the date when the goods should have been delivered. It is hereby agreed that suit shall not be deemed brought until jurisdiction have Suit shall not be deemed 'brought' unless jurisdiction is obtained over the Carrier by service of process or by an agreement to appear.

93 'It is hereby agreed that this Bill of Lading shall be construed, and the rights of the parties thereunder determined, wherever possible, according to the law of the United States of America'.

94 If any provision of this Bill of Lading is, or is held to be, invalid under the Carriage of Goods by Sea Act of the United States, or any law that is compulsory applicable, such provision shall, to the extent of such invalidity, but no further, be null and void. The terms and conditions of this Bill of Lading are separable, and if any term or condition is, or is held to be, invalid, null and void, or unenforceable, such holding shall not affect in any way the validity or enforceability of any other term or condition of this Bill of Lading.

95 National Contract Management Association (2013) 11 Journal of Contract Management <www.ncmahq.org>. Accessed 3 January 2015.

and evolving to become a tool for optimising ongoing business relationships.[96] Contracts have become central in international transactions.[97] Indeed, the number of contracts drawn has increased dramatically. Additionally, contracts have become particularly interdependent – especially in complex, integrated systems – and can therefore be of the utmost assistance.

**2.59** Lowe says that contracts put forth the rights and obligations of the parties to the contract and describe the responsibilities and procedural roles of those named within the contract, asserting that a common awareness of the distribution of risk within a contract is a key feature of 'harmonious, effective and efficient projects'.[98] Most pertinently for this discussion, contract serves to manage the risk of third parties and their contracts. As stated, however, contracts alone are not enough to limit risk. Insurance helps by transferring risk. In comparison with insurance of the past, the structure of risks covered by insurance today has expanded substantially. In marine insurance, the risks covered were mostly external in relation to the assured: perils of the sea, wars, pirates, robbers, and so forth. Currently the risks are of a different nature and internal to the carriage structure and the relationship between the parties performing the carriage.[99]

**2.60** Minichello likens insurance to grease; it lubricates the entire system to ensure it operates in a smooth manner. Transferring risks of liabilities, which can potentially arise out of a contract of carriage, is crucial.[100]

**2.61** Limitations of liability and protection clauses are perceived as tools to facilitate the transactions and negotiations between two parties of a business. The extension to third parties of this and other forms of legal protection has been necessary since third parties have been substantially utilised to circumvent the agreement between the parties. Protection clauses can be criticised because they allow negligent third parties to have the same protection as the parties of the contract.[101]

**2.62** It is believed that the protection of third parties from contract works and achieves its aim. However, the corporate reality intensifies the need for a scheme of partnership, outsourcing agreements, and corporate management separated by ownership. The systems in place today are much more complex than those of the past, in which it was easy to picture the divisions between companies working on the same project. In this situation the distinction of liabilities is also difficult to mark.[102]

96 PWC, 'Contract Management, Control Value and Minimise Risks' (2015) <www.idii.com/wp/MembaPwContractMgmt.pdf>. Accessed 18 January 2015.

97 Lorenz Kahler, 'Contract-Management Duties as a New Regulatory Device' (2013) 76 Law and Contemporary Problems 89.

98 Lowe (n. 27).

99 Lopuski (n. 26).

100 Minichello (n. 73).

101 As Sweeney specifies:

> The completed transaction from seller's warehouse to buyer's warehouse now involves other participants in the processing and movement of the goods-participants who are land based and whose services were either unnoticed or unused in the past, and it is these new non-maritime participants for whom the protections of the ocean carrier are sought to be extended by Himalaya clauses.
>
> Sweeney (n. 17)

102 Lord Diplock (n. 26).

## CHAPTER 3

# The factual context of shipping

### Multilateral common enterprise

**3.1** For the purposes of this book, the term 'multilateral common enterprise' is used to describe an informal venture between more than two parties. In order to flesh out this description, the definitions of 'joint venture' and 'joint enterprise' – both of which terms derive from partnership law and agency law – must first be addressed. 'Joint venture' refers to an established limited company, a partnership, or an unincorporated contractual association for a given purpose.[1] Hewitt provides some context:

> Joint venture refers to a range of collaborative business arrangements, the fundamental characteristics of a joint venture being collaboration between the participants involving a significant degree of integration between the joint ventures. The key element to be considered and agreed by the joint venturers is the degree and nature of that collaboration. Joint ventures may take the form of a contractual alliance, a partnership or a corporate joint venture.[2]

**3.2** A joint enterprise, on the other hand, is an informal joint venture that does not need an express business agreement nor an evidence of sharing profit and losses.[3] This book borrows the concepts of joint venture and joint enterprise in order to better illustrate a 'common enterprise' as featuring a collaboration between parties. The words 'common' and 'enterprise' have been selected because, in order to have a proper joint venture (or joint enterprise), there has to be a clear intention to carry out activities together. While all members of the multilateral common enterprise cooperate with each other in practice, they do not necessarily consider themselves to be part of the same project.

### The shipping context

**3.3** The factual context of today's shipping industry takes into consideration variables that were practically irrelevant only a few decades ago, such as

1 Greg Gordon, John Paterson and Emre Üşenmez, *Oil and Gas Law: Current Practice and Emerging Trends* (2nd edn, Edinburgh University Press 2007).

2 Ian Hewitt, *Joint Ventures* (3rd edn, Sweet & Maxwell 2005).

3 United States Legal Inc., 'Distinction between Joint Venture and Joint Enterprise' (2014) <http://jointventures.uslegal.com/distinction-between-joint-venture-and-joint-enterprise/>. Accessed 10 November 2015.

containerisation and multimodal operations, logistics, and supply chains. The key to the relationships between these processes is integration; not simply formal integration, but above all *informal, factual* integration. Integration, according to Panayides (quoting O'Leary-Kelly and Flores), is the extent to which otherwise separate parties cooperate to achieve mutually desirable ends. The definition, therefore, comprises elements governing the levels of collaboration, coordination, cooperation, and interaction.[4]

**3.4** The integration of transport into the rest of the supply chain began, ultimately, with the advent of containerisation and multimodalism. As a result of this integration, the carriage of goods by sea can no longer be construed as a single, well-defined leg of a multi-leg journey.[5] Instead, it must be taken rather as *a part* of the journey, where each party is not only vital in linking the journey's stages of transport together, but is also a stakeholder in this integrated system.[6]

**3.5** Today, transportation is the common thread running through the whole tapestry of production; from manufacturing, through delivery to the final consumers, and even returns. Careful coordination across the whole process is essential in maximising the benefit to all parties.[7]

**3.6** As Christopher explains, current business enterprises are changing strategies, eroding internal boundaries, and creating what he calls the extended enterprise, the arrival of which has changed competition between organisations.[8] Christopher defines a virtual enterprise as a series of relationships between partners, evolving into a confederation of organisations that agree common goals.[9] Fremont explains why this is so highly applicable to the shipping industry. The primary concern for the shipping companies is the logistics of the cargo. They therefore have interests in expanding their area of business, i.e., looking for integrated services. Taking this concept further, as Fremont suggests, the role of shipping related to port-to-port business is nowadays probably only secondary to the business of the whole chain.[10] Logistics and supply chains rely heavily on

4 Dong-Wook Song and Photis M Panayides, 'Global Supply Chain and Port/Terminal: Integration and Competitiveness' (2008) 35 Maritime Policy and Management 1, 73. Also from a governance perspective, it has been reported that due to rapid changes in technology, the competitive environment, firm strategies and other pressures are prompting many firms to seek continuing cooperative relationships with other firms. Peter Smith Ring, Andrew H Van De Ven, 'Structuring Cooperative Relationships between Organizations' (1992) 13 Strategic Management Journal 483–498.

5 As it was when the carriage of goods by sea was understood on a tackle-to-tackle basis.

6 A stakeholder is 'any group or individual who can affect or is affected by the achievement of the organization's objectives'. R Eduard Freeman and John McVea, 'A Stakeholder Approach to Strategic Management' (Darden Business School Working Paper No. 01-02, 2001). It is worth mentioning here the stakeholder theory which, since the beginning of the 1980s, has supported the idea that organizations should recognise the interests not only of shareholders, but also of stakeholders. In fact, this theory sees the support of the stakeholders as key to the success of the organization.

7 G Santosh Kumar and P Shirisha, 'Transportation: The Key Player in Logistics Management' (2014) 3 Journal of Business Management & Social Sciences Research 1.

8 Martin Christopher, *Logistics and Supply Chain Management* (2nd edn, Prentice Hall 2011) 265.

9 Ibid., 266.

10 Antoine Frémont, 'Empirical Evidence for Integration and Disintegration of Maritime Shipping, Port and Logistics Activities' (OECD/ITF Joint Transport Research Centre Discussion Paper No. 2009-1, 2008).

transportation. Approximately 33% of logistical costs are transport related, and thus it is central to the performance of logistics systems.[11]

**3.7** A carrier's focus on integration is likely to impact on its relationship with land operators. In the past, shipowners and ports tended to compete with one another; now the competition is mainly amongst players in the field of logistics. Van De Voorde contends that, today, the standalone competitiveness of these players is much less important than whether or not they are part of a high-performing logistics chain.[12]

**3.8** As previously stated, the exigency of integration would probably not have become so central had it not been for the container revolution that allowed transported of one container along the whole chain, and thus reduced costs.[13] Containerisation has created a chain of interests amongst the operators that handle the containers, i.e., logistics. According to Hummels, logistics 'involves a series of activities, including storage, inventory management, materials handling and order processing, and comprises physical activities (e.g., transport, storage, etc.) as well as non-physical activities (e.g., supply chain design, selection of contractors, freightage negotiations)'.[14] Furthermore, logistics management is an integrative process that seeks to optimise the flow of materials and supplies from the organisation to the customer.[15] It seems reasonable, therefore, that the parties of a chain would aim to optimise their logistical system. When a logistics chain comprises parties that do not belong to the same structure and that differ in nature, it can be problematic. Therefore, a common strategy is often absent when attempts to improve individual yet interdependent logistical systems are made.[16]

**3.9** Logistical activities are utterly dependent upon a solid transportation system. A good system will ease implementation, shrink costs, and increase quality.[17] Transportation is also central to the activities of logistics management, representing as it does the greatest cost in logistics systems. Thus, the overall performance of a logistics system can be deeply affected by the efficiency of its transport system. Even a powerful logistics strategy will not reach its full potential without careful linking of transportation.[18] In order to achieve a fully integrated system, parties in a logistics chain have to share inventory levels,

11 Yung-Yu Tseng, Wen Long Yue and Michael A P Taylor, 'The Role of Transportation in the Logistic Chain' (2005) 5 Proceedings of the Eastern Asia Society for Transportation Studies 1657.

12 Eddy Van de Voorde and Thierry Vanelslander, 'Market Power and Vertical and Horizontal Integration in the Maritime Shipping and Port Industry' (OECD/ITF Joint Transport Research Centre Discussion Paper No. 2009-2, 2008).

13 David Hummels, 'Transportation Costs and International Trade in the Second Era of Globalization' (2007) 21 The Journal of Economic Perspectives 3, 131.

14 Ibid.

15 Thomas R Leinbach and Cristina Capineri, *Globalised Freight Transport:* Intermodality, E-Commerce, Logistics and *Sustainability* (Edward Elgar, 2007) 142.

16 Ibid.

17 As stated by Tseng, Yue and Taylor (n. 11), transportation is key for the efficiency in business logistics and it expands other functions within the logistics network.

18 Ibid.

product characteristics, and available resources.[19] Logistics is, in fact, only one part of the supply chain process that 'plans, implements, and controls the efficient, effective forward and reverse flow and storage of goods, services, and related information between the point of origin and the point of consumption in order to meet customers' requirements'.[20] Woo defines a supply chain as 'a connected series of activities which are concerned with planning, coordinating and controlling materials, parts, and finished goods from supplier to customer'.[21] In the context of shipping, Woo then specifies that a maritime supply chain is a 'connected series of activities pertaining to shipping services which is concerned with planning, coordinating and controlling containerised cargoes from the point of origin to the point of destination'.[22]

**3.10** This book uses these definitions to create new boundaries within and without which third parties currently operate, arguing that the carriage of goods by sea is not an isolated business but instead integrated into a broader supply chain. Legal protection should consequently have the same rationale for all the parties involved and should be seen as part of the management of the supply chain. To that end, it should be part of what is called supply chain management.

**3.11** Supply chain management is a systems-based approach to viewing the channel as a whole rather than as a set of fragmented parts.[23] Parties within the management of a single supply chain in fact share the same mutual risk.[24] Christopher enhances the concept of network integration, arguing that any 'firm' lies at the heart of an independent network – 'a confederation of mutually complementary competencies and capabilities' – and each network functions as an integrated supply chain. Each of these supply chains is, inevitably, in competition with other supply chains. According to Christopher, this 'radically revised competitive structure' demands a very different approach from managers to the one adopted when more traditional models were dominant:

> To achieve market leadership in the world of network competition necessitates a focus on network management as well as upon internal processes. Of the many issues and challenges facing organisations as they make the transition to this new competitive environment, the following is perhaps most significant: traditionally members of a supply chain have never considered themselves to be part of a

19 Scott J Mason, P Mauricio Ribera, Jennifer A Farris and Randall G Kirk, 'Integrating the Warehousing and Transportation Functions of the Supply Chain' (2003) 39 Transportation Research Part E 141.

20 Tseng, Yue and Taylor (n. 11).

21 Su-Han Woo, 'Seaport Supply Chain Integration and Orientation, and their Impact on Performance' (PhD thesis, Cardiff University, 2010).

22 Ibid.

23 Lisa M Ellram and Martha C Cooper, 'Supply Chain Management, Partnership, and the Shipper – Third Party Relationship' (1990) 1 The International Journal of Logistics Management, 2.1, 2.

24 Woo (n. 21) lists the following as a feature for a supply chain management: 'mutually sharing information, mutually sharing risks and rewards, cooperation, the same goal and the same focus on serving customers, integration of processes and partners to build and maintain long-term relationships' 58.

> marketing network and so have not shared with each other their strategic thinking. For network competition to be truly effective requires a significantly higher level of joint strategy development. This means that network members must collectively agree strategic goals for the network and the means of attaining them.[25]

**3.12** The analysis above clearly shows the concepts of network and common interests. However, it also lends weight to the idea that parties of the supply chain in reality do not consider themselves to be part of the network.

**3.13** Essential to this network is the concept of sharing, in particular the sharing of information and plans necessary to make the channel more efficient and competitive.[26] Electronic commerce has played a crucial role in supporting and enhancing this sharing.[27] Referring to shipping, Chuah agrees that cargo management has become highly computerised, and that the parties involved in the chain share responsibility for it.[28]

**3.14** Given how closely aligned the various parties in the 'whole' channels have now become – particularly in the context of third parties in the carriage of goods by sea – affording them different legal protection according to historical differentiations seems an outdated approach. The default position ought to give protection to 'all the service providers who help the cargoes move', from the starting point to the final consumer.[29] This is the concept of multilateral common enterprise.

## Globalisation impact

**3.15** Globalisation itself had a profound impact on the formation of worldwide chains that extend well beyond maritime barriers. It is important, according to Stopford, to look beyond maritime operations to a broader, comprehensive perspective as the aim of a cargo owner is effectively to have a coverage of the whole distance, from origin to destination; not only for the sea leg.[30]

**3.16** Global supply chains allow people to move products to and from every corner of the world. As Drake reports, it is possible for a fish to be caught in the Mediterranean Sea and served in Japan several days later. A product manufactured deep in the interior of China can be delivered direct to a consumer in the American heartland within a week.[31] In this way, even consumers can be

25 Christopher (n. 8) 217.

26 Ibid. See also Shang-Min Lin, Andrew Potter, Stephen Pettit and Rawindaran Nair, 'A Systems View of Supply Network Integration in Maritime Logistics' (2014) 19th Logistics Research Network Conference (Huddersfield, 3–5 September 2014).

27 Lin et al., ibid.

28 Jason Chuah, 'Impact of the Rotterdam Rules on the Himalaya clause: the Port terminal Operators' Case' in D Rhidian Thomas (ed.), *The Carriage of Goods by Sea under the Rotterdam Rules* (Informa 2010).

29 Lin et al. (n. 26). However, it is worth repeating that this book does not aim to label this protection to specific third parties.

30 Martin Stopford, *Maritime Economics* (Routledge 1997).

31 Matt Drake, *Global Supply Chain Management* (Business Expert Press at 1, 2012).

considered part of a supply chain's management. Every time a consumer rates or comments on their recent service from a company such as Amazon, for example, they are helping to improve supply chain management.

**3.17** A supply chain is in essence a common enterprise, even if it is not legally identified as such.[32] As Jephson and Morgen define it, a supply chain is a 'network involved in the provision of product and service packages to a customer'.[33] Consider the creation and delivery of a basic t-shirt sold in the United States. Cotton grown in the United States is transported to China. After being spun into thread, the cotton is then woven into fabric used to make the t-shirts. The finished articles are then sent back to the United States where they are finally sold. Before reaching a consumer, each t-shirt essentially makes two trips across the world. That this happens at all implies not only that the cost of labour in China is substantially lower than in the United States (and potentially elsewhere), but also that the transportation of materials and products in both directions is reliable, cheap, and efficient.[34]

**3.18** This is by no means a fully representative case, but it illustrates neatly the idea that, in a supply chain, what matters most is management of involved parties; if this is done well, there are no geographical barriers. To cite another example, consider the complex supply chains of a tennis ball used at the Wimbledon tournament in England, for example:

- Raw materials from the United States, Greece, Japan, Thailand, South Korea, New Zealand, England, China, and Malaysia are all shipped to the Philippines, where the various constituent parts are turned into tennis balls.
- The balls are put into tins from Indonesia, and once packaged they are sent to Wimbledon.[35]

**3.19** Supply chains usually start with export-production – from, e.g., a mine, a refinery, a farm, or a manufacturer – followed by storage and land transportation phases. Next, there is typically a cargo-handling phase followed by the shipping portion of the journey. After the shipping comes the discharging, storage again, and then more land transport until the goods arrive at the importer. Between production and consumption, the cargo is usually handled 14 times.[36]

**3.20** The cargo handling phase is far from insignificant; it is not unusual for a manufacturer to relocate a processing plant (such as a steel mill) to a coastal site in order to avoid land transport of raw material. This is yet another example of companies belonging to the same multilateral common enterprise working

32 In reality, a supply chain is a *de facto* scenario without a proper regulation.

33 Chris Jephson and Henning Morgen, *Creating Global Opportunities: Maersk Line in Containerisation 1973–2013* (Cambridge University Press, 2014).

34 Drake (n. 31) 21.

35 'The 50,000 Mile Journey of Wimbledon's Tennis Balls' (*Warwick Business School*) <www.wbs.ac.uk/news/the-50000-mile-journey-of-wimbledons-tennis-balls/>. Accessed 13 February 2016.

36 Stopford (n. 30) 297.

together but without a common strategy; they are not officially part of the same corporation. Similarly, the cargo terminal – also without sharing in a common strategy with the other participants of the supply chain – tries to be as suitable as possible for the needs of its users.[37] Stopford says that the key word is *integration* and that what matters is that the transport system is designed as a whole.[38] It is argued that the whole supply chain not only transport has to be seen as a whole.

**3.21** Other examples abound, but the point is this: the supply chain of a product can, as we have seen, be very complicated. Without a high level of co-ordination between parties, such supply chains would be at best, financially unappealing, and, at worst, totally impractical.[39]

**3.22** Today, giant corporations (such as Amazon) often seek to create what they call a global supply chain, allowing one-click shipping for seamless international trade. Amazon has already registered in the United States as an ocean-freight forwarding business and aims to create a global delivery network that controls the flow of goods from factories in China and India to customer in the States and Europe. Third party carriers will constitute and organise this global network in the first instance, but once there is sufficient volume – and once Amazon is able to run operations unassisted – Amazon will attempt to displace them.[40]

### *Vertical integration*

**3.23** Recently, carriers have conducted extensive research into economies of scope.[41] Economies of scope in the carriage of goods by sea are translated to vertical integration between different operators of the same chain.

**3.24** Vertical integration describes the expansion of a firm's business activities into upstream or downstream activities. Some examples of vertical integration in transport are: connections established between traditional forwarders and

37 Ibid., 297.

38 Ibid.

39 Companies exist that specialise in the creation and streamlining of supply chain management, and these are known as network orchestrators. They usually work for companies that are seeking to outsource the management of their own supply chains to a specialist. Perhaps the most famous of these network orchestrators is the Hong Kong-based company Li & Fung, Drake (n. 31) 58.

40 Spencer Soper, 'Amazon Building Global Delivery Business to Take on Alibaba' (*Bloomberg*, 9 February 2016) <www.bloomberg.com/news/articles/2016-02-09/amazon-is-building-global-delivery-business-to-take-on-alibaba-ikfhpyes>. Accessed 29 February 2016.

41 See David J Teece, 'Economies of Scope and the Scope of the Enterprise' (1980) 1 Journal of Economic Behavior and Organization 3, 223. According to Teece, economies of scope are conceptually similar to economies of scale. Although economies of scale for a firm primarily refer to reductions in the average cost (cost per unit) associated with increasing the scale of production for a single product type, economies of scope refers to lowering the average cost for a firm in producing two or more products. The term and the concept's development are attributed to John C Panzar and Robert D Willig, 'Free Entry and the Sustainability of Natural Monopoly' (1977) 8 Bell Journal of Economics 1, 1; John C Panzar and Robert D Willig, 'Economies of Scope' (1981) 71 American Economic Review (Papers and Proceedings) 268.

road hauliers; semi-trailer operators and swap-body operators owning the load units and buying the haulage services from small hauliers; intermodal transport services organised by road transport companies, operating either in cooperation with other hauliers or independently.[42]

**3.25** When referring to carrier and third parties formal vertical integration happens in shipping in different ways: contractual berthing or volume agreements between a third party stevedore and the shipping line; minority shareholding of the shipping line in a terminal; joint ventures between the shipping line and a third party stevedore, often linked to the dedicated use of the terminal by the shipping line; and a dedicated terminal with at least a 51% shareholding by the shipping line or its terminal operating sister.[43]

**3.26** Matzuaka identifies the reasons for vertical integrations in the increasing market share that companies can gain entering in market related to the core one.[44] Fremont adds that this could also happen in order to reduce costs, exploiting better economies of scale or for a better relationship with the counterpart.[45] Panayides completes the concept stating that the operational integration of sea and inland transport was initiated by the need for greater efficiency and became feasible due to containerisation and technological developments.[46]

**3.27** The gargantuan manufacturing firms of the late-nineteenth century were the first to implement vertical integration. At the time, it was not unusual for big corporations to own most if not all stages of production; from raw materials to the finished product. In many cases, they would also own at least some segment of the distribution channel.[47]

**3.28** Narrowing to the shipping sector, vertical integration in terminal operations occurs in the dry bulk and general cargo markets as well as the container market.[48] The tanker market is a notable exception; here, vertical integration has taken place to a much lesser extent, probably as a result of the nature of the operations involved. Invariably, transfer superstructures are not required, save for pipeline connections with refineries and so forth; handling and production are usually taken care of by the same party.[49]

42 Thomas R Leinbach and Cristina Capineri, *Globalised Freight Transport: Intermodality, E-Commerce, Logistics and Sustainability* (Edward Elgar, 2007) 142. An example is the International Union for Road-Rail Combined Transport (UIRR).

43 Theo Notteboom and Jean-Paul Rodrigue, 'The Corporate Geography of Global Terminal Operators' (2011) 39 (2012) Maritime Policy and Management *3*, 249.

44 John Matsusaka, 'Takeover Motives during the Conglomerate Merger Wave' (1993) 24 RAND Journal of Economics, 3, 357; Cong Wang and Fei Xie, 'Corporate Governance Transfer and Synergistic Gains from Mergers and Acquisitions' (2007) 22 Review of Financial Studies 829.

45 Ibid.

46 Photis M Panayides, 'Economic Organization of Intermodal Transport' (2002) 22 Transport Reviews 4, 401.

47 Drake (n. 31) 6. As it can be deducted from this example, the main benefit of having a complete vertical integration system is the level of control that can be exercised over it.

48 Study on the Analysis and Evolution of International and EU Shipping. Department of Transport and Regional Economics, September 2015.

49 Ibid.

**3.29** Frequently, the level of integration is sufficient for the dividing line between once separate markets for logistics services to have been blurred or entirely eroded.[50] The advantages of vertically integrating systems were acknowledged in the early 1980s; sizeable investments were made in different modes and service capabilities, primarily by ocean carriers. Panayides identifies potential benefits for both carriers and shippers. For the former, this includes:

1. Increased business and market share
2. Survival in the competitive international environment: facilitation of management and coordination
3. Economies of scale and scope that can lead to lower cost structures and higher profits shared creativity along all stages of the logistical process
4. Capitalising on the relative advantages of the various transport modes and greater routing flexibility

**3.30** For the latter, this includes:

1. Improvements in service quality
2. Ease in transacting the business dealings
3. Simplified claims settlements
4. Filing, tracing of shipment, and paperwork needed for shipment
5. Increased control over shipment[51]

**3.31** It is relevant to note that most of the top terminal operating companies are subsidiaries of shipping companies. Maersk provides an appropriate illustration of a total transportation company that demonstrates high levels of vertical integration through all the steps of a supply chain.[52] Maersk is also active in road and rail and was also active (until 2005) in the air transport business. As the concept of supply chain management began to mature, Maersk became a pioneer in the development of containerisation in a broader context.[53]

**3.32** Towards the end of 1988, Maersk began evaluating a concept known as Maersk Materials Management (3M). The proposal was a computer-supported logistics system that would allow Maersk Line to broaden its role in transportation and logistics chains from supplier to ultimate receiver. The hope was that such a system would allow Maersk to actively participate on a profitable basis in all aspects of the land-based logistics and distribution: 'The industries of the 1990s will demand and force the integration of the various links in the

50 T Heaver, H Meersman and E Van de Voorde, 'Co-Operation and Competition in International Container Transport: Strategies For Ports' (2001) 28 Maritime Policy & Management 3, 293.

51 Ibid. This article is about intermodal transport, this book brings this forward.

52 See generally ITF Round Table, *Integration and Competition between Transport and Logistic Business* (OECD Publishing, 2010).

53 Jephson and Morgen, 179.

transportation chain, and the time when shipping lines, land transport organizations and ports could work independently will be gone'.[54]

**3.33** Maersk is just the main total transportation company, being also a precursor of it. However, the other main European carriers, – MSC (Mediterranean Shipping Company) and CMA-CGM (Compagnie Maritime d'Affrètement - Compagnie Générale Maritime) – have also entered the stevedore business.[55]

**3.34** Vertical integration in the shipping industry is achieved mainly through integration of shipping companies with terminal operations.[56] Vertical integrations are, however, only the latest attempt by liner carriers to pursue scope economies and network economies, on both the demand and the supply sides. Recently, the innovations in this sector have concerned the vertical expansion of carriers and their involvement in port activities and logistic functions.[57] Additionally, shippers ask for uniformity in the carriage in order to maintain high quality without causing delay or defect.[58]

**3.35** From the perspective of vertical integration, what has traditionally been considered a separate third party is now often linked with the carrier or the shipper from a corporate perspective. This again illustrates the importance that shipping companies attach to being involved in the terminal operating business, not so much for the sake of diversification, but rather to ensure that sufficient port capacity is available.

**3.36** The introduction of terminal handling charges represents the primary means through which vertical integration affects costs in shipping. The cost of sea freight includes the handling charges of terminal operators. More and more frequently, shippers will seek to secure 'all-in' rates that cover three basic elements: sea freight, surcharges, and terminal handling charges.[59] Such comprehensive rates allow the shipper to pay the carriers directly without necessarily being acquainted with the third parties involved. In the container market, therefore, the carrier's costs take into account the cost of third party involvement. This sheds some light on the reasons for certain market participants attempting to secure control over these chains, whether through mergers, acquisitions, or vertical and horizontal integration.[60]

**3.37** Lin et al. report that, in addition, those operators who choose to integrate vertically tend to include only the aspects that are relevant and easily

54 Ibid., 195.

55 Claudio Ferrari, Francesco Parola and Marco Benacchio, 'Network Economies in Liner Shipping: The Role of Home Markets' (2008) 35 Maritime Policy and Management 2, 127.

56 Richard W Palmer and Frank P Degiulio, 'Admiralty Law Institute Symposium: Terminal Operations and Multimodalism Terminal Operations and Multimodal Carriage: History and Prognosis' (1989–1990) 64 Tulane Law Review 281.

57 Ferrari, Parola and Benacchio (n. 55).

58 Renato Midoro and Francesco Parola, *Le Strategie delle Imprese di Linea nello Shipping ed Intermodalita: Dinamiche Competitive e Forme di Cooperazione* (Franco Angeli 2013).

59 European Commission, 'Terminal Handling Charges during and after the Liner Conference Era' (Competition Reports, produced by Ben Hackett on behalf of Raven Trading Limited, European Commission, Brussels 2009).

60 Van de Voorde and Vanelslander (n. 12).

incorporated. Sometimes, the operator will seek to take advantage of the resources (or acquire the services of their members) in the chain. By way of example, leading shipping carriers often invest in their terminal operators to secure long-term benefits.[61] Lin et al. also assert that freight forwarders are interested in owning and managing their own warehouses if needed, but tend not to own land transport fleets as they are harder to manage.[62]

Once links are forged between these various operational strands, they are usually strengthened to maximise productivity and minimise costs. The shipping company is thus in a position to improve the entire chain's productivity. Where vertical control has not been achieved by a shipping company, the efficacy of each action is dependent upon the relationship between shipping lines and terminal operators. Shipping companies will try, as a rule, to maximise control over the generalised cost of a given port call. If this proves hard to do, the most appropriate solutions would be sought, such as using a different port that will reduce the generalised cost.[63]

**3.38** Apart from the aforementioned – and apart from economies of scope achieved through vertical integrations – in some sectors where the hire rates are impossible to control because they are part of fixed tariffs (such as the liner/container sector) the only way to make a profit is by reducing costs with economies of scale.[64]

### *Horizontal integration*

**3.39** A paper on shipping analysis prepared by PwC for the European Commission reports that ports and the maritime industry compete as part of the supply chains to which they belong. Some of these alliances are formal, as in the case of the vertical integration of shipping companies with port terminals. The same report shows that:

1. The forms of control of the maritime industry and ports, however, are likely to become increasingly flexible as, in addition to mergers, recent developments include alliances, joint ventures, and dedicated handling activities.
2. Cooperation may involve carriers, terminal operating companies, port authorities, hinterland operators, and hinterland terminal operators.
3. It has been reported that 14 out of the top 20 container shipping companies have integrated vertically with port terminal operations, sometimes under an 'own brand' name.[65]

61 Lin et al. (n. 26).
62 Ibid.
63 Ibid.
64 Midoro and Parola (n. 58).
65 Study on the Analysis and Evolution of International and EU Shipping Final report September 2015. Department of Transport and Regional Economics, University of Antwerp.

**3.40** As mentioned previously, the integration into the supply chain of the carriage of goods by sea is made possible by the nature of modern ports. Within international logistics chains – and the networks associated with them – these ports serve as vital nodes. In isolation, a port's remote location means little; what matters today is the network that connects ports to consumers.[66]

**3.41** The greater the number and depth of long-term, co-operative relationships that a port has, the higher its level of integration in the supply chain.[67] On a smaller scale, a port can itself be viewed as a series of links – ship unloading, storage transport, storage, loading, and so forth – constituting a miniature supply chain of its own. The industry and marketplace now require that ports function as integrated nodes in the supply chain, bridging the gap between land and sea, not simply as sites to load and discharge cargo.[68] This evolution has built new relationships among operators on sea and on land.[69]

**3.42** A logistics chain's success is contingent upon the competitive strength of its seaports; the reverse is also true. The same logic is applicable to other players in maritime transport, such as shipowners, hinterland transport providers, and port undertakings; each is a stakeholder in the same venture.[70]

**3.43** It is known that stakeholders, as part of the supply chain, have a direct interest; port and terminal integration in supply chains impacts on stakeholder operations and the satisfaction of their customers.[71] According to Van de Voorde, this shift began in the middle of the twentieth century. Ports were considered prime locations for various industrial activities. As a result, they became significant links in the industrial chain as well as playing a role in trade and transport chains.[72]

**3.44** Ports now occupy a new position as centres for loading, in addition to serving as links between sea and land transport. This change allows carriers to select ports with the best facilities and most competitive costs, even if they are not the closest port to the cargo's ultimate destination.[73] Furthermore, the United Nations Conference for Trade and Development (UNCTAD) reports that the point at which the shipper considers the cargo delivered has

66 Kevin P Coyne and Renée Dye, 'The Competitive Dynamics of Network-based Businesses', 76, no. 10 (January–February 1998) Harvard Business Review, 99.

67 Song and Panayides (n. 4).

68 Ibid.

69 Some of these changes are as follows: (i) Carriers previously dealt with local companies or public ports, but now tend to deal with vast corporations with commensurately hefty negotiating power; (ii) Ports and their facilities have evolved in order to accommodate bigger vessels, and are now more technologically advanced; (iii) There is a distinction between 'pure' terminal function (e.g., stevedores) and shipping companies that entered the port industry. In this sense, the container has precipitated a change; cargo loading and discharging previously needed a labour force but now it requires a high level and extensive amount of technology, machinery. Accordingly, the carriage flow has to be a ruthlessly efficient process.

70 Van de Voorde and Vanelslander (n. 12).

71 Song and Panayides (n. 4).

72 Van de Voorde and Vanelslander (n. 12).

73 Midoro and Parola (n. 58).

changed.[74] Traditionally, this point was deemed to be at the port; on the dock, below the ship's hook. On this understanding, carriers were not responsible for or involved with the cargo prior to it being loaded on board his ship or after it was discharged. This point has now moved ashore. Shippers deliver goods to the carrier's container freight station for consolidation and loading into the carrier's container (in the event that the shipper has not already loaded the goods into a container beforehand). Then, either the shipper delivers the container to the carrier's container yard (usually close to the port) or sometimes the carrier will take delivery of the container at the shipper's factory.[75] Liu, referencing Drewry, points out that:

> The competition between container ports was for a long time not very intensive because ports are location specific. However, with the increasing proportion of transhipment traffic within the total container port traffic the geopolitically-sensitive nature of container ports has been altered, and competition among ports has intensified. Ports are now not only competing with nearby ports, but also with ports relatively far away. For example, the Port of Gioia Tauro (South Italy, Mediterranean Sea) competes with the Port of Rotterdam (West Netherlands, North Sea) for the continental European market.[76]

**3.45** This factual context facilitates the integration between players. An example of port integration is highlighted by the role of carrier-operated terminals (also known as dedicated terminals). These terminals are often used by ocean carriers as a way of securing and controlling terminal capacity in order to improve their service reliability.[77] Ports and their terminal operators are thus required to offer facilities that permit efficient, economic interface between vessels and inland transportation; without them, ports and terminals would struggle to compete in the containerised cargo market.[78] Carriers tend to focus their primary operations within a small number of ports as a result of their integration.[79] This integration also involves the shipper; they are all linked by customer-supplier relationships.[80]

**3.46** Ports play an expanded role in the new era of logistics insofar as they function as components of integrated global supply chain systems.[81] As far as container transport is concerned, the most significant port-related expenses tend

74 Report by the UNCTAD 'The Economic and Commercial Implications of the Entry into Force of the Hamburg Rules and Multimodal Convention' (1991) New York <http://unctad.org/en/Docs/tdbc4315rev1_en.pdf>. Accessed 23 September 2013.

75 Ibid.

76 Qianwen Liu, 'Efficiency Analysis of Container Ports and Terminals' (PhD Book, University College London 2010).

77 Palmer and Degiulio (n. 56).

78 Ibid.

79 Ibid.

80 Wayne K Talley, 'Maritime Transport Chains: Carrier, Port and Shipper Choice Effects' (2014) International Journal of Production Economics 151, 174.

81 Song and Panayides (n. 4).

to be the terminal handling charges and time-related costs.[82] Market participants are thus encouraged to strive for greater control over these chains.[83]

**3.47** Van de Voorde explains these structural evolutions within ports. Traditional stevedore firms have evolved into more complex terminal operator companies. Shipping companies, many of which have established their own terminal operating branch, often provide the external capital to do this. The shipping company can use these terminal operating companies as dedicated terminals, or they can take a more independent tack, e.g., acting as a multi-user terminal in order to improve utilisation rate.[84]

**3.48** It is not enough anymore simply to have control of a port. Because various parties are aiming to take over the entire supply chain, the border between where the hinterland starts and where it ends has been blurred. The result, according to Degiulio, is that proximity of a port to shippers and receivers is much less important than it has been in the past.[85]

**3.49** Ports have been described as bi-directional logistics systems; Ships deliver goods for distribution via land and inland waterways that carry the goods along the subsequent legs of the journey. At the same time, ports accept cargo delivered by land and water-based modes and convey them to ships for the ocean part of the journey.[86]

## Towards terminalisation

**3.50** Terminal operators are likely to be increasingly active in the supply chain in the future, and thus increasingly important.[87] The flow of freight is regulated primarily by transport terminals, who influence considerably the nature of supply chains in terms of location, capacity, and reliability.[88] Moreover, logistics service providers and shippers have begun to use terminals as facilities to store consignments cheaply.[89] Of particular relevance, according to Rodrigue and Notteboom, is the fact that terminals (rather than ports) are competitors in the struggle between ports. Though terminals are certainly in competition with one another, this competition is not exclusively for tangible assets, such as port infrastructure. Instead, terminals are competing mainly through their offer of services adding value to their users within the supply chains.[90] Also

82 Barry Zondag, Pietro Bucci, Padideh Gützkow and Gerard de Jong, 'Port Competition Modeling Including Maritime, Port, and Hinterland Characteristics' (2010) 37 Maritime Policy and Management: The Flagship Journal of International Shipping and Port Research 3, 179.

83 Van de Voorde and Vanelslander (n. 12).

84 Ibid.

85 Palmer and Degiulio (n. 56).

86 Song and Panayides (n. 4).

87 Jean-Paul Rodrigue and Theo Notteboom, 'The Terminalization of Supply Chains: Reassessing the Role of Terminals in Port/Hinterland Logistical Relationships' (2009) 36 Maritime Policy and Management: The Flagship Journal of International Shipping and Port Research 2, 165.

88 Ibid.

89 Ibid.

90 Ibid.

relevant here is the concept of the 'terminalisation' of supply chains; this captures the changing role of terminals as through-locations in supply chains.[91] For instance, a new trend – described as 'warehousing-derived terminalisation' – has emerged, and it concerns the fact that the role of warehousing has been transferred to the terminal. Today, therefore, a terminal is typically part of the supply chain as a depository as well.[92]

**3.51** After five decades of container-based shipping, ports and terminals are no longer simply passive players prone to restricting capacity, reliability, and efficiency. As markets, customers, and the needs of both evolve, the widening gap between supply chains and related logistics network structures is promoting a more intimate relationship between inland terminals and ports. Accordingly, logistics providers and terminal operators are revisiting their models for generating revenue, securing profits, and providing value to their customers, all of which is being done without neglecting the operational considerations of the terminals. In some cases, shippers and logistics providers use terminals to augment their distribution processes. This has given rise to the creation of extended distribution centres. Increasingly, inland terminals are being considered as the extended gates of seaport terminals; by moving cargo inland they often reduce the time at seaport terminals.[93]

### *Third parties involved*

**3.52** Here, it is appropriate to make an important distinction. On the one hand, there are categories of third party that relate to the carrier and the vessel because they function as employees or servants of the carrier. These were already part of the issue surrounding third party protection when the issue first arose, between the beginning and the middle of the last century. On the other hand, in recent years contemporary third parties have emerged, such as freight forwarders, terminal operators, non-vessel-operating common carriers, and inland carriers (these are mainly independent contractors). The first group is now in broad terms incorporated within the position of carrier. The role of parties within the second group is not subsidiary to the carrier but is rather a proper, defined, specific role in the chain. Thus, this role cannot be defined as a third party anymore.[94] This book defines third parties as 'the third part of the enterprise' to reflect the fact

91 Daniel Olivier and Brian Slack, 'Rethinking the Port' (2006) 38 Environment and Planning A, 8, 1409.

92 Notteboom and Rodrigue (n. 87).

93 Ibid.

94 The Rotterdam Rules apply a proper division of employees of the parties (including Master and Agents, who were previously considered third parties) and performing parties. Thus indicating that, strictly in this regards, the rules represent an improvement; see Carlo Corcione, 'The Evolution of Third Party Protection in Carriage of Goods by Sea: From the Himalaya Clause to the Himalaya Protection' (2014) 49 European Transport Law Journal 3, 271.

that they do not fit the classic perception of third parties.[95] That is to say, they are not, in carriage of goods by sea, 'a person or group besides the two primarily involved in a situation'.[96]

**3.53** The list of third parties is by no means exhaustive, but it is nevertheless important for understanding the involvement of third parties in the multilateral common enterprise.

### Terminal operators

**3.54** Terminal operators have been defined as the matching point between sea and land. The following assessment underscores their importance:

> In the eyes of the law, the terminal is the chameleon of the maritime industry. The law treats the terminal at various times, and occasionally at the same time, as an ocean carrier, an Interstate Commerce Commission (ICC) common carrier, a warehouse, a common-law bailee, an agent of an ocean carrier, an agent of an ICC common carrier, an agent of a cargo shipper, and an agent of a cargo consignee.[97]

**3.55** They can have liability and consequently protection as carrier, bailee, or as a third party. This makes them a crucial category in the multilateral common enterprise. As explained, terminal operators and shipping firms are currently closed related by vertical integration and therefore from an economic perspective (especially in the container marker), it is very difficult to differentiate this category of third party from the carrier.

**3.56** A Convention on the Liability of Terminal Operators in International Trade was produced by the United Nations Commission on International Trade Law (UNCITRAL) in April 1991. The convention applies to loss or damage to goods, identified objectively as involved in international carriage, when the goods are in the charge of the terminal operator for transport-related services.[98]

There has also been a convention on Terminal Operators Liability after a project started half a century ago by the International Institute for the Unification of Private Law (UNIDROIT) on warehousing contracts that had been concerned only with the safe-keeping aspects of the industry. Wide divergences in liability regimes were noted in the study, ranging from a strict and unlimited liability to total exculpation and non-liability.

**3.57** According to this convention, the definition of terminal operator excludes carriers.[99] Terminal operators have a delicate role in the chain, being very connected with maritime activities but substantially undertaking a land-based

95 As it has been elaborated in the past.

96 Oxford Dictionary, 'Third Party' (2015) <www.oxforddictionaries.com/definition/english/third-party>. Accessed 27 April 2015.

97 Chester D Hooper, 'Legal Relationships: Terminal Owners, Operators, and Users' (1989–1990) 64 Tulane Law Review 595.

98 Ibid.

99 J C Sweeney, 'Crossing the Himalayas: Exculpatory Clauses in Global Transport – *Norfolk Southern Railway Co. v James N. Kirby*' (2005) 36 Journal of Maritime Law and Commerce, 155.

job. Before deciding to establish uniformity, Hooper suggests that we ask: 'In relation to what does terminal liability need uniformity?'[100] Hooper considers two aspects of uniformity: first, uniformity in relation to other terminals; second, uniformity in relation to other modes of transportation.[101] He also defines the different features of the job of terminal operators as follows:

1. As agent of an ocean carrier
2. As a common carrier or freight forwarder
3. As a warehouse
4. As an agent of an Interstate Commerce Commission common carrier[102]

Hooper suggests that terminal operators need not look solely to the carrier's bill of lading to limit their liability for loss or damage to cargo.[103]

**3.58** The position of terminal operators is quite difficult to determine within the international legal framework, for the aforementioned reasons. Terminal operators are also protected by domestic law. In the United States, for example, they are protected by the Federal Maritime Commission (FMC), which controls the tariff of wharfage, dockage, warehouse, and other terminal facilities. They are also protected by the Uniform Commercial Code.[104] However, it should be restated here that this book does not look at the legal protection that third parties (as terminal operators in this case) can provide for themselves.

**3.59** Terminal operators can also face liability under bailment terms. The liability of the terminal operator as bailee is a matter of local law, which varies greatly by jurisdiction.[105]

**3.60** An article from the law firm Holman Fenwick and Willan observes that, currently, there is no international convention or national legislation which applies to traditional port services. Operators are free to govern their liabilities using contractual terms of their own negotiation. By comparison, terminal operators expanding into international distribution must accept the possibility that a convention will be applied; the Hague Rules or Hague-Visby Rules if by sea, the CMR if by road, the Montreal/Warsaw Rules if by air, or the Uniform Rules concerning the Contract for International Carriage of Goods by Rail if by rail. These conventions contain time bars, limits of liability, and defences that will probably be different to the contractual terms negotiated by terminal operators and, if any of the conventions are applicable by operation of law, it is not possible to contract outside of them.[106]

100 Hooper (n. 97).

101 Ibid.

102 Ibid.

103 Ibid.

104 Thomas R Denniston, Carter T Gunn and Alfred E Yudes, 'Liabilities of Multimodal Operators and Parties Other than Carriers and Shippers' (1989–1990) 64 Tulane Law Review 517.

105 Ibid.

106 HFW Ports & Terminals Group, 'Expansion into Logistics – A Risky Business' (*HFW Ports & Terminals Group*, January 2010) (Article first appeared in the December 2009 issue of

**3.61** This is accentuated by the fact that, presently, container terminals compete for more traffic with each other than do container ports. The emergence of global terminal operators means that the market share is now concentrated in the hands of a few global terminal operators; for example, PSA (PSA International Pte Ltd), APM (Arnold Peter Möller Maersk), and P&O.[107] This makes them vast corporations not only by means of horizontal integration but also through vertical integration with the carrier. There are several reasons for the flourishing of terminal operators:

1. Port privatisation
2. Increase in stevedoring costs
3. Increasing transhipment traffic
4. Horizontal integration[108]

Freight forwarders

**3.62** As previously discussed, the orthodox notion of the carriage of goods by sea is usually restricted to relationships between carrier and shipper. However, the contract is sometimes arranged by a freight forwarder, who can act as an intermediary between carrier and shipper. Freight forwarders, therefore, sit in a tricky position; depending on the facts, they can be intermediaries, independent contractors, agents, and even principals or carriers in a contract for the carriage of goods partly or totally by sea.[109]

**3.63** That freight forwarders can be appointed by both the carrier and the shipper complicates matters further. In these cases, freight forwarders might seek to avoid the carrier's liability but, on the other hand, without appropriate protection they can be sued in tort. Freight forwarders can act as the agent of the carrier signing or issuing the bill of lading to the shipper, and they can also

Port Strategy: Port strategy 'A Risky Business') <www.portstrategy.com/news101/administration/legal-and-insurance/expansion_into_logistics_-_a_risky_business>. Accessed February 2014.

107 Daniel Olivier, Francesco Parola, Brian Slack and James Wang, 'The Time Scale of Internationalisation: The Case of the Container Port Industry' (2007) 9 Maritime Economics and Logistics 1, 1.

108 Jean-Paul Rodrigue, 'Intermodal Transportation and Integrated Transport Systems: Spaces, Networks and Flows' (The 'Flowpolis: The Form of Nodal Space' Conference, Las Palmas de Gran Canaria, Spain, 2–4 November 2006). Rodrigue explains that:

> (a)s of 2005, global port operators accounted for over 58% of container port capacity and 67% of global containerised throughput. A horizontal integration structure is being set up as port holdings acquire the management of transport terminals in a wide array or markets. The main rationale behind the emergence of large port holdings includes: Financial assets ... Managerial expertise ... Gateway access ... (and) Leverage'. As mentioned previously, increased market power and reduction in costs are amongst the most important advantages of the horizontal integration.

109 H Edwin Anderson, 'The Status and Associated Liability of Ocean Freight Forwarders' (2009) 36 Transportation Law Journal 121.

act on behalf of the shipper when arranging the shipment of goods.[110] Although they sometimes fulfil a role similar to a non-vessel terminal operator, their legal status regarding the liability to the shipper is different. The case of *Scholastic Inc. et al. v M/V Kitano et al.* explored the main differences:

> [A freight forwarder] simply facilitates the movement of cargo to the ocean vessel. The freight forwarder secures cargo space [...] gives advice on governmental licensing requirements [and] proper port of exit and letter of credit intricacies, and arranges to have the cargo reach the seaboard in time to meet the designated vessel. A usual discussion is on the difference between a freight forwarder and an NVOCC, which, in contrast, does not merely arrange for transportation of goods, but takes on the responsibility of delivering the goods. The most fundamental difference between a freight forwarder and an NVOCC is that an NVOCC issues a bill of lading.[111]

**3.64** The case of *Scholastic Inc.* also offers another interesting insight:

> When the status of an intermediary as NVOCC or freight forwarder is disputed, the intermediary argues for freight forwarder status and its limited liability, while the plaintiff argues for NVOCC status and increased liability arising from the bill of lading.[112]

In order to better clarify the differences, the position of non-vessel-operating common carriers (NVOCCs) has to be addressed.

### Non-vessel-operating common carriers

**3.65** A NVOCC is a carrier who enters into a contract to carry goods but who does not operate or own the vessels providing the carriage. A multimodal freight forwarder can also be considered an NVOCC because, although using the services of sub-carriers, it is the 'principal' in the performance of the contract of carriage of goods.[113] In fact, Title 46 of the United States Code that contains the

110 Ibid. See also *Norfolk Southern Ry. v James N. Kirby, Pty Ltd. (Kirby)* (2004) 543 US 14. These are known as the main activities of a freight forwarder: (1) ordering cargo to port; (2) preparing and/or processing export declarations; (3) booking, arranging or confirming cargo space; (4) preparing or processing delivery orders or dock receipts; (5) preparing and/or processing ocean bills of lading; (6) preparing and/or processing consular documents or arranging for their certification; (7) arranging for warehouse storage; (8) arranging for cargo insurance; (9) clearing shipments in accordance with United States Government export regulations; (10) preparing and/or sending advance notifications of shipments or other documents to banks, shippers, or consignees as required; (11) handling freight or other monies advanced by shippers, or remitting or advancing freight or other monies or credit in connection with the dispatching of shipments; (12) coordinating the movement of shipments from origin to vessel; and (13) giving expert advice to exporters concerning letters of credit, other documents, licences or inspections, or on problems germane to the cargoes' dispatch. Title 46 Shipping Part 500 to End (Revised as of October 1, 2013): 46-CFR-Vol-9.

111 *Scholastic Inc. v M/V Kitano (Kitano)*, 362 F Supp 2d 449 Dist Court SD New York 2005.

112 Ibid., 458.

113 J Bes and N Lopez, *Bes' Chartering and Shipping Terms* (11th edn, Barker & Howard Ltd. 1992).

Shipping Act of 1984/1986, as amended by the Ocean Shipping Reform Act of 1998/1997, regulates ocean carriers and intermediaries and defines two kinds of ocean transportation intermediaries (OTIs): NVOCCs and ocean freight forwarders. The NVOCC has been defined as 'a common carrier that does not operate the vessels by which the ocean transportation is provided, and is a shipper in its relationship with an ocean common carrier'.[114]

**3.66** In contrast, Title 46 OTI states that a freight forwarder is:

> [A] person that (i) in the United States, dispatches shipments from the United States via a common carrier and books or otherwise arranges space for those shipments on behalf of shippers; and (ii) processes the documentation or performs related activities incident to those shipments.[115]

The United States Court of Appeal for the Ninth Circuit has given the following general description of what NVOCCs do: 'an NVOCC is an intermediary between the shipper of goods and the operator of the vessel that will carry the goods'. NVOCCs will typically combine various shippers' goods into a single shipment, contract with the vessel for the transportation of the goods, and deliver the goods to the vessel, normally in a sealed container. In this respect, NVOCCs perform a not dissimilar function to freight forwarders; both consolidate small shipments from multiple shippers into large, standardised units of cargo that can be loaded on and off ships and lorries or other types of transportation with relative ease.[116]

### Stevedores

**3.67** Although mainly operating as land workers, stevedores are one of the main groups to function as third parties in the carriage of goods by sea.[117] The stevedore is a person who loads and discharges goods from vessels. In the past they were known also as dockers or longshoremen.

A stevedore contract has been defined as maritime in nature and within admiralty jurisdiction to the extent that it relates to maritime activities. However, when a stevedore acts as a terminal operator, they may be exposed to land-based principles of negligence. It has also been reported that, if storage of cargo is merely incidental to the loading or unloading of a vessel, admiralty law will control. Many claims between owner and charterer refer to stevedore damage. Stevedore damage to vessels is commonplace when loading or discharging cargo.[118]

114 46 United States Code of Federal Regulations (CFR) 530.3 (f) (1).

115 46 CFR 515.2 (o)(1)(ii).

116 *All Pacific Trading, Inc. v Vessel M/V Hanjin Yosu* 7 F 3d 1427 (9th Cir. 1993) para 3.

117 Marva Jo Wyatt, 'Contract Terms in Intermodal Transport: COGSA Comes Ashore' (1991–1992) 16 Tulane Maritime Law Journal 177.

118 See generally <www.ukpandi.com/knowledge/article/stevedore-damage-1915/>. Accessed 3 January 2016; <www.nepia.com/media/72637/LP-Briefing-Stevedores.PDF>. Accessed 4 April 2014; <www.steamshipmutual.com/publications/Articles/Articles/Liability_Stevedores>. Accessed 18 March 2013.

**3.68** Stevedores, along with terminal operators, fall into the category of independent contractors. The stevedore's position is arguably already rather delicate; from the 'venture' between shipowner and charterer in the charterparty, the stevedores, according to the contract, could be appointed by the shipowner or the charterer. In this respects, it has been reported that the stevedore position is crucial because without a proper regulation between shipowner and charterer, the liability consequent a damage could create confusion between the parties.[119] In the contract *Shelltime 4*, for example, there is a specific clause titled Stevedores, Pilots, Tugs.[120] Another example comes from the NYPE 1946 form of time charter, which has a clause called Stevedore Damage.[121]

**3.69** Stevedore is a category of third party that has been involved extensively in claims regarding the carriage of goods by sea involving protection clauses. In this sense, they may be the category posing the highest risk. There is a long history of American cases of stevedores acting as third parties, the first being *Carle & Montanari, Inc. v American Export Isbrandtsen Lines, Inc.* This is the first United States case in which the stevedore was afforded the defence of a bill of lading's protection clause.[122]

**3.70** In support of this book's main arguments, it seems that the role of stevedores is currently highly integrated with other categories of parties working at the port.[123]

119 The Swedish Club, 'Slot Charter Insurance' (*The Swedish Club*, 2 September 2007) <www.swedishclub.com/upload/174/02.slot-charterer-insurance.pdf>. Accessed 11 October 2014.

120 Stevedores when required shall be employed and paid by charterers, but this shall not relieve Owners from responsibility at all times for proper stowage, which must be controlled by the Master who shall keep a strict account of all cargo loaded and discharged. Owners hereby indemnify Charterers, their servants and agents against all losses, claims, responsibilities and liabilities arising in any way whatsoever from the employment of pilots, tugboats or stevedores, who although employed by charterers shall be deemed to be the servants of and in the service of owners and under their instructions (even if such pilots, tugboat personnel or stevedores are in fact the servants of Charterers their agents or any affiliated company); provided, however, that (1) The forgoing indemnity shall not exceed the amount to which Owners would have been entitled to limit their liability if they had themselves employed such pilots, tugboats or stevedores, and (2) Charterers shall be liable for any damage to the vessel caused by or arising out of the use of stevedores, fair wear and tear excepted, to the extent that Owners are unable by the exercise of due diligence to obtain redress therefore from stevedores. Available to view at <https://shippingforum.files.wordpress.com/2012/08/shelltime-4-as-revised-20031.pdf>. Accessed 14 December 2015.

121 New York Produce Exchange Form (NYPE 46):

> A) The charterers shall be responsible for damage (fair wear and tear excepted) to any part of the sue Owners caused by stevedores. The Charterer shall be liable for all costs for repairing such damage and for any time lost. B) The Master or the Owners shall notify the Charterers or their agents and stevedores of any damage within 24 hours, failing which the Charterers shall not be responsible. C) Stevedore damage affecting seaworthiness shall be repaired without any delay before the vessel sails from the port where such damage was caused or discovered. Stevedore damage affecting the vessel's trading capabilities shall be repaired prior to redelivery, failing which the Charterers shall be liable for resulting losses. All other damage which is not repaired prior to redelivery shall be repaired by the Owners and settled by the Charterers on receipt of Owners' supported invoice.

122 Sweeney (n. 99).

123 Ibid.

Inland carriers

**3.71** The problem of inland carriers and protection in the carriage of goods by sea is that, in order to receive the protection of the carrier in the carriage of goods by sea, a third party has to carry out some of the carrier's duties or contract with the carrier. Prior to *Kirby*, the case law on the protection of rail and truck carriers by Himalaya clauses was conflicted.[124] The current position of an inland carrier is that they have protection if mentioned in the protection clause.

**3.72** The position of inland carriers is very complicated. Although fully involved in the multilateral common enterprise, the maritime community does not recognise them as a 'party' to be protected by the maritime regulations. This is particularly clear in the *travaux préparatoires* of the three major conventions on the topic; in all of them inland carriers have been deliberately left outside the protection of the convention.

## Conclusion

**3.73** This chapter establishes the basis for a multilateral perspective with regard to third party protection in the carriage of goods by sea. Put simply: protection should be viewed in the light of shipping's integration within the supply chain.

Traditionally, these third parties have not been formally recognised as part of the supply chain. Hence, there is a need for the concept – and definition – of a multilateral common enterprise. It is essentially a multilateral system of legal and commercial interests. Some of them, as explained above, are formal, as in the cases of vertical and horizontal integrations. Vertical integration is a form of dyadic formal enterprise; horizontal integration is pivotal to the understanding that third parties are now likely to be big corporations rather than weak parties with little or no bargaining power. Over the years, there has been substantial involvement in the shipping industry of third parties who were not previously mentioned, yet have a specific 'factual' role and depend neither on carrier nor shipper. In certain circumstances – e.g., in the case of freight forwarders and NVOCCs – these third parties can even be the *primary* link in the chain.

**3.74** An essential part of these changes should be the uniformity and harmonisation of the legal tutelage of the parties involved in the carriage. In order to achieve this, however, barriers of different national laws, different requirements, and different local approaches have to be overcome.[125]

124 Ibid. In *Taisho Marine & Fire Ins. Co. v Maersk Line, Inc.*, 796 F. Supp. 336 (1992) a road haulier was afforded such protection.

125 Panayides (n. 46).

CHAPTER 4

# Third party protection under the Hague/Hague-Visby Rules

## The background – the Harter Act

**4.1** The Harter Act[1] has been selected for this analysis even though it is not an international convention and is applicable only to carriage of goods from or between ports in the United States and foreign ports.[2] The reason for this is that the contemporary story of regulating the relationship between the parties interested in the venture and liabilities for cargo starts with the Harter Act. The act was the first attempt to draw a compromise between carriage and cargo interests.[3]

**4.2** The Harter Act is the predecessor of all modern international conventions regarding the carriage of goods by sea. The bilateralism of the shipping industry at that time is clearly reflected in the Act itself. It emerged from a peculiar factual context that existed between the shipowners and the cargo interests. Shipowners were financially solid and with such a high bargaining power were able to decrease liability against the cargo owners. They were able to insert substantial exculpatory clauses in the bill of lading, limiting their liability as much as possible. Tetley, quoting Scrutton, notes that the exemption clauses became 'all encompassing, so much so that it inspired one commentator to remark that there seems to be no other obligation on a shipowner than to receive the freight'.[4]

**4.3** Thus, the balance between the parties was substantially in favour of the carrier. As detailed by Reynolds in 1889, the Annual Report of the West of England P&I Club records the Club's committee congratulate its members on the lack of cargo-related claims, apparently the result of '*the now general adoption of the negligence clause; the premium reduction for use of this clause is*

1 1983. As stated by the Hague-Visby Rules, *Travaux Préparatoires* at 16, the first attempts to draft a uniform bill of lading were made by the ILA's Affreightment and International Bill of Lading Committee in 1882.

2 46 USC para 190.

3 The Harter Act 1893 was followed by other Common Law countries directly afterwards (Australia in 1904 with the Carriage of Goods Act, New Zealand in 1903 with the Shipping and Seamen Act and Canada with the Water-Carriage of Goods Act 1910).

4 William Tetley, 'Case Comment: The House of Lords Decision in *The Starsin*' (2004) 35 JMLC 121–139. See also Vanessa Rochester, 'The Lone "Carrier": An Analysis of the Implications of the General Reluctance to Hold Parties Involved in Sea Carriage Jointly and Severally Liable' (PhD thesis, University of Cape Town, 2014).

*therefore discontinued*'.[5] As Knaught points out, in certain areas and especially the North Atlantic, a typical shipowner would apparently exclude virtually all – or at any rate, a great deal – of his liability when carrying goods, 'when he liked, as he liked, and wherever he liked'.[6]

**4.4** Cargo and related interests (including trade, financial, and insurance concerns) worked to improve the situation and won passage of the Harter Act in 1893.[7] The act strikes a balance between the fact that the carrier was not allowed to contract out of liability for due diligence as regards seaworthiness and care of cargo, but was not liable for negligence in navigation and management of the ship.[8] The main aim of the Act was to equalise the bargaining power of the two parties and allocate risk more appropriately.[9] As Evans points out, the Harter Act was the solution to the issue of the common law rules of liability in the United States that effectively held carriers strictly liable for any damage to cargo that occurred during shipment.[10]

**4.5** After a brief overview of the Act, it must be noted that almost nothing in the Harter Act concerns third parties and this is because, at the time of its drafting, the only parties entitled to have relevance to the carriage were the carrier and the shipper; contemporary shipping was a bilateral activity.

**4.6** The Act defines the term 'carrier' to include 'the owner or the charterer who enters into a contract of carriage with a shipper'.[11] This definition does not include any other party who may play one of the carrier's duties under the contract for the carriage of goods by sea. Problems arise because nothing in the Harter Act extends limitation and liability from the carrier to a third party (even though warehousemen or stevedores often enter in a contract with the carrier for that period).[12] In fact, while the carrier in that period was responsible for the goods, a cargo owner could have sued a carrier's sub-contractor or servant.[13] Apart from the owner/manager of the vessel, the only category of third party inserted in the Harter Act is the agent and the master of the vessel, but their responsibility is restricted to loading, stowage custody, care, and delivery. Nothing outside the strict role of the ship and the people involved is mentioned.

5 Francis Reynolds, 'The Hague Rules, the Hague-Visby Rules, and the Hamburg Rules' (1990) 7 MLAANZ Journal, 16.

6 Arnold Knauth, *The American Law of Ocean Bills of Lading 116* (4th edn, Baltimore 1953).

7 Harter Act 1893, 27 Stat 445 (codified at 46 USC Appendix 190–196).

8 Marva Jo Wyatt, 'Contract Terms in Intermodal Transport: COGSA Comes Ashore' (1991–1992) 16 Tulane Maritime Law Journal 177.

9 See Grant Gilmore and Charles Black, *The Law of Admiralty* (2nd edn, The Foundation Press 1975).

10 See I L Evans, 'The Harter Act and Its Limitations' (1910) 8 Michigan Law Review 8, 637.

11 Harter Act, 46 U.S.C. § 190.

12 William Tetley, 'Chapter 1, Application of the Rules Generally' (*Euro Marine*, no date) <www.euro-marine.eu/hague-VisbyRules.html>. Accessed 29 June 2014.

13 As per, amongst the others, *Adler v Dickson (The Himalaya)* (1954) 2 Lloyd's Rep 267; (1955) 1 QB 158; *Scruttons Ltd. v Midland Silicones Ltd. (Scruttons)* (1961) 2 Lloyd's Rep 365.

## Third parties in the Hague/Hague-Visby Rules and the COGSA of the United States (1924–1968)

**4.7** After the Harter Act, the need to allocate the risk and balance in the relationship between carrier and shipper became more pressing.[14] The result, in 1924, was the birth of the Hague Rules.[15] Enacted in the United States as the Carriage of Goods by Sea Act, or COGSA[16] and subsequently the Visby Protocol,[17] the Hague Rules were the first international regimes regarding the topic and remain the primary international tools for risk allocation between the Harter Act and the as yet unratified Rotterdam Rules.[18]

**4.8** Within the Hague Rules (as within the Harter Act), the protection of third parties in the carriage of goods by sea concerned only the carrier and shipper. The basic relationship between vessel interests and cargo interests is clearly stated in the *travaux préparatoires*, in which the committee mainly considered the law of the carriage of goods by sea to be 'the law governing the relations of shipowners and cargo owners with regard to carriage by sea under bills of lading'.[19] Narrowing the focus to third parties, the provisions of the Hague Rules are even more 'ship-related', being concerned only with tackle-to-tackle approaches; literally, from loading onto the ship to unloading from the ship. Article 1 stipulates that the contract of carriage (to whom the rules apply) only applies to the bill of lading[20] and regulates the relationship between the carrier and the holder of the bill of lading.[21] Article 1(e) regulates the tackle-to-tackle provision by saying that 'carriage of goods covers the period from the time when the goods are loaded on to the time they are discharged from the ship'.[22]

**4.9** This provision is unclear and highly controversial. It has the potential to create problems for the carrier and then for any other category of third parties working for said carrier. Although the Rules are expansive enough to cover the period from 'when the goods are loaded on, to the time they are discharged', a limitation is then created in the wording 'to and from the ship'. This is a problem because goods are usually managed by the carrier or one of his auxiliaries before and after what is called the hook-to-hook phase.

14 In this respect – as per Diplock, 'Conventions and Morals: Limitation Clauses in International Maritime Conventions' (1969–1970) 1 Journal of Maritime Law and Commerce 525 – the role of the conventions is essentially defining and limiting the liabilities of parties.

15 International Convention for the Unification of Certain Rules of Law Relating to Bills of Lading, 25 August 1924.

16 USC, Title 46a, Ch 28, Carriage of Goods By Sea <www.law.cornell.edu/uscode/html/uscode46a/usc_su p_05_46_10_28.html>. Accessed 1 August 2015.

17 Protocol to Amend the International Convention for the Unification of Certain Rules of Law Relating to Bills of Lading, 23 February 1968, 1977 Great Britain.

18 With the exception of the Hamburg Rules adopted in 1978, but less travelled by major shipping countries.

19 Delegation of the United Kingdom, Hague-Visby Rules, *Travaux Préparatoires*, 23.

20 Or any similar that is also included in a charterparty.

21 Article 1(b).

22 Article 1(e).

**4.10** In the time that elapsed between the ratification of the Hague Rules and the emergence of the Visby Protocol, carriage started to evolve[23] but third parties outside the scope of the bill of lading could only rely on domestic protection.[24] However, the fact that shipping was moving ashore was already clear from the *travaux*, where it appears that shipping companies at that time were much more focussed on their activities at sea and wanted to limit their liability only to the sea leg.[25] Furthermore, the problem of the restricted scope of application was noted in the *travaux préparatoires*:

> It is true that the shipowner can negotiate his own terms as every other trader, on the other hand it is true that if not regulated, all the responsibilities (included third parties) will be regulated randomly. The next point, and it is one to which the British shipowner attaches the greatest importance, is that the Rules control only the actual sea carriage. They are applicable only from the time the goods reach the ship's tackle. The shipowner is left as free as, but no freer than, every other trader, to make his own terms in regard to all other services he renders as collecting, receiving, distributing, and as forwarding agent, or in any other capacity.[26]

**4.11** Between the coming into force of the Hague Rules and, later, the Visby Protocol, case law regarding third parties underwent an impressive evolution: the cases of *Adler v Dixon*,[27] *Scrutton*,[28] and *The Eurymedon* in the United Kingdom,[29] and the case of *Herd*[30] in the United States. These cases had an undeniable impact on the Visby Protocol.[31] It is appropriate to highlight here that these cases provide evidence that the Hague Rules did not protect any party independent from the carrier, leaving the cargo interests able to circumvent the limitation of liability with the carrier in tort or suing someone else.

**4.12** During the *travaux* of the Hague Rules, the sub-committee was aware that attempts had been made, often successfully, to avoid the limitations and exemptions of the bill of lading convention in different ways. Thus, in some countries a contracting party may sue not only in accord to contract but also tort. If sued in tort, the carrier may therefore find themselves deprived of the benefit of limitation and of the one-year prescription period, and so on. Alternatively, the plaintiff may prosper by suing under tort those other than the carrier

23 Containerisation started in the 1960s.

24 See the concept of bailment in *Elder, Dempster & Co. Ltd. v Paterson, Zochonis & Co. Ltd. (Elder Demspter)* (1924) AC 522 (HL).

25 In the *Travaux Préparatoires* (n. 19) at 33 it is stated,

> Speaking quite broadly, I take it that as the liners extended their shore organisations and undertook many duties beyond those of carrying by sea, they found it absolutely necessary to limit the responsibilities they assumed as against the freights they charged.

26 *Travaux Préparatoires* (n. 19) 37.

27 The Himalaya (n. 13).

28 Midland Silicones (n. 13).

29 (1975) AC 154, 169.

30 Herd & Co. v Krawill Machinery Corp. 359 US 297, 1959 AMC 879 (1959).

31 Reynolds explains that the Hague-Visby Rules arose from defects in the Hague Rules (Reynolds, The Hague Rules, the Hague-Visby Rules, and the Hamburg Rules).

(e.g., the master, the agent, a member of the crew, etc.). In order to avoid the possibility of bypassing the contract and legislation based on the convention, the sub-committee to the Comité Maritime International recommended that the following new Article be adopted:

1. Any action for damages against the carrier, whether founded in contract or in tort, can only be brought subject to the conditions and limits provided for in this Convention.
2. If such an action is brought against a servant or agent of the carrier or against an independent contractor employed by him in the carriage of goods, such servant, agent, or independent contractor shall be entitled to avail himself of the defences and limits of liability which the carrier is entitled to invoke under this Convention. The aggregate of the amounts recoverable from the carrier, his servants, agents, and independent contractors in the employment of the carrier, in that case, shall not exceed the limit provided for in this Convention.[32]

**4.13** Taking into account this suggestion, the Visby protocol inserted Article 4 bis, which regulates third party protection. The Article states that if an action is brought against a servant or agent of the carrier (they specify that this does not have to be an independent contractor) the servant or the agent is entitled to the same defence and limits of liability of the carrier.[33] This is in line with the period of application that does not cover loading or discharging. Naturally, the carrier's liability for third parties is confined to master, crew, servants, and agents.[34] As noted, the Article clearly excludes independent contractors from the provision.[35] As first stated by Carver and later reported by Chuah:

> It is difficult to be satisfied that the self-contradictory words servant or agent of the carrier (such servant or agent not being an independent contractor) mean anything but a servant who does not work on a self-employed basis. If one acts on another's behalf as an agent, not being a servant, under contract, one must be an independent contractor.[36]

32 *Travaux Préparatoires* (n. 19) 596.

33 Article 4 bis. This concerns the limitation of liability and time bar that third parties (through the carrier) wish to achieve. They are specified in Article 4, which states that the limits under the Hague-Visby Rules are 66,667 SDR per package or unit and 2 SDR per kilogram. Regarding the time bar, the Hague-Visby rules discharge carrier and ship from all liability in respect of the good unless suit is brought within one year (Article 3).

34 Article 4bis (2). See Carlo Corcione, 'The Evolution of Third Party Protection in Carriage of Goods by Sea: From the Himalaya Clause to the Himalaya Protection' (2014) 49 European Transport Law Journal 3, 271.

35 This is because the rules were meant to be only for the benefit of the parties and as such also the protection of third parties is related to their benefit.

36 Jason Chuah, 'Impact of the Rotterdam Rules on the Himalaya Clause: The Port Terminal Operators' Case' in D Rhidian Thomas (ed.), *The Carriage of Goods by Sea under the Rotterdam Rules* (Informa 2010).

**4.14** In order to explain the rationale behind the exclusion of independent contractors, vicarious liability of the carrier for their auxiliaries has to be further explored. The concept of the shipowner as vicariously responsible for their servant and agents comes from the early days of the preparatory work of the Hague Rules. It is quite impressive in this respect to note that the second paragraph of the first preparatory work available for research of an international convention on the carriage of goods by sea should state the concept of the shipowner being liable for his servants:

> The shipowner, should be liable for the faults of his servants in all matters relating to the ordinary course of the voyage, such as the stowage, the right delivery of the cargo, and other matters of this kind; The shipowner shall be responsible that his vessel is properly equipped, manned, provisioned, and fitted out, and in all respects seaworthy and capable of performing her intended voyage, and for the stowage and right delivery of the goods. He shall also be responsible for the barratry, faults and negligence, but not for errors in judgment, of the master, officers and crew.[37]

**4.15** Taking into account that the rationale is the carrier's vicarious liability for his master, officers, and crew and their benefit, the Hague/Hague-Visby Rules (during their preparation) often differentiated who is employed by the carrier and who is not.

**4.16** In these regards, the terms 'agent' and 'servant' have been discussed in the *travaux*, and the idea of mentioning each singular category of third parties was put emphatically forward by Tetley, representing Canada:

> The term 'agents' is extremely broad, whilst the term 'servants' could mean almost any one, including a surveyor who certainly is providing service. In other words, this par. (2) is a source of innumerable log cases and confusion. I think this Committee or the Committee formed for redrafting must very carefully decide which persons in particular are being included. Do you include the stevedores? Do you include stevedores who are actually employees of the line? Let us suppose the French Line takes a cargo to Montreal and the crew does not see to the discharging but the stevedores, who are not independent contractors but actually employees of the French Line. Are those stevedores covered? Do you intend to cover stevedores? That is the problem. There will be another disadvantage to a company which does not use independent stevedores but its own stevedores in certain ports which is quite possible, incidentally, in many ports of Canada and many ports of the world. Therefore, I do not know if it is the duty of this Committee or of the minor Committee which has been formed to do the drafting but they must, I think, disregard this word 'servant', disregard this word 'agent', these words 'independent contractor' and say exactly who you mean. Do you mean the Master, do you mean the Mate, all the officers, all the crew? Do you mean the pilot? Do you mean any stevedores? Or do you mean independent stevedores? Whom do you mean? Otherwise this will be a perfect cause and source of litigation.[38]

37 *Travaux Préparatoires* (n. 19) 611.
38 Ibid.

**4.17** The answer to Tetley's concern is given in another passage of the *travaux* that shows the intention and the need to protect only the parties related to the carrier, because they are the only ones carrying the responsibility of the job:

> While the general principles set out above meet with the approval of the full Sub-Committee a minority wishes to put on record that they cannot adhere to these provisions as far as independent contractors are concerned. In their view a contractor who is independent of the carrier should not, by the mere fact that he performs duties which might have been performed by the carrier himself, become entitled to avail himself of the limitation and exceptions of the Convention. A distinction should be drawn between, on the one hand the carrier, his servants or agents and on the other, the independent contractor. The servants and agents should be protected for social reasons and should have the benefits of the Convention whereas, in the view of the minority, these reasons do not apply to the independent contractor who should thus not have this benefit.[39]

**4.18** In order to make matters even clearer, the United Kingdom delegation, responding to Tetley during the *travaux*, stated that 'agent' and 'servant' are exactly the right words to separate parties who are employed by the carrier, and parties who are appointed for a specific job. In the words of Miller:

> The suggestion is that we suppress the words 'servant or agent' and instead of them substitute a list of the servants or agents whom we mean by that. I am very much afraid that if this is put to the vote we shall have to be opposed to it. The phrase 'servants and agents' has been used in many, many conventions. It has been used in the Limitation of Liability Convention, it is used, if I remember rightly, in the Nuclear Ship Convention. It is the way we designate persons who are employed by the shipowner, distinguishing persons employed regularly by the shipowner in contradistinction to those employed as independent contractors to do one particular job. No one could possibly argue that your servants or domestic staff are not your preposés, but when you come to build a house you employ in the loose sense of the word a contractor to build it and you pay him for it. No one could say that he is a servant, he is an independent contractor. Like the elephant it is very difficult to define, but you know it when you see it.[40]

**4.19** This again shows the difference between those employed by the carrier and those not employed by the carrier. Since the carrier was vicariously liable for his assistant and was therefore vulnerable, the protection of third parties must be viewed from their perspective. The rationale for third party protection being fully linked to the parties' interests is explained in the comment of the British Maritime Law association during the *travaux*:

> It has been said by some of the National Associations why should a cargo owner not be able to pursue his action against the man who has been negligent, such as the Chief officers: the officer in charge of the cargo, or the officer of the watch in case of a collision, the officer of the watch who gave a wrong order? To those who put forward this argument, it is from a practical point of view nonsense.

39 Ibid., 598.
40 Ibid., 609.

What does the carrier want? What he thinks he can get, but I doubt very much whether he thinks he can get £100,000 worth out of the chief officer in charge of the cargo, or the chief engineer who is negligent. He knows them well not to be rich and he knows very well that unless the carrier stands behind the unfortunate officer, he will not get his shipment's worth. That is the practical reason for these actions and there is no injustice in saying to the cargo owner:

> we have made a bargain with you which is now embodied in the Hague Rules whereby we agree, we the carrier agree only for you to be allowed certain exemptions. But you, the cargo owner are not to get round that by saying: my chief officer is responsible and making me pay through him.

That is what anybody engaged in the shipping agency business knows. there are numerous cases in which that has been done and the result of this is that the ship-owner has had to pay far beyond the limit to the cargo owner because the action was taken again. the carrier, servants or agents should be protected for the reasons that I have given. Actions brought against servants or agents are, in practical effect, against the carrier himself. We do not, however, support that this should include independent practice for the reason that the carrier can protect himself by contract. The action was against the carrier and therefore he had to be protected. But we do ask that the carrier be protected from or against his own servants or agents which, in practice, really is confined to actions against his sea-going servants, that is officers serving in his ship and we also think that if there could possibly arise a case in which loss or damage to cargo was caused by the owners' own agents on shore – and I personally cannot think of such a case arising – that should be covered also. It is mainly the officers serving in his ship.[41]

**4.20** Shipping has changed in the meantime and that which was considered not possible by the British association began to be possible in practice. As previously mentioned, according to the Hague Rules, the only party performing the carriage was the carrier. The Rules make no provisions relating to the consequences of performance of the whole (or a part of the carriage) by a sub-carrier. As a consequence, the cargo claimant may sue the sub-carrier only in tort. The same applies with the Hague-Visby Rules. Article IV *bis* rule 2 of the Hague-Visby Rules provides that the defences and limits of liability provided for in the Rules shall extend to a servant or agent of the carrier as long as the servant or agent is not an independent contractor; i.e., sub-carrier.[42]

**4.21** Since the passage of COGSA,[43] however, the shipping industry has evolved; carriers are not the only ones exposed to such differences in liability law related to the carriage of goods at sea.[44] The Visby Protocol sought to keep pace with industry evolutions by giving attention to the advent of containerisation

41 Ibid., 600.

42 The Warsaw Convention also applies only to contractual carriers, as well as the CMR and COTIF-CIM.

43 As anticipated, the Carriage of Goods by Sea Act ('COGSA') is the United States enactment of the International Convention Regarding Bills of Lading, commonly known as the 'Hague Rules'.

44 Jean-Paul Rodrigue and Theo Notteboom, 'The Terminalization of Supply Chains: Reassessing the Role of Terminals in Port/Hinterland Logistical Relationships' (2009) 36 Maritime Policy and Management: The Flagship Journal of International Shipping and Port Research 2, 165.

in the international carriage of goods.[45] This movement ashore has revealed a crucial distinction: a participant that may be considered a third party in one international convention (e.g., a maritime related one) might in a different sector (e.g., road, rail or air) be deemed a carrier.[46] Hence, the industry's desire to expand the legislative framework.

## Conclusion

**4.22** Reviewing the Harter Act and Hague/Hague-Visby Rules, it is clear that the aim of both is to protect their parties (carrier and shipper). In this bilateral approach, the protection of third parties (if any exists) is construed in relation to the protection of the main parties and the vicarious liability of the parties for them as well as the commercial convenience.

**4.23** At the beginning of the nineteenth century – when, for the first time, the transport industry felt the need to allocate loss and protect parties involved in the carriage of goods by sea – there were only two parties involved and all legislative efforts were focussed on them. When the Harter Act and Hague Rules were written there was no representative of third parties at the table of negotiations. As a result, neither the Harter Act nor the Hague Rules have made any significant difference to the protection of third parties. In the intervening years, the industry and the world, more broadly, have changed dramatically.

45 Fernanda Ruiz, 'Legal Study of Sea Carrier Limitation of Liability According to Brazilian Law in Comparison to the Hague-Visby Regime' (2010) 1 Lawinter Review 1, 144.

46 Wyatt (n. 8).

CHAPTER 5

# Third party protection under the Hamburg Rules

## The Hamburg Rules and multimodalism

**5.1** The factual context of the shipping industry changed substantially between the drafting of the Hague Rules and the Hamburg Rules.[1] Containerisation revolutionised the carriage of goods by sea, and re-shaped the shipping industry as a whole. As Wyatt notes, the ability of containers to travel between different modes of transport (the foundation of multimodalism) further complicated the relationship between shippers and other parties.[2] Despite their versatility, containers can present more problems, especially if cargo is damaged or lost. Determining not only who is liable but also during which leg of the multimodal chain[3] the cargo was damaged or lost, and, consequently, which liability scheme is applicable, is now a difficult task.[4]

**5.2** The need arose, therefore, for a new convention that reflected the changing industry. In the 12 years between 1968 and 1980, two conventions and one protocol had been drafted. Considering that the international community was quite silent for the 44 years between the Hague Rules and the Visby Protocol, this relatively high level of activity can be reasonably construed as a response to demand from the international community for clarification and updates. Haak lists the failures of trying to solve the issue of multimodalism:

- 1967 Genoa Rules and 1969 Tokyo Rules
- 1972 Transport Combine de Merchandise
- 1980 Multimodal Transport Convention by the United Nations[5]

**5.3** The Hamburg Rules came into force on 1 November 1992 and were ratified despite not receiving full support from the international community. To

1 Adopted in Hamburg on 31 March 1978, the Hamburg Rules were drafted largely as an answer to the concerns of developing nations that The Hague rules were not adequate.

2 Marva Jo Wyatt, 'Contract Terms in Intermodal Transport: COGSA Comes Ashore' (1991–1992) 16 Tulane Maritime Law Journal 177.

3 Multimodal shipment is defined as the movement of cargo from point to point by various transportation modes on a single bill of lading, referred to as a through bill of lading.

4 See generally Wyatt (n. 2); Thomas R Denniston, Carter T Gunn and Alfred E Yudes, 'Liabilities of Multimodal Operators and Parties Other than Carriers and Shippers' (1989–1990) 64 Tulane Law Review 517.

5 Krijn Haak and Marian Hoeks, 'Intermodal Transport in the Field of Conflicting Conventions' (2004) 10 Journal of International Maritime Law 5.

date, 34 states have ratified the rules; a significant show of acceptance, but insufficient adoption to give uniformity.[6]

**5.4** The states that have ratified the Hamburg Rules are principally small developing countries. It is pertinent to mention here that, of the 20 states that became signatories to the Hamburg Rules, Barbados and Kenya were the only two to have signed either the Hague or the Hague-Visby Rules.[7]

**5.5** The Hamburg Rules represent a significant development in the industry's understanding of responsibility for cargo. Under tackle-to-tackle conventions, Wyatt explains, the parameters of the carrier's liability under the contract of carriage were easier to establish. However, carriers in that period were often engaged with multimodal activities. As the industry evolved to take a more port-to-port approach, responsibility for cargo during handling became a rather grey area. The aim of the UNCITRAL was to overcome this dissonance. For the purposes of this book, categories such as stevedores and terminal operators will be left unexamined.[8]

**5.6** The scope of application of the Hamburg Rules—and consequently the period of carrier responsibility[9] under them—has therefore been extended from tackle-to-tackle to port-to-port. The extension has been defined in accordance with modern cargo transport, in which shippers are normally not located immediately opposite the quay.[10]

**5.7** In relation to the carriage of goods by sea, the reference to multimodal contracts present in Article 1(6) of the Hamburg Rules merits discussion. This article essentially states that, when there is a multimodal contract of carriage, the Hamburg Rules apply only to the sea leg. The convention is the only sea carriage instrument that takes the possibility of multimodal carriage into account, thus recognising that a multimodal contract does not exclude the sea contract. The application of the liability regime of the Hamburg Rules covers the period during which the carrier is in charge of the goods at the port of loading and ending at the port of discharge.[11]

6 Francesco Berlingieri, 'A Comparative Analysis of the Hague-Visby Rules, the Hamburg Rules and the Rotterdam Rules' (Paper delivered at the General Assembly of the AMD, Marrakesh, 5–6 November 2009).

7 Albania, Austria, Barbados, Botswana, Burkina Faso, Burundi, Cameroon, Chile, Czech Republic, Dominica Republic, Egypt, Gambia, Georgia, Guinea, Hungary, Jordan, Kazakhstan, Kenia, Lebanon, Lesotho, Liberia, Malawi, Morocco, Nigeria, Paraguay, Romania, Saint Vincent and The Grenadines, Senegal, Sierra Leone, Syria, Tunisia, Uganda, Tanzania, Zambia. <www.uncitral.org/uncitral/en/uncitral_texts/transport_goods/Hamburg_status.html>. Updated as of 17 August 2016.

8 Wyatt (n. 2).

9 Article 4, Period of Responsibility, 'The responsibility of the carrier for the goods under this Convention covers the period during which the carrier is in charge of the goods at the port of loading, during the carriage and at the port of discharge'.

10 UNCTAD, 'The Economic and Commercial Implication of the Entry into Force of the Hamburg Rules and Multimodal Convention' 1991 TD/B/C.4/315/Rev 1 ('the UNCTAD Report'). In the same period another Convention was drafted, mainly dedicated to multilateral transport. In this Convention the same period of responsibility is stated as follows,

> Under the MTO instead, the period of responsibility has been extended to cover the entire period during which the goods are in the change of the MTO. The convention simply brings the legal regime into line with current commercial practice.

11 Iara Costa Conrado, 'Multimodal Aspect of the Rotterdam Rules: A Critical Analysis of the Liability of the MTO' (PhD thesis, Lund University, 2011).

## Third party protection and the Hamburg Rules

**5.8** The Hamburg Rules consider the contract of carriage by sea as being when the carrier undertakes to carry goods by sea from one port to another.[12] Additionally, the Hamburg Rules cast the responsibility of the carrier more expansively than the Hague-Visby Rules. It is nonetheless confined to the periods of time during which the carrier is in charge of the goods at the port of loading, during the carriage, and at the port of discharge.

**5.9** In terms of action to be considered, the Hamburg Rules introduced a new element not present in the Hague-Visby Rules; the carrier (and consequently his third parties) is liable not only for loss or damage, but also for delay.[13]

**5.10** Furthermore, the Hamburg Rules introduce the concept of an 'actual carrier', which, in turn, introduces the concept of multilateral performance of the carriage.[14] The article states that, in a case where the performance has been assigned to an actual carrier, the carrier is still responsible for the all carriage (including for the part performed by the actual carrier).[15] Both the carrier and actual carrier are liable and their liability is joint and several.[16]

**5.11** Article 10 of the Hamburg Rules is, in practice, a precursor to the performing parties (and maritime performing parties) provisions of the Rotterdam Rules. However, the article does not precisely state that the defences and limitations of the carrier are extended to the actual carrier. As per the proposal of the United States mentioned in the *travaux préparatoires*:

> The United States (para. 38) notes that the 'carrier' and the 'actual carrier' are distinguished under article 10 of the draft Convention. Further, paragraph 2 of this article, which imposes responsibility on the actual carrier, does not state that the latter is entitled to the same benefits and limitations of liability to which the carrier is entitled under the draft Convention. Nor is such an entitlement referred to in any other article of the draft Convention. In order to clarify that the actual carrier has the same entitlement as the carrier, the United States proposes (para. 38) that the following words be added at the end of the first sentence of this paragraph: 'and the defences and limitations of liability provided to the carrier according to the provisions of this Convention shall also be applicable to the actual carrier for the carriage performed by him'.[17]

**5.12** Regarding the limitation of liability, the Hamburg Rules increase the Hague-Visby Rules' limitation to 835 SDR per package or unit and 2.5 per kilogram.[18] As previously stated, the Hamburg Rules regulate (for the first time)

12 Article 1(6) also specifies that,

> a contract which involves carriage by sea and also involves carriage by sea and carriage by some other mean is deemed to be a contract of carriage by sea for the purposes of this Convention only in so far as it relates to the carriage by sea.

13 Article 5(1).
14 Article 10, liability of the carrier and actual carrier.
15 Or part of it.
16 Article 10(4).
17 Hamburg Rules, *Travaux Préparatoires* at 55.
18 Article 6(1).

the delay in delivery. As per Article 6 (b), this is limited to an amount equivalent to two and half times the freight payable for the goods delayed, but does not exceed the total freight payable under the contract of the carriage of goods by sea. The time bar set by the Hamburg Rules is two years.[19]

**5.13** Fujita explains that the Warsaw Convention of 1929—replaced by the Montreal Convention in 1999—also imposes liability for air carriage on contractual carriers.[20] The same applies to the Convention on the Contract for the International Carriage of Goods by Road (CMR), 1956.[21]

**5.14** In the Hamburg Rules, the carrier is responsible for the action of his servants or agents.[22] In contrast, the Hague-Visby Rules do not mention independent contractors at all. This leaves room for misinterpretation and, in doing so, creates complexity. In the decades preceding the Hamburg Rules, there was an increase in the number of cases in which cargo owners sued independent contractors instead of the carrier, and the independent contractors subsequently requested a Himalaya clause. In the Hamburg Rules, third party protection is regulated by Article 7(2), which states that:

> If such an action is brought against a servant or agent of the carrier, such servant or agent, if he proves that he acted within the scope of his employment, is entitled to avail himself of the defences and limits of liability which the carrier is entitled to invoke under this Convention.

**5.15** The UNCTAD report on the economic and commercial implications of the multimodal convention and of bringing the Hamburg Rules into force suggests that this rule aims to protect the carrier. The *ratio* is that shippers could sue agents and servants of the carrier under domestic laws. As often happens in the commercial world, the carrier might be bound under his contract with the agents or servants to hold them harmless from claims by the cargo interests. Therefore, without Article 7(2), the carrier could be, although not in a direct way, subject to liabilities beyond those incorporated in the Convention.[23]

**5.16** Berlingieri elaborates upon the rationale behind Article 7(2), highlighting the benefit to the carrier:

> Claims against servants and agents of the carrier are normally actions in tort because the servants and agents are not parties to the contract. This rule is intended to protect the carrier. Without such a provision, cargo interests could be entitled to claim compensation under national law from agents and servants of the carrier in cases where the carrier would be able do disclaim liability owning to his ability to invoke defences under the Hamburg Rules; or, the cargo interests might be able to

19 Article 20.

20 Convention for the Unification of Certain Rules Relating to International Carriage by Air, Signed at Warsaw on 12 October 1929, quoted in Tomotaka Fujita, 'Performing Parties and Himalaya Protection' (2009) Colloquium on the Rotterdam Rules 21 September 2009.

21 Convention on the Contract for the International Carriage of Goods by Road (CMR) (Geneva, 19 May 1956) quoted in Fujita, ibid.

22 Article 5(1).

23 The UNCTAD Report (n. 365) 187.

claim higher amounts of compensation than could be recovered from the carrier under the Hamburg Rules. The carrier might be bound under his contract with agents or servants to hold them harmless from claims by the cargo interests. Thus, without a provision such as that in Article 7 (2) the carrier could be indirectly subject to liabilities beyond those contained in the Hamburg Rules.[24]

**5.17** The Hamburg Rules do not specifically exclude independent contractors; to do so was regarded as superfluous, even ambiguous. 'Independent contractor' is primarily a common law term. In the common law system, however, servants and agents are never independent contractors. Chuah specifies that:

> The Hamburg Rules attempt to improve on the Hague-Visby Rules by specifically deleting the reference to independent contractors. Article 7 rule 2 provides that if an action is brought against a servant or agent of the carrier in respect of damage, loss or delay, that third party shall be entitled to avail himself of the defences and limits of liability which the carrier is entitled to invoke under the Rules. The question should not be perceived as a matter of fact but of law; the concept of an independent contractor will be evaluated on the basis of the applicable law of the contract.[25]

**5.18** According to Liang, any third parties under the Hamburg Rules – whether they be servants, agents, or independent contractors – are on the same footing. They are able to enjoy the same defences and limitations as the carrier. Likewise, there can be no dispute as to whether the servants of an independent contractor can enjoy the same defences and limitations as the carrier under the Hamburg Rules. As a result, Liang argues, the Himalaya clause is not needed under the Hamburg Rules.[26] This is seen as imprecise. Failing to address the term 'independent contractors' leaves a degree of uncertainty. Case law on the topic has shown that, with some exceptions, Courts have placed enormous emphasis on exactly who the provision aims to protect. The words 'independent contractor' has frequently been judged as too generic.

## Conclusion

**5.19** When dealing with third parties, the approach of international conventions from the last century leans towards bilateralism. The issue, however, has now evolved.

**5.20** This evolution started with the need to regulate the relationship between carrier and shipper, a need met initially by the Harter Act and subsequently by the Hague Rules and associated protocols. The arrival of multimodalism in the

24 Berlingieri (n. 6).

25 Jason Chuah, 'Impact of the Rotterdam Rules on the Himalaya Clause: The Port Terminal Operators' Case' in D Rhidian Thomas (ed.), *The Carriage of Goods by Sea under the Rotterdam Rules* (Informa 2010).

26 Chen Liang, 'Benefits and Burdens of Third Parties under Exception Clauses in Bills of Lading' (1999) 24 Tulane Maritime Law Journal 225.

1970s heralded further significant developments and an ensuing acknowledgement from the industry that regulation of this area needed updating.

**5.21** Up to that point, the motivation for third party protection was simply protecting the carrier. Those third parties were related to him, and they were therefore protected both for practical reasons and for vicarious liability. The Hamburg Rules improved the situation by citing the actual carrier. Additionally, the various categories of third parties have also evolved. Previously, the issue was limited to third parties such as first officers and captains; now the scope is much broader.

**5.22** Although many countries have yet to ratify them, the Hamburg Rules may improve third party protection. They take into consideration the position of the actual carrier, providing that all the provisions of the Convention governing the responsibility of the carrier also apply to the responsibility of the actual carrier for the carriage performed by them.[27] Similar provisions have been adopted by other international conventions related to other modes of carriage.[28] The Hamburg Rules provide that the period of responsibility of the carrier covers the period during which the carrier is in charge of the goods at the port of loading, during the carriage, and at the port of discharge. Nevertheless, the situation was still far from resolved:

> None of the existing instruments applies to the whole contract period when the carrier undertakes to take the goods in charge at the door of the shipper and to deliver them at the door of the consignee, as gradually has become more and more frequent with the advent of containers.[29]

**5.23** Thus, the need for a new convention – the Rotterdam Rules.

27 Article 10(2).

28 Article 270 of the Uniform Rules Concerning International Carriage of Goods by Rail 1980; Appendix to the Convention Concerning International Carriage by Rail, as amended by the Protocol of Modification of 1999 COTIF-CIM; Budapest Convention on the Contract for the International Carriage of Goods by Inland Waterway, 2000 CMNI (Article 4); Article 39 of The Convention for the Unification of Certain Rules for the International Carriage by Air 1999; The Montreal Convention 1999.

29 Berlingieri (n. 6).

CHAPTER 6

# Third party protection under the Rotterdam Rules

## The shadow of multimodalism

**6.1** It is anticipated that the Rotterdam Rules will still emerge as a convention focussing largely on the relationship between carrier and shipper. The performing party is simply someone who performs any of the carrier's obligations.[1] It is argued that the geographic approach proposed by the Rotterdam Rules does not do justice to the concept of the multilateral common enterprise.

**6.2** When the Rotterdam Rules were first drafted, the shipping landscape differed substantially to the times when previous papers had been drafted; most of the issues that the Hague, Hague-Visby, and Hamburg Rules sought to address had been solved. At the inception of the Rotterdam Rules, however, new problems had arisen that needed to be resolved by the international maritime community.[2] The issue most relevant to this book is the fact that, as a result of the container revolution, there are now parties involved in the carriage that previously were not. These parties are not secondary to the carrier and the shipper; they are primary actors.

**6.3** Furthermore, there is no longer only one category of third parties performing carriage but rather a variety of categories. Hence, the creation in the Rotterdam Rules of a general definition, i.e., 'performing parties'. This term both acknowledges and enforces through an international regulation one of this book's primary arguments: that carriage is 'performed' by many parties and not only by the carrier.

1 With the respect to the receipt, loading, handling, stowage, carriage, care, unloading, or delivery of goods.

2 In the United States, a draft text for an amended COGSA had already been made. In this context in fact, the International Chamber of Shipping outlines that:

> It will be recalled that this lacuna led to the initiative in the US in the early nineties to modernise the US COGSA of 1936, resulting in a draft text for an amended US COGSA. This caused great concern, because it represented regionalism which would have caused chaos to international trade and the Industry. The US was ultimately dissuaded from pursuing this initiative in favour of the proposal to develop an international, and uniform, solution under the aegis of UNCITRAL and since then, the US has been fully engaged in the successful negotiation of a new Convention.

Reported by the position paper of Chamber of Shipping: 'The Convention on Contracts for the International Carriage of Goods Wholly or Partly by Sea (The "Rotterdam Rules")' <www.uncitral.org/pdf/english/texts/transport/rotterdam_rules/ICS_PositionPaper.pdf>. Accessed 4 April 2013.

**6.4** The *travaux préparatoires* for the Rotterdam Rules involved not only carrier, shipper, and insurances of both parties but, for the first time, representatives of third parties as well.[3]

**6.5** Compared to previous conventions, a greater number of states and institutions were interested in the drafting of the Rotterdam Rules.[4] Other associations such as the International Federation of Freight Forwarders Associations (FIATA), the International Shipowners' Association (ISA), and the International Group of Protection & Indemnity Clubs (IGP&I) wield significant influence over international maritime circles. These organisations can affect maritime legislation on both a national and an international level, particularly where the parties that they seek to protect are concerned.

**6.6** The need for a new convention was voiced as early as 1996. At its 29th session, the UNCITRAL considered a proposal for its work programme to include a review of current practices and laws in the area of the international carriage of goods by sea, with a view to establishing the need for uniform rules where no such rules existed, and with a view to achieving greater uniformity of laws.[5]

**6.7** In the same session, the Commission decided on the involvement of the international organisations representing the commercial sectors involved in the carriage of goods by sea; including the Comité Maritime International (CMI), the International Chamber of Commerce (ICC), the International Union of Marine Insurance (IUMI), the aforementioned FIATA, the International Chamber of Shipping (ICS), and the International Association of Ports and Harbours.[6]

**6.8** In the 32nd session of the Commission, 1999, it was stated that the aim of the convention was uniformity and harmonisation.[7] The commission resolved that:

> The purpose of its work was to end any multiplicity of the regimes of liability applying to the carriage of goods by sea and to adjust maritime transport law in order to better meet the needs and realities of international maritime transport practices.[8]

**6.9** Inevitably the Rotterdam Rules emerged from the ashes of failed multimodal conventions. In doing so, it represented an acceptance of sorts that a real

3 Amongst others, FIATA (FIATA Position on the UN Convention on Contracts for the International Carriage of Goods Wholly or Partly by Sea (The 'Rotterdam Rules')' (UNCITRAL 11, Doc. MTI/507 Annex II August 2009) <www.uncitral.org/pdf/english/texts/transport/rotterdam_rules/FIATApaper.pdf>. Accessed 1 September 2011) and CLECAT. CLECAT represents European freight forwarders, logistics service providers and customs agents. CLECAT, position paper 'RE: 2008 – United Nations Convention on Contracts for the International Carriage of Goods Wholly or Partly by Sea – the 'Rotterdam Rules'' Brussels, 11 May 2009.

4 When the Hague, Hague-Visby, and Hamburg Rules were drafted, completed, and ratified, the European Union did not even exist.

5 United Nations Commission on International Trade Law, 'Report of the Working Group on Transport Law, 9th Session' (New York, 15–26 April 2002 A/CN.9/510).

6 Ibid.

7 Ibid.

8 Ibid.

solution to multimodalism had not been found. In this way, the Rotterdam Rules are a compromise between the need for a pure multimodal convention, the failure of the precedents, and the intention of parties and delegations to have their scope of application and limitation limited to the sea.

**6.10** The expansion of door-to-door operations has not gone uncontested. The CMI argued that earlier efforts at a multimodal legislative convention – namely the United Nations Convention on International Multimodal Transport of Goods (1980) – were not successful; their concern was that including multimodal transport in the draft instrument might compromise the acceptability of the new instrument.[9]

**6.11** In the same period, a study of the feasibility of the multimodal carriage was prepared by the United States.[10] As a result it was noted that the legislative regime applicable to maritime export-import operations should not treat the maritime leg in isolation and disregard the broader door-to-door transport operation. Moreover, the report stated that a new convention should respond to the reality of containerisation and multimodalism, technological instruments, and improvement of logistics.[11]

**6.12** Echoing this support for a new convention, organisations such as Baltic and International Maritime Council (BIMCO) and the International Group of P&I Clubs (IGP&I) argued that there would be little value added by developing another unimodal regime; it would, they argued, be remiss to ignore door-to-door transport. Providing that carriage by sea is contemplated at some stage, the provisions of the instrument should apply to the full scope of the carriage.[12]

**6.13** The representatives of P&Is therefore declared that adoption of 'a network system approach in the context of door-to-door carriage [is] an approach that respects the unimodal regimes and with which we agree'.[13]

**6.14** The result is a highly compromised 'wet' multimodal regime. The Rotterdam Rules govern door-to-door transport and what is already called 'wet multimodal transport', i.e., any multimodal transport that includes a maritime leg.

**6.15** As previously stated, the convention acknowledges that the simple bilateral concept of carriage has expanded. The expression 'under a contract of carriage' should be replaced with 'in the context of transport operations' or 'in

9 Ibid.

10 UNCTAD Secretariat, 'Review of Maritime Transport, 2003' (United Nations Conference on Trade and Development, Geneva UNCTAD/RMT/2003).

11 United Nations Commission on International Trade Law, 'Report of the Working Group on Transport Law' (n. 389).

12 United Nations Commission on International Trade Law, 'Report of Working Group III (Transport Law) on the Work of Its Tenth Session: Comments from the Representative of the International Chamber of Shipping and the Baltic and International Maritime Council on the Scope of the Draft Instrument' (Thirty-sixth Session Vienna, 30 June–11 July 2003 A/CN.9/525) Annex 1, 36.

13 Ibid. Comments from the representative of the International Group of Protection & Indemnity Clubs' Annex 2, 37.

performing the transport operations', in order to more clearly indicate the relation of different performing parties to the 'contract of carriage'. It was specified, however, that the performing party was not a party to the contract of carriage between the shipper and the contracting carrier.[14]

**6.16** The CMI discussion also highlights the need for a regime that includes a carriage of goods by sea stage, regardless the other modes of transport:

> Since much sea transportation in the containerised field involves movement by more than one mode of transport, it is often difficult, if not impossible, to see whether the movement on land is subsidiary to that by sea. It is therefore considered by many that any future instrument should contain provisions applicable to the full scope of carriage irrespective of whether or not the movement on land may be deemed subsidiary to that by sea, providing carriage by sea is contemplated at some stage.[15]

**6.17** The Rotterdam Rules involve compromise, the extent and significance of which has been cited as a concern during the preparatory work. Germany's delegates raised serious concerns:

> . . . about the broad scope of the draft convention and, in particular, the establishment of special rules applying to multimodal transport contracts that provided for carriage by sea, which would lead to a fragmentation of the laws on multimodal transport contracts. To avoid that outcome, her delegation wished to see the draft convention applied solely to maritime transport contracts.[16]

**6.18** From a different view, the delegation of the United States argued that the 'maritime plus' approach was best suited to the manner in which the business community operated.[17] As explained by representatives of UNECE: 'The extension of the liability coverage from the tackle-to-tackle carriage under the Hague-Visby Rules or port-to-port carriage under the Hamburg Rules to door-to-door carriage is said to respond to the reality of containerised transport of goods'.[18]

**6.19** However, the merits of an approach such as this are debatable because the instrument does not consider the views of the parties involved in modes of transport other than sea, nor those of the shippers, who create the initial demand for the transport. Instead, it only reflects the view of the maritime transport-related interests.[19]

14 United Nations Commission on International Trade Law 'Report of the Working Group on Transport Law' (n. 388).

15 Comité Maritime International (CMI) Yearbook 2000, 113 <http://comitemaritime.org/Uploads/Yearbooks/Yearbook+2000.pdf>. Accessed 24 January 2014.

16 United Nations Commission on International Trade Law, 'Summary Record of the 865th Meeting' (Forty-first Session 2008A/CN.9/SR.865).

17 Ibid. Only transport by sea.

18 United Nations Economic Commission for Europe and Inland Transport Committee, 'Possibilities for Reconciliation and Harmonisation of Civil Liability Regimes Governing Combined Transport' (Thirty-seventh Session, 18 and 19 April 2002 TRANS/WP.24/2002/5).

19 Ibid.

**6.20** To date, 25 nations[20] have signed the rules. There have been only four ratifications.[21]

## Third party protection under the Rotterdam Rules

**6.21** The Rotterdam Rules have a more expanded scope of work and the contract of carriage is considered as a contract in which a carrier, against the payment of freight, undertakes to carry goods from one place to another.[22]

**6.22** The multilateral aspect of the convention and the involvement of third parties is shown immediately; as Article 12 states, the period of responsibility of the carrier for the goods under this convention begins when the carrier or a performing party receives the goods for carriage and ends when the goods are delivered.[23]

**6.23** Moreover, having affirmed that the carrier is liable for the breach of its obligation under this convention, Article 18 of the Rules[24] specifies that this breach can be caused by an act or an omission by three different categories of party: first, any performing party (thus delineating the concept of a network of people working together)[25]; second, the master and the crew of the ship[26]; and third, employees of the carrier or a performing party.[27] Last, it addresses any other person that performs or undertakes to perform any of the carrier's obligations under the contract of carriage.[28] This provision is residual, as it does not place any party performing the job beyond the carrier's responsibility. It provides, however, that the central party of the convention is the carrier. As the last sentence of the article states: 'to the extent that the person acts, either directly or indirectly, at the carrier's request or under the carrier's supervision or control'. Therefore, it recognises an enterprise of parties who nevertheless operate under the carrier's direction.

**6.24** Like the Hamburg Rules, the Rotterdam Rules also regulate (together with loss or damage) liability for delay.[29] Regarding the limitation of liability,

20 Armenia, Cameroon, Congo, Democratic Republic of Congo, Denmark, France, Gabon, Ghana, Greece, Guinea, Guinea Bissau, Luxembourg, Madagascar, Mali, Netherlands, Niger, Nigeria, Norway, Poland, Senegal, Spain, Sweden, Switzerland, Togo, United States of America <www.uncitral.org/uncitral/en/uncitral_texts/transport_goods/rotterdam_status.html>. Accessed 20 December 2018.

21 Spain in 2011, Togo in 2012, Congo in 2014, Cameroon in 2017 updated as of December 20, 2018.

22 The Article 1 definition also specifies that it is compulsory for the contract to provide for a sea leg and that it may have a leg by another mode of carriage.

23 Period of responsibility of the carrier.

24 Liability of the carrier for other persons.

25 Article 18(a).

26 Article 18(b) in line with The Hague and Hamburg Rules where the carrier is responsible for his immediate employees.

27 Article 18(c), extending vicarious liability to all the employees of the performing parties and eliminating the difference between the party itself and its employees.

28 Article 18(d).

29 Article 17. While Article 60 specifies that

> Subject to article 61, paragraph 2, compensation for loss of or damage to the goods due to delay shall be calculated in accordance with article 22 and liability for economic loss due to delay is limited to an amount equivalent to two and one-half times the freight payable on the

the Rotterdam Rules increase it to 875 SDR per package or unit and 3 SDR per kilogram. The time bar is two years.[30]

**6.25** In terms of third parties, the Rotterdam Rules expand the concept of actual carrier with the idea of 'performing parties'. A performing party is a person, other than the carrier, who performs or undertakes to perform any of the carrier's obligations under a contract of carriage. The obligations are in respect to specific actions that have been listed as follows: receipt, loading, handling, stowage, carriage, keeping, care, unloading, and/or delivery of the goods.

**6.26** In order to be qualified as a performing party such a person has to act either directly or indirectly at the carrier's request or under the carrier's supervision or control.[31] The Working Group noted that the purpose of the definition of 'performing party' was to regulate three different issues:

1. Governing parties that performed the carrier's activities under a contract of carriage, usually sub-contractors, and their joint and several liability with the contracting carrier
2. Regulating the vicarious liability of the performing party for its employees or others working in its service
3. In conjunction with drafted Articles 4 and 19, protecting the so-called 'Himalaya clause' for such employees, agents, or sub-contractors[32]

**6.27** The transformation from actual carrier to performing party[33] has been a work in progress, beginning with the CMI's preparatory work and continuing with the UNCITRAL work. During the first draft prepared by the CMI, the definition was of a performing carrier and not a performing party:

> A person who performs, undertakes to perform, or procures to be performed any of a contracting carrier's responsibilities under a contract of carriage, to the extent that the person acts, either directly or indirectly, at the request of, or under

goods delayed. The total amount payable pursuant to this article and article 59, paragraph 1, may not exceed the limit that would be established pursuant to article 59, paragraph 1, in respect of the total loss of the goods concerned.

30 Article 62.

31 Article 6(b) 'Performing party' does not include any person that is retained, directly or indirectly, by a shipper, by a documentary shipper, by the controlling party or by the consignee instead of by the carrier.

32 United Nations Commission on International Trade Law, 'Report of Working Group III (Transport Law) on the Work of Its Nineteenth Session' (Fortieth Session Vienna, 25 June–12 July 2007 A/CN.9/621).

33 For the definition of 'performing party' it is useful to follow some of the reasoning from the CMI (CMI Yearbook 2001, 539 <www.comitemaritime.org/uploads/yearbooks/ybk_2001.pdf>. Accessed 4 January 2014) as follows, The 'performing party' definition is limited to those who are involved in the carrier's core responsibilities of carriage, handling, custody, or storage of the goods. Thus, ocean carriers, inland carriers, stevedores, and terminal operators, for example, would be included under either 'performing party' definition. In contrast, a security company that guards a container yard, an intermediary responsible only for preparing documents on the carrier's behalf, and a ship yard that repairs a vessel (thus ensuring seaworthiness) on the carrier's behalf would not be included.

the supervision or control of, the contracting carrier, regardless of whether that person is a party to, identified in, or has legal responsibility under the contract of carriage.[34]

**6.28** The *Comité* states that the term 'performing carrier' does not include any person (other than the contracting carrier) who is retained by a shipper or consignee, or is an employee, servant, agent, contractor, or sub-contractor of a person (other than the contracting carrier) who is retained by a shipper or consignee.[35]

**6.29** In comparison to the Hamburg Rules, the class of 'performing carriers' not only includes the contracting carrier's sub-contractors but also the entire line of subsidiary persons; parties who perform the contract (i.e., the sub-contractor's sub-contractors, that party's sub-contractors, and so on, indefinitely).[36]

**6.30** The definition immediately provides an important clarification; that 'performing carriers' are only those who work, directly or indirectly, for the contracting carrier. If the cargo's interests have a servant or agent performing a task that would otherwise be the contracting carrier's responsibility under the contract of carriage, that servant or agent does not thereby become a performing carrier.[37]

**6.31** After having established the general concept of performing party, it should be noted that only a specific category of a performing party is liable under the convention, namely, a 'maritime performing party'.[38]

**6.32** Article 19 of the Rules explains that the maritime performing party – in essence, a performing party that operates exclusively between port of loading and port of discharging[39] – is liable while in custody of the goods and at any time to the extent that it was participating in the performance of any of the activities contemplated by the contract of carriage.[40] This article specifically excludes from the provision master, crew of the ship, and employees of the carrier or of maritime performing parties.[41]

**6.33** Traditional transport conventions have focussed on the liability of the carrier.[42] On the contrary, according to the Rotterdam Rules (pursuant to Article 19)[43] a maritime performing party is subject to the obligations and liabilities imposed on the carrier's defences and limits of liability as provided for

34 CMI Yearbook 2000 (n. 15) 117.

35 Ibid.

36 Ibid., 118. Probably one of the first definitions of performing party.

37 Ibid., 119.

38 Which is essentially a concept similar to the actual carrier of the Hamburg Rules.

39 'Maritime performing party' means a performing party to the extent that it performs or undertakes to perform any of the carrier's obligations during the period between the arrival of the goods at the port of loading of a ship and their departure from the port of discharge of a ship.

40 Article 19(h)(iii).

41 Article 19(4).

42 Tomotaka Fujita, 'Performing Parties and Himalaya Protection' (2009) Colloquium on the Rotterdam Rules 21 September 2009.

43 Liability of a maritime performing party.

in this Convention. However, the Rotterdam Rules limit this liability to the port of loading and the port of discharge.[44] It was noted that the definition of 'maritime performing party' referred back to the definition of 'performing party' and thus also includes employees, agents, and sub-contractors. It was suggested that, as formulated, the definition could have the unintended effect of allowing any possible contractual liability of a maritime performing party under the contract of carriage to be imposed directly on an employee, agent, or sub-contractor. Similarly, it was held that the definition of 'performing party' should be reconsidered in order to avoid such an unintended consequence.

**6.34** In response, it was explained that the reason that the definition had been framed so broadly was in order to avoid the privity of contract problem that had arisen in the jurisprudence with respect to Himalaya clauses. This allowed for such protection under the clause only for sub-contractors, but not for those further down the chain of contracts.[45]

**6.35** In exchange for their liability under the convention and pursuant to Article 4, the maritime performing party receives the same defence and limitation of liability of the carrier (whether in contract, tort or otherwise).

**6.36** During the draft, the committee supported the provision establishing that the general policy behind Paragraph 4 was to afford employees, agents, and sub-contractors of the carrier and maritime performing parties the full protection of the rights, defences, and limits of liability available to the carrier under the drafted convention for any breach of contractual obligations or duties. In the event that an action under the draft convention was made directly against it, a protection, which was often sought through the insertion of 'Himalaya' clauses in transport documents, would be offered.[46]

**6.37** It is evident from these distinctions that those drafting the Rules wished to draw a clear geographic distinction between someone who works at the port and someone who does not. In one of the first drafts of the convention, the notion of 'non-maritime performing party' was also drafted in order to make the difference even clearer: 'Non-maritime performing party' means a performing party who performs any of the carrier's responsibilities prior to the arrival of the goods at the port of loading or after the departure of the goods from the port of discharge'.[47]

**6.38** In contrast to previous conventions where the rationale for the protection of third parties was the carrier's vicarious liability and the carrier's benefit; the rationale for third party protection under the Rotterdam Rules has changed from benefiting the carrier to benefiting third parties. The reason is that specific categories of performing parties (maritime) have the same liability of the carrier.

44 Article 19(b).

45 United Nations Commission on International Trade Law 'Report of Working Group III' (n. 389).

46 Ibid.

47 United Nations Commission on International Trade Law, Working Group III (Transport Law)' (13th Session New York, 3–14 May 2004 A/CN.9/WG.III/WP.36).

In this case, the rationale for the protection of the maritime performing party is that they have the same liability as the carrier, and they therefore must have the same limitation. The second category defined by the Rotterdam Rules includes employees of the carrier and maritime performing parties, together with master, crew, and people working onboard. As Fujita states, they need a different justification because they are not liable under the convention. In this case the justification is purely economic; they depend on the carrier or maritime performing party, and therefore it would mean that the cargo owner could still null the provision, suing the employee of the carrier instead of the carrier.[48] This feature supports an important argument here; specific categories of third parties are freed from carrier dependency and become part of the business.

**6.39** Berlingieri explains that, when considering whether and to what extent the sub-contractors of the carrier (called 'performing parties') should be subject to the Rotterdam Rules and liable to be sued by the shipper or consignee, it was decided that it would be convenient to do so only in respect of services rendered at sea or in the ports. Therefore, the notion of a 'maritime performing party' was created, thereby incorporating in the Rotterdam Rules the principles on which the Himalaya clause is based.[49] It is important to note that the parties under the convention pursuant to Article 20 are jointly and severally liable.[50]

**6.40** In the Rotterdam Rules different categories of third parties (grouped into the general category of maritime performing party) are, for the first time, protected. This confirms not only the Rotterdam Rules' acceptance of the concept of multilateralism, but also how integrated and sophisticated the world of trade has become. It should also be acknowledged that the role and responsibility of a shipper are completely different from that stated in the Harter Act or Hague Rules, wherein it was limited only to someone who entered into a contract with the carrier. The role of shipper is now much more involved, in accordance with the fact that carriage is now a network of interests.[51]

48 See generally Fujita (n. 42).

49 Francesco Berlingieri, 'A Comparative Analysis of the Hague-Visby Rules, the Hamburg Rules and the Rotterdam Rules' (Paper delivered at the General Assembly of the AMD, Marrakesh, 5–6 November 2009).

50 Article 20 states that,

> 1. If the carrier and one or more maritime performing parties are liable for the loss of, damage to, or delay in delivery of the goods, their liability is joint and several but only up to the limits provided for under this Convention. 2. Without prejudice to article 61, the aggregate liability of all such persons shall not exceed the overall limits of liability under this Convention.

51. Article 34 also regulates liability of the shipper for its third parties as follows,

> The shipper is liable for the breach of its obligations under this Convention caused by the acts or omissions of any person, including employees, agents and sub-contractors, to which it has entrusted the performance of any of its obligations, but the shipper is not liable for acts or omissions of the carrier or a performing party acting on behalf of the carrier, to which the shipper has entrusted the performance of its obligations.

Chuah (n. 53) further enhances the role of the shipper in the Rotterdam Rules and its involvement in the carriage operations: 'In a tackle-to-tackle type of arrangement, it is

**6.41** Article 4, paragraph 2 of the Rotterdam Rules (applicability of defences and limits of liability) states that:

> Any provision of this Convention that may provide a defence for the shipper or the documentary shipper applies in any judicial or arbitral proceeding, whether founded in contract, in tort, or otherwise, that is instituted against the shipper, the documentary shipper, or their sub-contractors, agents or employees.[52]

**6.42** In this context, says Smeele, the independent contractor is not a maritime performing party – even though the Rotterdam Rules enable parties to the contract of carriage to agree that cargo loading, discharging, handling, and stowing are to be performed by the parties interested in the cargo – and therefore that the cargo owners may delegate the performance of these duties to an independent contractor.[53]

## Issues regarding third party protection

**6.43** As Fujita clearly explains in the colloquium on the Rotterdam Rules: 'There are many people other than the carrier who are involved in transport of goods'.[54] This is acknowledged by the Rotterdam Rules but, as previously stated, the Rules have given rise to two categories, distinguished according to where they perform their services. If services are performed in the port area and/or during the voyage between the ports of loading and discharge, protection is granted by the Rotterdam Rules. If services are performed outside of the port area or sea voyage, no protection is granted by the Rules, but provisions of other international unimodal conventions or national law will still apply.[55]

**6.44** As Baldwin notes, through Article 4(1), the Rotterdam Rules extend the scope of the carrier's protection to maritime performing parties, the master,

probable that the port terminal operator actually is the *shipper's* independent contractor. Under the Rotterdam Rules, the shipper is indebted to the carrier a number of significant duties including the duty to deliver cargo packed in an appropriate manner, the duty to cooperate with the Carrier and the duty to provide relevant handling instructions. The shipper will be liable for breaches caused by the acts or omissions of any person, including employees, agents, and sub-contractors, to which it has entrusted the performance of any of its obligations'.

52 Article 4, para 2.

53 Frank Smeele, 'The Maritime Performing Party in the Rotterdam Rules 2009' (2011) European Journal of Commercial Contract Law 1. Chuah specifies that 'In the circumstances, the Rotterdam Rules leave it to the shipper and his employee agent or independent contractor to make provisions for a Himalaya clause' (Jason Chuah, 'Impact of the Rotterdam Rules on the Himalaya Clause: The Port Terminal Operators' Case' in D Rhidian Thomas (ed.), *The Carriage of Goods by Sea Under the Rotterdam Rules* (Informa 2010)), 1, 72–86.

54 Fujita (n. 42).

55 See David Moran Bovio, 'Ocean Carriers' Duty of Care to Cargo in Port: The Rotterdam Rules of 2009' (2008) 32 Fordham International Law Journal 4, 1160. Many legal systems have differentiated further within the group of independent contractors of the carrier and have created separate categories and protective rules for sub-carriers, stevedores, pilots, and other independent contractors.

crew, and other categories performing services on board the ship. These, however, may not be servants or agents of the carrier: for instance when the carrier is a time charterer and to employees of the carrier or of a maritime performing party.[56]

**6.45** Article 1(7)(d) and Article 19(1)(b) state that the definition and liability of an MPP apply only 'during the period between the arrival of the goods at the port of loading [...] and their departure from the port of discharge'.

**6.46** It is clear, therefore, that the definition of a port – along with its boundaries and delimitation – are crucial to the implementation of the Rotterdam Rules. Atamer suggests that cargo owners will now focus on investigating where the landside limits of the port are to be drawn.[57]

**6.47** The concept of a 'port' has inevitably changed since the Harter Act. Logistics have connected ports with inland infrastructure. Numerous ports are nowadays in the process of being privatised. Hence, two considerations arise: first, owing to the port's logistics, a geographical dimension of the port can be expanded in the future; second, the privatisation of ports is likely to encourage a commercial perspective on the dimensions of a port, rather than a geographical view based on state or territory.

**6.48** Today, the private sector plays an important role in port management. The concept of a port is evolving from what was once a specific area under state control into something more akin to a managed company.[58] Private investments are integral in helping ports operate at maximum efficiency.[59] The Rotterdam Rules leave boundary regulation up to the relevant national law. So, as far as the Rotterdam Rules are concerned, the 'port phase' of the goods is one of many identifiable during the transport process. Determination of the limits of each transport section is possible only on a case-by-case basis. Any arbitration will be influenced by the geography of the port in question, the modality of the goods, other details of the contract, and, most importantly, the law regulating the port.[60] Chuah is concerned that:

> The word 'port' is not explicitly defined. This lack of a definition would seem to be intentional but problematic. A question is whether cargo consolidation areas would also count as the port area. In the light of the increasing need for cargo consolidation near a port, it seems unrealistic to make an artificial distinction between inland and port without looking at the logistic chain.[61]

56 Kevin Baldwin, 'COGSA Carriers' (2010–2011) 35 Tulane Maritime Law Journal 391.

57 Kerim Atamer, 'Construction Problems in the Rotterdam Rules Regarding the Performing and Maritime Performing Parties' (2010) 41 Journal of Maritime Law and Commerce, 4.

58 Holman Fenwick Willan, 'Global Investment in Ports and Terminals' (June 2011) <www.hfw.com/downloads/HFW%20Ports%20and%20Terminals%20Report%20%5BA4%5D%20February%202013.pdf>. Accessed 9 February 2013.

59 Ibid.

60 Bovio (n. 55).

61 Chuah (n. 53).

**6.49** The difficulty in defining the port area emerged also during the working group that in fact shows:

> Concerns were raised, however, that in the case of very large or geographically proximate ports, or different ports that were administered under a single authority, it would be very difficult to determine whether a performing party were performing its services 'exclusively within a port area', and thus very difficult to determine who qualified as 'maritime performing parties.' Support was expressed for those concerns, including some support for the suggestion that the Working Group might wish to consider excluding altogether inland carriers from operation of the draft convention. In response, it was noted that the Working Group had previously agreed to leave the determination of what constituted a 'port' to local authorities and the judiciary, since views on that topic differed widely according to geographic conditions.[62]

**6.50** In their final version, the Rotterdam Rules therefore incorrectly rely on the geographic approach. Analysis of the Working Group, however, clearly shows that another 'functional' approach was considered in creating the definitions of a 'maritime performing party'.[63] There are no specific references to this functional approach, but within the first draft of the CMI one can identify a more conceptual approach to dealing with the issue. At the time, the CMI expressed the concept that a performing carrier (the original definition for a performing party) should be generally entitled – without differentiating the categories according to the geographic aspect of their job – to the same rights as the contracting carrier. The CMI continues, stating that this gives performing carriers the benefits of a broad Himalaya clause without the need to include a Himalaya clause in the contract of carriage or the transport document.[64] It is clear that, in this sense, the geographic distinction was not supposed to be included in the Rules at that time.

**6.51** Another solution proposed during the preparatory work (and one that could be commercially viable) was channelling the liability to only the main

62. United Nations Commission on International Trade Law, 'Report of Working Group III (Transport Law) on the Work of Its Tenth Session: Comments from the Representative of the International Chamber of Shipping and the Baltic and International Maritime Council on the Scope of the Draft Instrument' (Thirty-sixth Session Vienna, 30 June–11 July 2003 A/CN.9/525) Annex 1, 36.

63 According to the Report of Working Group III (Transport Law) on the work of its 12th session (Vienna, 6–17 October 2003 A/CN.9/544), para 30 states

> By way of presentation, the Working Group heard that two approaches had been envisaged in creating the definitions, namely, a functional approach and a geographical approach. The geographical approach had been chosen as the simpler of the two. It was proposed that the geographical area for the definition could be the 'port', although it was conceded that a definition of 'port' could pose considerable difficulties, and would likely be defined with reference to national law.

Para 31 states

> There was general agreement in the Working Group that these definitions were a good basis for continuing the discussion on how to define maritime and non maritime performing parties. There was general agreement that a geographical approach to the definition was appropriate, and there was support for the suggestion that inland movements within a port should be included in the definition of a maritime performing party, as, for example, in the case of a movement by truck from one dock to the next.

64 CMI Yearbook 2000 (n. 34) 135.

party of the convention. Here, it is relevant to report the position of the International Chamber of Shipping. In the CMI *travaux préparatoires:*

> The ICS proposes that the convention should only deal with the liability of the contracting carrier. Whether or not the carrier in some cases sub-contracts part of the transportation to another carrier and in another cases performs the whole carriage should not change the legal position of the shipper. The ICS argues that channeling the liability only to one party will avoid multiparty suits that are usually very protracted and difficult to settle. The ICS then suggests that the contracting carrier will then decide whether exercise his right of recourse against its contractors. Finally ICS reports that also the shippers representatives expressed the preference for the convention to deal only with the liability of the contracting party.[65]

**6.52** In this respect, the proposal had the support of the IGP&I that reinstated the concept:

> The IG reiterates its belief that liability under the DOI should be 'channelled' to the contracting carrier alone and that the liability and protection of performing parties should be addressed through contractual indemnities. The concept of providing for the liability of performing parties as defined, seems to be an unnecessary complication of a regime the objective of which should be to simplify in so far as possible the carriage of goods involving a sea leg.[66]

**6.53** The International Group also reported the example of the International Conventions on Civil liability for Oil Pollution Damage (CLC) where the concept of channelling liability to a single party in international convention has proved to be successful.[67] The NitLeague and the World Shipping Council follow the same rationale:

> The Instrument should not provide a right to sue a party performing the obligations of the carrier (see CMI Draft Articles 6.3.2(a)(i) and (ii). The right of suit for cargo claims should be solely against the carrier issuing the contract of carriage. Agreement to a higher liability limit or greater responsibilities by the contracting carrier should not be binding on a performing party, unless the performing party agrees to such higher limit or responsibility. Supplemental Submission Performing Parties. The parties agreed that the Instrument should not provide a right to bring an action for cargo loss or damage against a party that performs the obligations of the contracting carrier. Rather, all such actions must be commenced against the contracting carrier. The contracting carrier is responsible for the acts and omissions of any party that performs the duties of the carrier (including sub-contractors and agents of performing parties.[68]

**6.54** Though the channelling of responsibility represents an interesting alternative, its lack of implementation renders it only theoretical. In practice, the less

65 CMI Yearbook 2001, 139 <www.comitemaritime.org/uploads/yearbooks/ybk_2001.pdf>. Accessed 8 January 2014. The International Chamber of Shipping aims to have only the contracting carrier in the instrument and not the performing carriers.

66 Ibid., 459.

67 Ibid.

68 Same for NITL and WSC. See CMI Yearbook 2001, ibid., 139.

desirable geographic approach has been adopted. Chuah contends that favouring a geographic test of what constitutes the maritime side of its coverage is contrary to how the shipping industry views cargo logistics.[69]

**6.55** Furthermore, Atamer draws attention to problems hidden behind the definitions and wording of performing parties and maritime performing parties. First, Articles 1(6)(a)(i) (for performing parties) and 1(7)(a)(i) (for maritime performing parties) refer to such parties as any *person* other than the carrier. The term 'person' does not offer clear guidance on whether or not legal entities are supposed to be included in this group.[70] Second, any person described in Article 12(2) who fails to act according to the 'carrier's request, supervision, or control' is denied the carrier's vicarious liability and is therefore unable to be held liable as a maritime performing party under Article 19.[71] Third, any person involved solely in 'keeping' the goods does not, on a literal interpretation, qualify as a performing party nor as a maritime performing party.[72]

**6.56** Smeele expresses discomfort at the idea of excluding independent contractors who simply assist in the performance of others' carriage or cargo-related obligations without undertaking any of these obligations themselves. The same is true for independent contractors who perform other of the carrier's duties under a contract of carriage that are related to carriage or cargo-handling only indirectly, such as issuing and arranging documentation for transport; equipping, supplying, and crewing the ship; and exercising due diligence to keep the vessel in a seaworthy state.[73]

**6.57** Smeele goes on to point out the uncertainty within the Rules of the position of other parties, such as: suppliers of containers, ship repair yards, and repairers who perform the carrier's duty to exercise due diligence to make and maintain the cargo holds in which the cargo is to be carried.[74]

**6.58** The confusion regarding the definitions of port and the different positions of maritime or non-maritime performing parties has also influenced the approval of various categories of third parties. Without aiming to provide an exhaustive list, it is helpful here to provide examples in the form of inland carriers, port terminals, and freight forwarders.

### *The position of inland carriers*

**6.59** The position of the inland carrier[75] is one of the most controversial. The proposal of the United States regarding the definition of 'maritime performing

69 Chuah (n. 53).
70 Atamer (n. 57).
71 Ibid.
72 Ibid.
73 Smeele (n. 53).
74 Ibid.
75 During the preparatory work the term 'inland performing party' was also proposed as alternative for the words 'inland carrier'. United Nations Commission on International Trade Law Thirty-seventh session (New York, 14 June–2 July 2004 A/CN.9/544).

party' during the Working Group helps to better understand the position. The proposal states that:

> It has been suggested that the definition of 'maritime performing party' (draft article 1 (7) of the draft convention) should be edited to clarify that a rail carrier, even if it performs services that might be considered the carrier's responsibilities after the arrival of the goods at the port of loading or prior to the departure of the goods from the port of discharge, should be considered a non-maritime performing party.[76]

**6.60** From this suggestion some understanding can be drawn. Countries with a strong tradition of carriage of goods by rail – the United States, for instance – are reluctant for a rail carrier to be classed as a maritime performing party, even if they perform carriers' responsibilities.[77] In the final version, this suggestion is slightly different: 'An inland carrier is a maritime performing party only if it performs or undertakes to perform its services exclusively within a port area'.[78] It can be very difficult not to include an inland carrier in the definition of 'performs or undertakes to perform any of the carrier's obligations during the period between the arrival of the goods at the port of loading of a ship and their departure from the port of discharge of a ship'. In a door-to-door contract, an inland carrier can go beyond the line of a port and, if goods are damaged, the fact that they have exceeded a line makes the difference in terms of protection that they can rely on. This test is purely geographical and not make room for commercial perspectives.

**6.61** As previously stated, establishing what does and does not constitute a port area is a complicated process. Thanks to multimodal carriage, logistics, and new needs within the industry, the meaning of the term 'port' is in flux. In a few years, today's inland carrier could be a maritime performing party as a result of the geographic expansion of ports.[79]

**6.62** Moreover, amid such confusion, the inland carrier might prefer to keep its position as a non-maritime performing party and keep the protection that the CMR allows. According to Clarke, 'CMR, it has been said, works well enough … There is little evidence that road carriers, their customers or trade organizations that represent them today want change'.[80]

**6.63** Conversely many inland carriers, if sued directly in tort, are likely to benefit from an international convention governing transport, such as the CMR.

76 United Nations Commission on International Trade Law, 'Transport Law: Preparation of a Draft Convention on the Carriage of Goods (Wholly or Partly) (by Sea): Proposal of the United States of America on the Definition of 'Maritime Performing Party'' (Nineteenth Session New York, 16–27 April 2007).

77 It is also relevant to know that the United States signed the Rotterdam Rules on the first day, indicating their support (however no ratification has been made).

78 Article 1(7) Rotterdam Rules.

79 See Holman Fenwick Willan, 'What Impact Will the Rotterdam Rules Have on Shipowners?' July 2010. This article first appeared in the July 2010 issue of Britannia News Conventions Supplement and is reproduced with their kind permission <www.britannia.co.uk>. Accessed 9 February 2013.

80 Bevan Marten, 'Multimodal Transport Reform and the European Union: A Treaty Change Approach' (2011–2012) 36 Tulane Maritime Law Journal 741.

There are countries, however, to which no international convention applies, and in which national law may not provide protection against a claim in tort to an inland carrier. Therefore, third parties might need contractual protection – i.e., from a Himalaya clause – that avoids significant liability for a rail carrier, as in *Kirby*.[81] Thus, in this instance, any attempts to replace the Himalaya clause with what has been called 'Himalaya Protection' under the Rotterdam Rules will surely fail.

**6.64** The decision to exclude the inland carrier from the Rotterdam Rules appears to have emerged from the Working Group. According to their report, it was proposed that rail carriers should be excluded from the definition of 'maritime performing party' even when performing services within a port. In support of this, certain quarters suggested that such an exemption was warranted, given the practical reality; though rail carriers might appear similar to other inland carriers – in that they collect cargo or deliver it for carriage within a port area – rail carriers differ dramatically from other inland carriers. Ultimately, their services exist almost solely for the purpose of moving goods great distances into or out of a port, not simply moving goods from one place to another within a port.[82]

**6.65** This explains the intention of excluding only the rail carrier, and it is seen as fundamentally wrong because it excludes a category of third party solely because they overrun the port boundaries.

### *The position of terminal operators*

**6.66** Terminal operators represent another controversial category. They fall within the definition of a 'maritime performing party' and therefore jointly and severally liable with the carrier under the Rules for loss or damage insofar as the occurrence causing such loss or damage meets the requirements of Article 19(1)(b). Terminal operators have no liability under the Hague, Hague-Visby, and Hamburg Rules – a terminal operator is not an 'actual carrier' – and they have expressed concern at being brought within the scope of a mandatory regime.[83]

**6.67** Terminal operators are significantly affected by the Rotterdam Rules; being liable under the new convention will substantially affect their risk profile. Under the convention, shippers and cargo interests will almost certainly bring more insurance claims against port terminal operators. Moreover, the claim scenario is likely to differ dramatically for global terminal operators lacking a contractual relationship with cargo interests: 'That funnel will disappear. Instead of the carriers being the front line of claims, it will be the terminal operators themselves'.[84]

81 Peter Jones, 'The Utility of Himalaya Clauses under the Rotterdam Rules' (*Paterson MacDougall LLP*, 2009) <www.forwarderlaw.com/library/view.php?article_id=587>. Accessed 15 August 2015.

82 United Nations Commission on International Trade Law (n. 5).

83 The United Nations Convention on the Liability of Operators of Transport Terminals in International Trade 1991 is not yet in force.

84 The National Association of Marine Surveyors, Inc. 'President's Message' (*NAMSGlobal*, 2010) <www.namsglobal.org/assets/92/20100127webnews.htm>. Accessed 15 December 2014.

**6.68** Legal counsel for Hutchison Ports UK has described the current arrangement – in which cargo interests and port operators have no direct interaction – as 'a situation we very much like', citing a dearth of claims emanating from cargo interests directly.[85] Under the Rotterdam Rules, terminal operators become a 'maritime performing party' nonetheless, having joint and several liability.[86] According to Hutchison, cargo interests will be able to 'cherry pick' the parties against whom they seek to bring a claim: 'Our view is that they will like to bring their claim against Hutchison, a major terminal operator. Our ability to limit our liability is fettered'.[87]

**6.69** Similarly worrying is the reality that cargo interests claiming against the port terminal operator have no contractual relationship with them. Consequently, there is no commercial relationship to protect and therefore scant incentive for the cargo interests settle cases swiftly.[88] If the Rotterdam Rules are enforced, terminal operators will, for the first time, be subject to a mandatory convention.[89]

**6.70** Finally, as Chuah reports, in contrast to the Himalaya clause, Articles 4 and 19 do not provide for an indemnity but merely the extension of the carrier's defences and limitations of liability rights to the maritime performing party. Therefore, port terminal operators (as well as all the other third parties) may therefore still ask for an indemnity through a protection clause in the contract.[90] Given all of the above, it is easy enough to see why terminal operators have shown little support for the Rules.

### *The position of freight forwarders*

**6.71** Freight forwarders are frequently engaged in various capacities in seaports. They will rely, therefore, according to their specific activity, on the protection afforded to them as a maritime performing party.

**6.72** In answer to this question (i.e., whether freight forwarders fall within the definition of 'maritime performing party') the CMI stated that the Rotterdam Rules apply to some of these and not to others:

- If, for instance, freight forwarder undertakes to carry the goods to its customer, it is a carrier under the Rotterdam Rules.
- If a freight forwarder enters into a contract with a sub-carrier in its own name, it is a shipper under the Rotterdam Rules.
- If a freight forwarder enters into a contract with a carrier on behalf of a customer (as an agent), it is not the carrier or the shipper under the Rotterdam Rules and is not liable as such.

85 Holman Fenwick Willan, 'Terminal Operators Face Claims 'Front Line' in Rotterdam Rules' February 2010. This article first appeared in the February 2010 issue of the Lloyd's List and is reproduced with their kind permission <www.lloydslist.com>. Accessed 9 February 2013.

86 Ibid.

87 Ibid.

88 Ibid.

89 Ibid.

90 Chuah (n. 53).

- When freight forwarder provides services as a stevedore, for instance. As regards the contractual relationship between the freight forwarders (acting as stevedores) and the carrier, the contractual relationship is not affected by the Rotterdam Rules because they do not apply to the contract between the carrier and the maritime performing party, unless that contract satisfies the definition of 'contract of carriage' (Article 1(1)) (this is apparently not the case here).
- As regards the forwarder's relationship with the shipper or consignee, the Rotterdam Rules make the carrier and the maritime performing party jointly liable towards the shipper and consignee.[91]

**6.73** The CMI continues saying that the fact that the freight forwarder, acting as a maritime performing party, is subject to the Rotterdam Rules would probably constitute an advantage rather than a disadvantage, because it guarantees that the freight forwarders enjoy defences including the short time-bar and the right of limitation of its liability. At present, in cases where it may be sued in tort, it would be liable without limitation irrespective of the contractual terms.[92]

**6.74** FIATA has declared a rather different perspective, stating that freight forwarders are 'adversely affected by the liability regime applicable to maritime performing parties'.[93] Specifically, they raise three separate issues. First, freight forwarders acting as stevedores and warehousemen, who under the Rotterdam Rules enjoy freedom of contract, will be categorised as performing parties and therefore subject to carriers' liability regimes. Second, any move towards ratification are likely to be opposed in countries where the state controls or owns the interests of stevedores or warehousemen. Third, the introduction of maritime law will be resisted by multi-purpose cargo terminals operating as centres of distribution in logistical operations. In conclusion, FIATA argues that any implementation of the Rotterdam Rules is likely to substantially increase the administrative load placed on freight forwarders.

**6.75** In support of this, the Freight Forwarders association European Association for Forwarding, Transport, Logistics and Customs Services (CLECAT)has provided a strong view on the Rotterdam Rules, as explained in the following report:

> While neutral towards all transport modes, our Members are amongst the main users of maritime transport (or shipping) services, they would thus be directly affected by the possible entry into force of the above mentioned international conventions, which we will refer to as 'Rotterdam Rules' (RR) hereinafter.[94]

**6.76** The Rotterdam Rules will not, according to CLECAT, offer any advantages for its members. They cite the expanding complexity of the situation, as

91 CMI Yearbook 2000 (n. 15).
92 Ibid.
93 FIATA (n. 3).
94 CLECAT (n. 3).

well as the increasing expense of insurance and protection under the regime. CLECAT has called upon nations and EU institutions – particularly those whose stevedore and warehousing enterprises are government-owned – to refrain from ratifying the Rules in order to avoid increasing the exposure of these states to tort claims.[95] These claims tend to be not only unlimited in nature but also lacking the background offered by the convention in relation to the contractual carrier and potentially other maritime entities party to the occurrence and ensuing claims.

**6.77** The limitations of the Rotterdam Rules are relatively low. However, due to the package limitation – which is usually relevant for multimodal carriage of containers – the limitation figures for the Rules are often higher. The Rotterdam Rules, by contrast with the CMR, are more convenient for the cargo claimant, but only if the package weighs fewer than 109 kilograms. Furthermore, any shipper may be able to multiply the 'per package' factor simply by adding the content of the container into the transport document.[96]

**6.78** Until category associations such as CLECAT and FIATA are persuaded of their advantages, the Rotterdam Rules will face a strong opposition in terms of approval from freight forwarders.

## Conclusion

**6.79** The shore is no longer the place at which the line is drawn. The question now is this: is the port still a good place to draw a line?

**6.80** Under the Rotterdam Rules, the carrier is responsible for different third parties. However, while the carrier is responsible for a substantial chain of third parties, not all of them receive the same protection.

**6.81** The Rotterdam Rules have provisions similar to those of the Hague-Visby Rules and the Hamburg Rules in respect of the servants and agents of the carrier. However, with the adoption of the notion of maritime performing parties they have widened the category of persons to whom they apply and clearly provide that all such persons are also subject to the obligations and liabilities of the carrier. The action against them is, therefore, clearly in contract. This provision shows one of the most controversial aspects of the Rotterdam Rules; the fact that only the maritime performing parties have the same obligation as the carrier. Therefore, some categories of party involved in the carriage of goods by sea might hope that the Rotterdam Rules will not be ratified, because they wish to avoid this liability. This point is crucial and bears reiteration: the Rotterdam Rules, in one way or another do not approach third party protection in an adequate way.[97]

95 Ibid.

96 FIATA (n. 3).

97 Not only third parties categories are completely different nowadays. Furthermore their protection is given with different reasons. For example the employees of the carrier receive protection according to their status, while the performing parties for their area of work.

CHAPTER 7

# Third party protection under English law

**7.1** As one of the leading English cases has expressed, and many other commentators have already corroborated, 'Denying validity to the clause would be to encourage action against servants, agents, and independent contractors in order to get round exemptions'.[1] This is because cargo owners can also sue parties other than contracting parties in tort.[2] Third party protection has, however, been a contentious issue not only in English law in general, but also in maritime law.

**7.2** The majority of shipping contracts are governed by English Law. Under this, a person that has not entered into a contract cannot benefit from it.[3] As reported by Spurin (referring to *White v Jones*[4] and *Henderson v Merrett Syndicates*[5]): 'The mere fact that a contractual relationship exists does not prevent a litigant suing in either contract or in tort and selecting the course of action which provides the best procedural advantages or the most appropriate remedies'. At the same time, however, Spurin suggests 'the terms of a contract can exclude a tortious duty of care, preventing such an action. This is most likely to happen where a contract contains exclusion clauses and limitation clauses'.[6]

**7.3** English law has for a long time been reluctant to accept that parties outside the contract (i.e., third parties) can receive protection from it.[7] However, in the shipping world there exists a need to extend this protection. Consequently, the industry has for many years used different 'tools'[8] to permit this protection.[9]

1 *The Eurymedon* (1975) AC 154, 169; Jill Poole, *Contract Law* (12th edn, Oxford University Press 2014); Robert Merkin, *Privity of Contract, Privity of Contract: The Impact of the Contracts (Right of Third Parties) Act 1999* (Oxford, Taylor & Francis 2013) 67.

2 Tort is not based on the existence of contractual rights and relationships; rather it is based on the existence of a duty owed by one party to another.

3 This is related to the concepts of privity and consideration.

4 *White v Jones* (1995) UKHL 5.

5 *Henderson v Merrett Syndicates* (1994) 3 All ER 506.

6 Corbett *Spurin*, 'The Liability of Carriers to Cargo Owners' (Ch 5, The Nationwide Academy for Dispute Resolution (UK) Ltd. 2004) <www.nadr.co.uk/articles/published/shipping/005CHAPTERFIVETRADE4.pdf>. Accessed 27 March 2014.

7 English Courts have been less inclined than the United States Courts to extend protection to parties outside the contract. As it will be further detailed, however, not always.

8 Such as protection clauses.

9 As detailed by Macmillan,

> A and B contract and A excludes or limits the liability that would otherwise arise on the part of B. A extends the benefit of this exclusion or limitation term to C, who is usually the

## Third party protection and the obstacle of privity and consideration

**7.4** The extension of protection from the two parties of a contract to a third party has been an ongoing evolutionary process, especially in the carriage of goods by sea. The problem lies – especially for common law but even more so for English Law – in dealing with the old principles of privity and consideration. Privity is an obstacle because 'an agreement is only enforceable as between the parties to the agreement. Third parties to an agreement cannot legally enforce benefits accruing to them from the agreement, nor can they have burdens thrust upon them by others'.[10] More specifically, 'an agreement must be supported by consideration, so that both parties provide or promise to provide something valuable in money or services, benefit or detriment in exchange for the like consideration of the other party'.[11]

**7.5** In 1861, the case of *Tweddle v Atkinson* established what became known in the English legal system as the 'third party rule'.[12] In *Drive Yourself Hire Co. (London) Ltd v Strutt*,[13] Lord Denning commented:

> It is often said to be a fundamental principle of our law that only a person who is a party to a contract can sue on it. I wish to assert, as distinctly as I can, that the common law in its original setting knew no such principle. Indeed, it said quite the contrary. For the 200 years before 1861 it was settled law that, if a promise in a simple contract was made expressly for the benefit of a third person in such circumstances that it was intended to be enforceable by him, then the common law would enforce the promise at his instance, although he was not a party to the contract.[14]

**7.6** The thrust of Lord Denning's comment is that third parties to a contract should not derive any right from that agreement. *Dunlop Pneumatic*[15] is a leading case in determining the contemporary meaning of the concepts of privity and consideration. In it, Lord Haldane states:

> My Lords, in the law of England certain principles are fundamental. One is that only a person who is a party to a contract can sue on it. Our law knows nothing of a jus quaesitum tertio arising by way of contract. Such a right may be conferred by way of property, as, for example, under a trust, but it cannot be conferred on a stranger to a contract as a right to enforce the contract in personam. A second

agent, employee or sub-contractor of B. Should A sue C, C can avail himself of the exclusion or limitation of liability clause found in the A-B contract where this clause covers the liability in question.

Catharine MacMillan, 'A Birthday Present for Lord Denning: The Contracts (Rights of Third Parties) Act 1999' (2000) 63 The Modern Law Review 5, 721–738, 726

10 On the topic of privity the leading case is *Dunlop Pneumatic Tyre Co Ltd. v Selfridge & Co Ltd.* (1915) AC 847.

11 On the topic of consideration leading cases are *Thomas v Thomas* (1842) 2 QB 851, and *Tweddle v Atkinson* (1861) EWHC QB J57.

12 *Tweddle v Atkinson* (n. 11).

13 *Drive Yourself Hire Co. (London) Ltd. V Strutt* (1954) 1 QB 250.

14 Ibid., 272.

15 *Dunlop* (n. 10) 853.

principle is that if a person with whom a contract not under seal has been made is to be able to enforce it consideration must have been given by him to the promisor or to some other person at the promisor's request. These two principles are not recognised in the same fashion by the jurisprudence of certain Continental countries or of Scotland, but here they are well established.[16]

**7.7** Consideration is an old and well-established concept in English Law.[17] Lord Denning famously described the doctrine of consideration as 'too firmly fixed to be overthrown by a side-wind'.[18] The following statement is also of relevance here:

> A person wishing to enforce an agreement must show that they have brought something to the bargain which has 'something of value in the eyes of the law', either by conferring a benefit on another person or incurring a detriment at their request.[19]

**7.8** Lord Somervell, in the case *Chappel & Co*, stated that:

> Even though the bargain is selling a house for as little as a peppercorn and the seller 'does not like pepper and will throw away the corn'.[20]

**7.9** What is 'brought to the bargain' can be anything of value that the parties of the agreement consider adequate enough to render the contract valid. If only one party offers consideration, the agreement is not legally a binding contract. Consideration in its fundamental form expresses the concept of *quid pro quo*. Only one who gives something to the contract can enforce a promise and therefore only a person who has provided consideration can enforce a contract. It is said that, in order to be enforceable, a contract must be 'met with' or 'supported by' consideration.

**7.10** Although undeniably important, Hallebeek concedes that 'the rule of consideration has not been a significant restriction given the willingness of Courts to recognise nominal consideration as sufficient and to infer the existence of consideration on relatively flimsy evidence'.[21] Hallebeek goes on to say that the real problem stems from the 'parties only' rule, where only parties to a contract have rights in it. As he explains, the rule does not adequately sustain the realities of complex commercial transactions. Looking at the contract as a 'single transaction between two individuals' does not work in an industry such

16 Ibid.

17 In *Dunlop Pneumatic* Lord Dunedin questioning consideration said that is: 'possible for a person to snap his fingers at a bargain deliberately made … not in itself unfair and which the person seeking to enforce it has a legitimate interest to enforce', *Dunlop* (n. 10) 853.

18 *Central London Property Trust Ltd. v High Trees House Ltd.* (1947) KB 130.

19 See *Thomas v Thomas* (n. 11), and *Currie v Misa* (1875) LR 10 Ex 153 (Lush L J) 162: 'A valuable consideration, in the sense of the law, may consist either in some right, interest, profit or benefit accruing to the one party, or some forbearance, detriment, loss or responsibility given, suffered or undertaken by the other'.

20 *Chappell & Co. Ltd. v Nestle Co. Ltd.* (1960) AC 87 (Lord Somervell).

21 Jan Hallebeek and Harry Dondorp, *Contracts for a Third-party Beneficiary: A Historical and Comparative Account* (Martinus Nijhoff Publishers 2008) 116.

as shipping, where interactions are seldom binary, and usually involve a network of actors.[22] In bringing the two concepts of privity and consideration, the former restricts who can enforce an agreement to those have brought the latter to the bargain.

**7.11** Consideration for a promise can be the performance of a contractual duty owed to someone other than the promisor.[23] Contextualising it in the carriage of goods by sea, it can be argued that it has to be a duty of the carrier performed by the third party.

**7.12** The relationship between employer and employee is an important aspect of the relation between privity and consideration. In most cases, even if the employer is the contractual party, the employee is usually the one performing most of the obligations arising under the contract.[24] This was the case in the now famous example of the employees and the crew of the carrier in *Adler v Dixon: The S.S. Himalaya.*[25] This type of situation has often involved indicating in the contract which categories of people could be construed as parties to the contract; a task usually achieved using a protection clause. According to Tetley, a protection clause can only affect the rights and responsibilities of the parties if its underlying contract is operative. In the case of Himalaya clause, the underlying contract only becomes active to protect the stevedore and terminal operator when the latter begins to perform obligations as referred in the contract of carriage.[26]

**7.13** Since third parties in the carriage of goods by sea are not privy to the contract of carriage, they have typically encountered difficulties in benefiting from such exclusion clauses. This was the case in *Scruttons v Midland Silicones.*[27]

**7.14** Privity and consideration have never sat comfortably in the commercial world. In *Smith and Snipes Hall Farm Ltd v River Douglas Catchment Board*, Lord Denning stated that a third party can enforce a promise made for his benefit 'provided that he has a sufficient interest to enforce it'.[28] The need for a promise to provide consideration in order to enforce a promise was firmly established by the beginning of the eighteenth century. Merkin highlights Lord Mansfield's criticism of this arrangement, in which Mansfield argues that the role of law should be to facilitate rather than inhibit commercial practice.[29]

**7.15** The history of the doctrine of privity of contract in twentieth-century English Law has been defined as 'one of fluctuation between the doctrine and

22 Ibid.

23 See *Shadwell v Shadwell* (1860) EWHC CP J88, confirmed by *The Eurymedon* (n. 1).

24 Robert E Forbes, 'Practical Approaches to Privity of Contract Problems' (2002) 37 Canada Business Law Journal 357.

25 *Adler v Dickson (The Himalaya)* (1954) 2 Lloyd's Rep 267; (1955) 1 QB 158. It should be noted that under UCTA 1977 and the Athens Convention 1974 it is not possible to exclude liability for death or personal injury under English Law.

26 William Tetley, 'Limitation, Non-responsibility and Disclaimer Clauses' (1986) 11 Maritime Law 203.

27 *Scruttons Ltd. v Midland Silicones Ltd. (Scruttons)* (1961) 2 Lloyd's Rep 365.

28 (1949) 2 KB 500.

29 Merkin (n. 1) at 9.

pragmatism'[30] and has always been fought on different grounds. Under English law, and with the exception of clauses in contract as *a device* and international conventions, privity and consideration in the carriage of goods by sea have often been circumvented using the concept of bailment and the concept of agency – as a tool for accepting the protection clause – and also more recently the Contract (Right of Third Parties) Act 1999.

## Bailment

**7.16** Apart from the mechanism of protection clauses in contract, bailment law offers an alternative means to afford protection to third parties. Bailment occurs when there is a delivery or transfer of a chattel (or item of personal property) by one person (the bailor) to another (the bailee) with a specific mandate which requires the identical item to be delivered up to the bailor or to be dealt in a particular way by the bailee.[31] The concept of agency is expressed in the next paragraph, but for an immediate distinction, bailment is different from agency insofar as:

1. The bailee merely exercises, with leave of the bailor, certain powers over the bailed property but, unlike the agent, the bailee does not represent the bailor.
2. The bailee cannot enter into contracts on the bailor's behalf, although he may have the power to do things which are reasonably incidental to his use of the goods which he holds (e.g., to have the property repaired) and thereby make the bailor liable to a third party.[32]

**7.17** With this immediate difference appropriately framed, the focus can shift to the concepts of bailment, bailment on terms, and sub-bailment relevant to third party protection in the carriage of goods by sea. Particular attention is given to the relationship between the cargo owner (bailor), the carrier of the vessel (the bailee), and the shipowner of the vessel under a charterparty (the sub-bailee) in receiving the goods under the terms of the bill of lading or any other third parties in the position of sub-bailee.

**7.18** It is argued here that an analysis of bailment and bailment on terms are topics of paramount relevance for the protection of third parties in the carriage of goods by sea under statutory law systems. This is because, with protection clauses, the relationship that bailment creates has been applied to protect third parties (including but not limited to shipowners).[33] Moreover, bailment has

30 Merkin (n. 1) at 10. The ruling of Devlin J in *Pyrene v Scindia Navigation Co. Ltd.* (1954) 2 QB 402 also provides support for the condemnation of privity.

31 L S Sealy and R J A Hooley, *Commercial Law: Text Cases and Materials* (4th edn, Butterworths 1999).

32 Ibid.

33 A famous and current example is *The Mahkutai* (1996) AC 650, where the shipowners sought to rely on both the Himalaya clause and the principle of bailment on terms.

two aspects in common with the protection clauses: first, the same difficulty in dealing with the concepts of privity and consideration; second, the same commercial approach towards the law, i.e., meeting the expectation of the parties.

**7.19** Lord Denning explains sub-bailment on terms in *Morris v C. W. Martin & Sons Ltd*, but it should be noted that this case does not relate to shipping.[34] As Lord Denning explains, the principle of sub-bailment of terms is when A, the owner of the goods bails his goods to B, the bailee, who then sub-bails the goods to C, the sub-bailee, under a contract containing exemption clauses limiting or excluding C's liability. Thus, in an action by A against C for the loss or damage to the goods, A will be bound by the exemption clauses contained in the contract between B and C even though A was not a party to that contract. Regarding *Morris v Martin*, Lord Denning said:

> If the owner of the ship accepts goods for carriage on a bill of lading contained exemption condition … the owner of the goods is bound by those conditions if he impliedly consented to them as being in the known and contemplated form.[35]

**7.20** *Morris* was an 'inland' case relating to fur, but through it Lord Denning nonetheless created an important authority for the carriage of goods by sea. His establishment of the doctrine of sub-bailment on terms has subsequently been recognised by a variety of authorities[36] and academics.[37]

## The *Elder Dempster* case

**7.21** The case of *Elder Dempster* is the precursor to all contemporary cases revolving around the aforementioned issue. Before the advent of the Himalaya clause, the only remedy available for a third party – in the case of *Elder Dempster*, the shipowners – was appealing on bailment on terms. In *Elder Dempster*, the shipowners tried to rely on a clause in a bill of lading to which they were not privy. Both the Court of Appeal and the House of Lords allowed the shipowner to rely on carrier limitation of liability. However, the reasons provided differed.

34 (1966) 1 QB 716.

35 Ibid.

36 *China Pacific S.A. v Food Corporation of India* (1982) AC 939, 957–958; *Compania Portorafti Commerciale S.A. v Ultramar Panama Inc. (No. 2)* (1990) 2 Lloyd's Rep 395; *Dresser U.K. Ltd. v Falcongate Freight Management Ltd.* (1992) QB 502; *Hispanica de Petroleos S.A. v Vencedora Oceanica Navegacion S.A. (No. 2)* (Note) (1987) 2 Lloyd's Rep 321; *Johnson Matthey & Co. Ltd. v Constantine Terminals Ltd.* (1976) 2 Lloyd's Rep.215; *Singer Co. (U.K.) Ltd. v Tees and Hartlepool Port Authority* (1988) 2 Lloyd's Rep. 164; and by the Privy Council in *Gilchrist Watt and Sanderson Pty. Ltd. v York Products Pty. Ltd.* (1970) 1 WLR 1262 and *Port Swettenham Authority v T W Wu and Co. (M) Sdn. Bhd.* (1979) AC 580.

37 Joseph Chitty, *Chitty on Contracts* (26th edn, Vol. 2, Sweet and Maxwell 1989) 115, para. 2653; Sir Guenter *Treitel* QC, *Treitel on Contract* (8th edn, Sweet and Maxwell 1991) 558–560; N Palmer, 'Sub-Bailment on Terms' (1989) Lloyd's Maritime and Commercial Law Quarterly 466; A P Bell, *Modern Law of Personal Property in England and Ireland* (Butterworths 1988) and A P Bell, 'Sub-Bailment on Terms' in N E Palmer and E McKendrick (eds.), *Interests in Goods* (Ch 6, LLP 1993) 178–180.

In the Court of Appeal, Scrutton L.J. qualified the shipowner as agent of the charterer and therefore entitled to the same protection of the charterer against the cargo owner.[38]

**7.22** The main issue in *Elder Dempster* was whether the fault was due to unseaworthiness or bad stowage. Given the vast amount of literature regarding the concept of unseaworthiness, it is perhaps unsurprising that the decision became long and somewhat controversial. Of particular pertinence here, however, is the issue that the Lords addressed last; 'a further question' as defined by Viscount Cave[39] or even more explicitly by Lord Sumner,[40] 'a final argument'.

**7.23** Lord Sumner led the speech, agreeing that the shipowners had received the goods as bailees on the terms of the bill of lading.[41] Both judges of the Court of Appeal and the House of Lords shared the view that the reason for protecting the shipowner is to give justice to the commercial expectation of the bill of lading:

> Were it otherwise there would be an easy way round the bill of lading in the case of every chartered ship; the owner of the goods would simply sue the owner of the ship and ignore the bill of lading expectations, though he had contracted with the charterer for carriage on those terms and the owner had only received the goods as agent for the charterer.[42]

**7.24** In the opinion of Viscount Finlay, 'it would be absurd that the owner of the goods could get rid of the protective clauses of the bill of lading … by suing the owner of the ship in tort'.[43]

**7.25** In *Elder Dempster*, the House of Lords held that the damage was to be attributed to bad stowage and as a result, the time charterers were protected by the bill of lading exception.[44] However, the cargo owners had also sued the shipowners in tort. Consequently, the question arose as to whether the shipowners were also protected by the exception contained in the bill of lading, to which they were not parties. Essentially, the case illustrates the following concept:

**7.26** If a cargo owner (bailor) places the goods on a chartered vessel under a bill of lading issued by a carrier (bailee), the shipowner of the vessel receives the goods under the terms of the bill of lading (sub-bailee). If the cargo owner sues the shipowner for a breach of duty in tort or bailment, the shipowner can rely on the exemptions set out in the bill of lading. Therefore, as stated in Elder Dempster,

38 *Elder, Dempster & Co. Ltd. v Paterson, Zochonis & Co. Ltd. (Elder Demspter)* (1924) AC 522 (HL).

39 Ibid., 533.

40 Ibid., 564.

41 Ibid. As stated by Lord Sumner:

> (i)t may be, that in the circumstances of this case the obligations to be inferred from the reception of the cargo for carriage to the United Kingdom amount to a bailment upon terms, which include the expectations and limitations of liability stipulated in the known and contemplated for of bill of lading.
>
> 564–565

42 Ibid., 441, 442 (Scrutton L.J.).

43 Ibid., 548.

44 On this point differing from a majority of the Court of Appeal.

the reception of goods by the shipowner under the terms of the contract between the cargo owner and the carrier maybe referred to as 'bailment on terms'.[45]

**7.27** The authority of *Elder Dempster* has rarely been followed and received much criticism. In the Australian case of *Wilson v Darling Island Stevedoring & Lighterage Co.*, for example, Fullagar J. explains:

> In my opinion, what the Elder Dempster case decided, and all that it decided, is that in such a case, the master having signed the bill of lading, the proper inference is that the shipowner, when he receives the goods into his possession, receives them on the terms of the bill of lading. The same inference might perhaps be drawn in some cases even if the charterer himself signed the bill of lading, but it is necessary to consider any such question.[46]

**7.28** Fullagar J. seems to disagree entirely with the rationale in *Elder Dempster*, placing more importance upon the simple fact that he who damages pays. He argues that the case shows 'a curious, and seemingly irresistible, anxiety to save grossly negligent people from the normal consequences of their negligence'.[47]

**7.29** This concept was embraced by Viscount Simonds in the concluding sentence of his speech in *Midland Silicones*[48] and elaborated upon more recently by Tetley in his article, 'The Himalaya clause revisited'.[49] Despite the criticism it has attracted, Bingham L.J. (in *Dresser U.K. Ltd. v Falcongate Freight Management Ltd.*) acknowledged the decision in *Elder Dempster* as 'a pragmatic legal recognition of commercial reality'.[50]

**7.30** In the Court of Appeal,[51] Scrutton L.J.[52] rejected the claim against the shipowners on a suggested principle of vicarious immunity. This principle was relied on by the shipowners in argument before the House of Lords[53] and was accepted[54] by Viscount Cave,[55] Viscount Finlay,[56] and Lord Sumner.[57]

45 *Elder, Dempster* (n. 38).
46 (1956) 1 Lloyd's Rep 346, 365 (Aust HCt).
47 Ibid., *Elder, Dempster* (n. 38) has been also criticised by Carver, *Carriage by Sea* (13th edn, Stevens & Sons Ltd. 2005) paras 717–719; Thomas Edward Scrutton, *Scrutton on Charterparties and Bills of Lading* (19th edn, Sweet & Maxwell 1984) 251, n. 36, 458, n. 47 and Paul Todd, *Modern Bills of Lading* (2nd edn, Blackwell Law 1990) 99.
48 *Midland Silicones* (n. 27); also in *The Mahkutai* (n. 33).
49 Tetley (n. 27).
50 (1992) QB 502, 511.
51 (1923) 1 KB 420, 441–442.
52 Who alone considered the damage was to be attributed to bad stowage rather than unseaworthiness.
53 (1924) AC 522.
54 Ibid., 534.
55 With whom Lord Dunedin ibid., 548, Lord Carson ibid., 565 agreed.
56 Ibid., 548.
57 Ibid., 564.

> in the circumstances of this case the obligations to be inferred from the reception of the cargo for carriage to the United Kingdom amount to a bailment upon terms, which include the exceptions and limitations of liability stipulated in the known and contemplated form of bill of lading.
>
> Lord Dunedin, 548 and Lord Carson, 565 agreed

**7.31** The reason that the shipowner in *Elder Dempster* could be considered a sub-bailee lies in Scrutton L.J.'s doctrine of vicarious immunity, a concept that can be found in the expression of the conventions on the carriage of goods by sea regarding the relationship between carrier and his servant, agents, and sub-contractors.[58]

## Agency law

**7.32** Agency is another tool to circumvent the problem of privity and consideration in order to provide full justice to contractual clauses.[59] The concept of agency has been defined as an exception to the doctrine of privity, where an agent may contract on behalf of his principal with a third party and form a binding contract between the principal and third party.[60] Agency allows one to move consideration from a third party (sub-contractor of one of the two parties of the contract) to a contractual party.

**7.33** In law there are many definitions of agency. What is appropriate here is the concept of 'representation':

> Agency is the relationship between two persons when one, called the agent, is considered in law to represent the other, called the principal, is such a way as to be able to affect the principal's legal position in respect of strangers to the relationship by the making of contracts or the disposition of property.[61]

**7.34** It is pertinent to mention that such assent can be expressly stated or implied:

> Agency is the fiduciary relationship which exists between two persons, one of whom expressly or impliedly manifests assent that the other should act on his behalf so as to affect his relations with third parties, and the other of whom similarly manifests assent so to act or so acts pursuant to the manifestation.[62]

**7.35** To summarise, agency is the relationship that exists between two persons, one of whom consents that the other should act on his behalf. In other words, agency enables one person to enter a contract on behalf of another.[63]

58 For instance, Article 4 bis of the Hague-Visby Rules scheduled to the Carriage of Goods by Sea Act 1971.

59 The fact is that contracts often provide for a benefit to be conferred upon a third party as a primary or secondary intention of the agreement. Such benefits can be financial or other, or an exclusion of liability and/or an indemnity in favour of a third party, such as a director, officer, or employee of a contracting party.

60 *Midland Silicones* (n. 27).

61 Gerald Henry Louis Fridman, *The Law of Agency* (7th edn, Butterworths 1996) 11.

62 Francis Martin Baillie Reynolds and William Bowstead, *Bowstead and Reynolds on Agency* (18th edn, Sweet & Maxwell 2006) Article 1(1).

63 See *Municipal Council v Prabhu Narain*, AIR 1968 Raj 297; P Ramanatha Aiyar, *The Major Law Lexicon* (Wadhwa and Company 2010); Cane Conaghan, *The New Oxford Companion to Law* (Oxford University Press 2008); Roger Billins, *Agency Law* (Longman 1993); A C Pritchard, 'United States v O'Hagan: Agency Law and Justice Powell's Legacy for the Law of Insider Trading'

**7.36** Fundamentals of agency law demonstrate lack of consistency with any doctrine of privity. The idea of a principal enforcing a contract between the agent and a third party made for the principal's benefit does not sit comfortably with the assertion that a contract between two parties cannot confer rights or liabilities on a third party, even if the third party is the intended beneficiary. It is particularly at odds with the rule that the agents may themselves incur liabilities and obtain rights under the contract with the third party if the agent has signed the contract in a manner that indicates personal liability.[64]

**7.37** Agency is essential for modern trade. Contracts are often drawn up by intermediaries; a practice that is even more common in shipping.[65] Agency is an important exception to the doctrine of the privity of contract. It is argued that the agency rule in English law was also expressed in the leading case of *Dunlop Pneumatic*: 'English law knows nothing of a *jus quaesitum tertio*'. Lord Haldane refers to agency in the last part of his summary of the concept of privity and consideration.[66] Agency is Haldane's third fundamental principle; privity and consideration being the first and second, respectively:

> A third proposition is that a principal not named in the contract may sue upon it if the promisee really contracted as his agent. But again, in order to entitle him so to sue, he must have given consideration either personally or through the promise, acting as his agent in giving it.[67]

**7.38** However, Haldane refers only to third parties who wish to sue and not third parties who seek protection.

**7.39** The concept of agency was developed primarily for the sake of commercial convenience and, therefore, it is considered a tool to allow third party protection.

**7.40** An agent may be either a servant or an independent contractor.[68] Forbes explains that the law of agency relies on a general principle: an agent may

(1998) 78 Boston University Law Review 13; Randy E Barnett, 'Squaring Undisclosed Agency Law with Contract Theory' (1987) 75 California Law Review 1969.

64 Merkin (n. 1) at 32.

65 There are a wide variety of circumstances in international trade where agents are involved. In particular, import and export agents make contracts of carriage, stevedoring and storage on behalf of clients and carriers may act as agents for stevedores, as in *The Eurymedon* case (n. 1).

66 Reported in paragraph 4.2 related to third party protection and the obstacle of privity and consideration.

67 *Dunlop* (n. 10) 753.

68 As it has been discussed, essentially, a servant is one who gives his service to another and there is a contract of employment between the two parties (e.g., in the maritime context a master is a servant). An independent contractor provides services for another. In this respect it is reported that a very recent decision of the Supreme Court of the United Kingdom expanded the definition of charterer's agent. *NYK Bulkship (Atlantic) NV (Respondent) v Cargill International SA* (Appellant) (2016) UKSC 20. In this case the word 'agent' has been extended to persons or subcontractors to whom the charterers' rights are made available downstream in the carriage chain or to whom perform the charterers' obligations. To the extent that they are 'availing themselves of the facility contractually derived either directly or indirectly from the charterers' *such subcontractors are the 'agents'*. <www.supremecourt.uk/cases/docs/uksc-2014-0143-press-summary.pdf>. Accessed 10 September 2016.

contract with another party on behalf of his or her principal. As a result the principal, not the agent, is liable to perform the contract and is entitled to the benefit of the contract. This is also the case where the other party does not know that the agent is representing the undisclosed principal.[69]

**7.41** According to Forbes, agency seems to function best when a set of relationships already extant precipitate a need for the creation of third party rights. This scenario might take place as a result of previous agreements between the contracting party and the third party, or where contracting parties aim for rights under the contract to be transferred on to the third party and the contracting parties make precise provision for how to achieve it.[70]

## The cases of *Scrutton* and *The Eurymedon*

**7.42** Agency in the carriage of goods by sea has been stated and substantially elaborated by two cases: *Midland Silicones Ltd v Scruttons Ltd* and *The Eurymedon*. Both cases put forward the principle now known as 'agency theory'.

**7.43** In 1961, in *Midland Silicones v Scruttons Ltd.,* the English House of Lords turned away from the perspective taken in *Elder Dempster* and reestablished the classic approach to privity. The Lords argued that to do away with a fundamental and elemental principle of law such as privity requires an Act of Parliament following due consideration of its merits and demerits. Almost 40 years later, their argument will be accepted by the English parliament.[71]

**7.44** According to Viscount Simonds, the case of *Scrutton* raised the question of whether the appellants – stevedores who admitted their negligence caused damage to certain cargo (consigned to the respondents under a bill of lading, 26th March, 1957) – could take advantage of a provision for limitation of liability contained in that document.[72]

**7.45** In the *Scrutton* case, the answer was positive providing that four conditions, as set by Lord Reid, were met.

> I can see a possibility of success of the agency argument if (first) the bill of lading makes it clear that the stevedore is intended to be protected by the provisions in it which limit liability, (secondly) the bill of lading makes it clear that the carrier in addition to contracting for these provisions on his own behalf, is also contracting as agent for the stevedore that these provisions should apply to the stevedore, (thirdly) the carrier has authority from the stevedore to do that, or perhaps later ratification by the stevedore would suffice, and (fourthly) that any difficulties about consideration moving from the stevedore were overcome. And then to affect the consignee it would be necessary to show that the provisions of the Bills of lading Act, 1855, apply.[73]

69 Robert E Forbes, 'Practical Approaches to Privity of Contract Problems' (2002) 37 Canada Business Law Journal 357.

70 Ibid.

71 *Midland Silicones* (n. 27).

72 Ibid.

73 Ibid. The Bill of Lading Act 1855 is an Act regulating the bill of lading.

**7.46** Lord Reid's speech, although refusing the allowance of protection to third parties in that specific instance, allowed the Himalaya clause to extend the defences of the carrier to servants, agents and independent contractors engaged in the loading and unloading process.[74] In particular, and referring to *Elder Dempster*, Lord Reid stated:

> It can be hardly be denied that the ratio decidendi of the Elder Dempster decision is very obscure. A number of eminent judges have tried to discover it, hardly any two have reached the same result, and none of the explanation hitherto given seems to me very convincing [...] I must treat the decision as an anomalous and unexplained exception to the general principal that a stranger cannot rely for his protection on provisions in a contract to which is not a party.[75]

**7.47** The primary problem in Lord Reid's agency theory is establishing that 'consideration' has passed from the stevedore to the shipper. *The Eurymedon* provided the answer a few years later.[76] The Privy Council held that the consideration was the discharge of the goods by the stevedore for the benefit of the shipper: 'The performance of these services for the benefit of the shipper was the consideration for the agreement by the shipper that the appellant (stevedore) should have the benefit of the exemptions and limitations contained in the bill of lading'.[77]

**7.48** Though similar to *Scrutton, The Eurymedon* case was not the same. The facts of the case are briefly summarised here:

- A contract of carriage existed, incorporating the Hague-Visby Rules.
- A Himalaya clause was drafted, essentially with the intent to avoid the outcome of *Scrutton.*
- The clause claimed to afford protection for the carrier and agents and independent contractors of the carrier and those who engaged by him.
- Stevedores were expressly included.
- Cargo was damaged during unloading.
- The consignee sued the stevedores.
- The stevedores won because the Court held that the stevedores were entitled to the benefit of limitation clauses.

**7.49** The distinction between *Scrutton* and *The Eurymedon* lies in the fact that the stevedores in *Scrutton* were not clearly included in the contract of carriage and the bill of lading as they were in *The Eurymedon* case. In *Scrutton*, there was no agency relationship because the carriers did not know at time of contract who the stevedores were to be. The shipowners in *The Eurymedon* made two separate contracts with the shipper and the stevedore company, which entitled the latter to rely on protection by the exclusion clause in respect of damage to

74 *Midland Silicones* (n. 27) 376.
75 Ibid., 377.
76 *The Eurymedon* (n. 1).
77 Ibid., 154–155.

cargo. Since the shipowners were agents of the stevedores, the stevedores were principal parties to the stevedore part of the contract with the shipper. Furthermore, the Court held in *The Eurymedon* that there was valid consideration.

**7.50** On the one hand, *The Eurymedon* reinforced the dicta of Lord Reid in *Scrutton*, establishing four requirements that must be met in order for a stevedore to benefit from the clauses of limitation that apply to the carrier against the shipper:

1. The bill of lading must make clear the carrier's intention to protect the stevedore.
2. The carrier makes clear that he is contracting for the stevedores' protection as well as for its own.
3. The authority of the carrier to act for the stevedore, whether antecedent or by ratification, must be declared.
4. There should be consideration from the stevedore.

**7.51** On the other hand, in doing so *The Eurymedon* completed the contractual procedure to give full protection to third parties.

**7.52** The performance of these services for the benefit of the shipper was the consideration for the agreement by the shipper that the appellant (stevedore) should have the benefit of the exemptions and limitations contained in the bill of lading. The Privy Council concluded that the stevedores provided consideration for the benefit conveyed by the clause simply by discharging the cargo from the vessel.

**7.53** According to Tetley, Lord Reid did not solve the problem; there was no consideration passing from the stevedore to the shipper:

> In my view, the consideration found by Lord Wilberforce for Lord Reid's agency theory and the presumed benefit to society and commerce are doubtful. It is my view that, only if the carrier himself also undertakes to discharge the goods and care for them after discharge, may he be able to benefit his servants or independent contractors by his contract with the shipper. Nor can anyone entitled to benefit under a Himalaya clause receive greater exemptions than those to which an original party to the contract is entitled.[78]

**7.54** In *The Eurymedon*, the Court 'upheld the efficacy of a Himalaya clause to confer upon the stevedores the benefit of defences and immunities contained in the bill of lading'.[79] By wrestling with established contract law – namely the

78 Tetley (n. 26).

79 This would be subsequently reaffirmed by the Privy Council in the case called *Port Jackson Stevedoring Pty. Ltd. v Salmond and Spraggon (Australia) Pty. Ltd. (The New York Star)* (1981) 1 WLR 138. In *The New York Star* the Court had to deal with an Australian decision where the Court did not allow the stevedoring contractor of the protection because the act took place after discharge. The Privy Council reversed with a very functional approach towards the contract of carriage and held that the contract ends not when the carrier ends his responsibility but where the goods are delivered to the consignee and therefore allowed the protection to the stevedore.

doctrines of consideration and privity – the case established *The Eurymedon* principle: 'the carrier acts as agent for independent contractors in contracting liability exemptions'. The necessary bilateral contract between the stevedore and the cargo-owner is created by the stevedore performing the stevedoring services.

**7.55** The Court in *The Eurymedon* held that the discharging of cargo by the stevedore could be deemed consideration for the artificial contract between the consignor and the stevedore. However, the discharging was requested for the execution of a separate contract; the stevedoring contract between the carrier and the stevedore.[80]

**7.56** The commercial incentives to back up the justification of the Himalaya clause in this case[81] were similar to those outlined almost 50 years earlier by Lord Wilberforce in *Elder Dempster*:

> In the opinion of their Lordships, to give the appellant the benefit of the exemptions and limitations contained in the bill of lading is to give effect to the clear intentions of a commercial document, and can be given within existing principles. They see no reason to strain the law or the facts in order to defeat these intentions. It should not be overlooked that the effect of denying validity to the clause would be to encourage actions against servants, agents and independent contractors in order to get around exemptions (which are almost invariable and often compulsory) accepted by shippers against carriers, the existence, and presumed efficacy, of which is reflected in the rates of freight. They see no attraction in this consequence.[82]

**7.57** *The Eurymedon* makes clear that, in many cases, the bill of lading issued by the carrier includes a Himalaya clause conferring to the carrier's sub-contractors the benefit of all terms benefiting the carrier by providing that in accord to such terms, the carrier enters into the bill of lading contract not only on his own behalf but also as agent for the sub-contractors. Such a clause protects a sub-contractor in certain circumstances by giving rise to a contract between the owner of the goods and the sub-contractor whereby the sub-contractor receives the benefit of clauses contained in the carrier's bill of lading.[83]

**7.58** From *Elder Dempster* to *The Eurymedon*, it became clear that there was a need to extend protection to third parties, and the principles of bailment (*Elder Dempster*) and agency (*Scrutton* and *The Eurymedon*) were used to achieve this extension. However, the concept of protection clauses through agency from the carrier and bailment were further enhanced in the 1990s when two famous cases regarding the carriage of goods by sea addressed the concept of bailment and protection clauses of third parties (in these cases, shipowners).[84] The cases of

80 For an example of an implied contract see Chen Liang, 'Benefits and Burdens of Third Parties Under Exception Clauses in Bills of Lading' (1999) 24 Tulane Maritime Law Journal 225.

81 Criticised by Tetley (n. 26) 11.

82 *The Eurymedon* (n. 1).

83 Ibid.

84 In a different way.

*The Mahkutai*[85] and *The Pioneer Container*[86] asked again whether a third party is entitled to receive protection from a contract of which he is not part.[87] Once more the Courts took completely different routes.

## The cases of *The Mahkutai* and *The Pioneer Container*

**7.59** *The Mahkutai* and *The Pioneer Container* have several features in common.

1. In both cases the defendant was a shipowner of a cargo vessel. The Mahkutai in the homonym case and the KH Enterprise in *The Pioneer Container* (which was the sister vessel of the KH Enterprise).
2. Both of these cases deal with concepts of bailment and protection clauses as raised by the respective shipowners.
3. In both cases the type of protection was an exclusive jurisdiction clause set out in the bill of lading.
4. Last, both cases were appealed to the Privy Council with Lord Goff of Chieveley delivering the judgement.

**7.60** What is substantially different, is the outcome that sees the shipowners of KH Enterprise, in *The Pioneer Container*, being held entitled to rely on the exclusive jurisdiction clause. The opposite outcome was reached in *The Mahkutai* with the Privy Council dismissing the shipowner's appeal.

**7.61** Without delving too much into the facts of the two cases, it is worth mentioning that in *The Pioneer Container* case, the cargo owners had engaged carriers to ship goods by sea under bills of lading that gave the carriers authority to sub-contract the whole or part of the carriage of the goods on 'any terms'. The carrier sub-bailed the goods to the shipowners for carriage on board their vessel for part of the voyage.[88]

**7.62** *The Mahkutai*[89] was a case in which the shipowners carrying cargo shipped under charterers' bills of lading sought to claim the benefit of a Himalaya clause in the time charterers' bills of lading or to invoke the principle of bailment on terms.[90] The question was whether a shipowner on a chartered vessel could share the same rights and liabilities of the carrier. Cargo owners instituted proceedings in the High Court of Hong Kong against the shipowners, who were claiming damages for breach of contract, breach of duty, or negligence. On application by the shipowners, the judges declared that the shipowners – although not parties to the bill of lading – were entitled to invoke the exclusive

85 *The Mahkutai* (n. 33).
86 *KH Enterprise v Pioneer Container (The Pioneer Container)* (1994) 2 AC 324.
87 Curiously, Lord Chievely was present in both.
88 *The Pioneer Container* (n. 86).
89 *The Mahkutai* (n. 33).
90 However, by these means they were seeking to invoke not an exception or limitation in the ordinary sense of those words, but the benefit of an exclusive jurisdiction clause.

jurisdiction clause either as a contractual term or as one of the terms on which the goods had been bailed to them.

**7.63** At the Court of Appeal, the cargo owner argued that the shipowners were not party to the bill of lading and therefore could not rely on the exclusive jurisdiction clause contained in the bill of lading. The only parties privy to the bill of lading were the cargo owner and the carriers (i.e., charterers). The cargo owner specified that they brought an action against the respondents in bailment and negligence and therefore the jurisdiction clause under the bill of lading did not apply.[91] The Court of Appeal of Hong Kong reversed the decision of the High Court by a majority.[92]

**7.64** The judges of the Court of Appeal based their decision on the assumption that the goods had been shipped on board the shipowner's vessel pursuant to a bill of lading containing a Himalaya clause whereby the shipowners, if sub-contractors, were expressly to be entitled to the benefit of some of the terms in the bill of lading but not of the exclusive jurisdiction clause. Therefore, that clause was not an implied term on which they had taken the goods into their custody because a bailment on terms, which included such point, would be contrary to the express provisions of the bill of lading.[93]

**7.65** The rationale of the shipowner's argument is illuminated by their legal representatives Peter Gross Q.C. and Duncan Matthews:

> Given the adherence of English law to the doctrine of considerations and privity of contracts, the problem is: whether A contracts with B on terms which purports to protect C, and in circumstances where C voluntarily takes into his custody A's goods, C can take the benefit of those terms when sued in tort by A. The shipowners are entitled to rely on the terms of the bill of lading, including the exclusive jurisdiction clause, because they received the cargo as bailees (sub-bailees) on those terms.[94]

**7.66** According to the shipowners' representatives, the shipowners' rights and liabilities against the shippers and their assigns are those to which the shippers have consented in the bill of lading contract with the carrier. That contract includes the exclusive jurisdiction clause.[95] Moreover, according to their representatives', the shipowners are entitled to rely on the terms of the bill of lading by operation of the Himalaya clause, because the four requirements presented by Lord Reid in the Scrutton case had been met.[96]

**7.67** Moving to *The Pioneer Container* appeal, Sydney Kentridge QC and George Legatt argued on behalf of the cargo owner that the doctrine of bailment

91 See also on the same point, *Gadsen v VCSC* (1977) 1 NSWLR 575 and *Air New Zealand Ltd. v The Ship Contship Americana* (1992) 1 NZLR 425. In both cases the Court of New South Wales and New Zealand declared the shipowners liable in negligence.

92 *The Mahkutai* (n. 33).

93 Ibid.

94 Ibid., 730.

95 Ibid., 652.

96 Ibid., 653.

and sub-bailment are contrary to the principle of law that a person cannot be bound by the terms of a contract to which they are not party,[97] thus raising the same debate of privity and consideration against commercial expectation.[98]

**7.68** Therefore they concluded: 'There is no need to stretch principles of law to give protection to a sub-bailee when he can protect himself, if not by insurance then by contracting an indemnity with the intermediate bailee'.[99]

**7.69** Conversely, as expressed by Michael Thomas Q.C. and Anthony Dicks on behalf of the shipowners:

> Two relationships are governed by the terms of the bill of lading, namely, the agreed contractual provisions as between the defendants and the shipowners and the terms of the sub-bailment of the plaintiff's goods. A contract is formed by agreement. A bailment is formed by a transfer of possession independently of contract. Upon accepting possession of another's goods, a bailee may stipulate the terms affecting his liabilities, those terms will bind not only the immediate bailor, but also those who are privy to the bailment, including those with superior rights to possession who have consented to the bailment.[100]

**7.70** In both cases, the two principles invoked by the shipowners – bailment on terms and third parties benefiting by a term in a contract – are products of developments in English law during the present century.[101] According to the judgement in *The Mahkutai*, the two principles seem to have a common aim:

> Recognising some form of modification of, or exception to, the strict doctrine of privity of contract to accommodate situations which arise in the context of carriage of goods by sea, in which it appears to be in accordance with commercial expectations that the benefit of certain terms of the contract of carriage should be made available to parties involved in the adventure who are not parties of the contract.[102]

**7.71** In *The Mahkutai*, the cargo owners argued that shipowners were not entitled to the benefit of the exclusive jurisdiction clause in the bill of lading through the agency of the carrier, nor could they rely on the Himalaya clause because they were not servants, agents, or sub-contractors of the carrier.[103]

**7.72** Regarding bailment, they considered consent an essential element of bailment on terms. An owner of goods is bound by the conditions of a sub-bailment only if he or she has expressly or impliedly consented to the bailee making a sub-bailment on those terms. The cargo owners in *The Mahkutai* case did not consent to the bailment to the shipowners due to the terms of the bill of lading.[104]

97 Such as the case of *Midland Silicones* (n. 27).
98 *The Pioneer Container* (n. 86).
99 Ibid., 329. See also *Gillespie Bros. & Co. Ltd. v Roy Bowles Transport Ltd.* (1973) Q.B. 400.
100 Ibid. See also *Morris* n. 34 and Norman Palmer, 'Ambulatory Bailments' (1983) 36 Current Legal Problems 1, 91
101 Ibid.
102 *Midland Silicones* (n. 27); *The Eurymedon* (n. 1) and *Port Jackson Stevedoring Pty. Ltd. v Salmond and Spraggon (Australia) Pty. Ltd. (The New York Star)* (1981) 1 WLR 138.
103 *The Mahkutai* (n. 33), Richard Aikens QC and Alan Roxburgh.
104 Ibid.

**7.73** In *The Pioneer Container* case, Lord Goff of Chieveley followed the doctrine of sub-bailment on terms as stated by Denning in *Morris*. He affirmed that, as far as English law and the law of Hong Kong are concerned, a technical problem arises for shipowners who carry goods in situations where there is no contractual relationship between the shipowners and certain cargo owners. This is because English law still adheres strictly to the principles of privity of contract and consideration. Lord Goff asks whether this adherence should continue with the same strictness, highlighting the opinions of judges of great authority and distinction who were in no doubt that it should be so maintained. Goff concludes, however, by pointing out that, in the present case, the question is whether the law of bailment can be invoked by the shipowners to circumvent this difficulty.[105]

**7.74** This begs a question raised in *The Pioneer Container* case: should it be a prerequisite of a bailment that the bailor should have consented to the bailee's possession of the goods? Bell, cited in *The Pioneer Container* judgement, argues that it should:

> If the owner seeks to hold a sub-bailee responsible to him as bailee, he has to accept all the terms of the sub-bailment, warts and all; for either he will have consented to the sub-bailment on those terms or, if not, he will (by holding the sub-bailee liable to him as bailee) be held to have ratified all the terms of the sub-bailment.[106]

**7.75** Palmer[107] and Tay[108] disagree, arguing that a person who voluntarily takes another person's goods into his custody holds them as bailee of that person (the owner), and that they can only invoke, for example, terms of a sub-bailment under which the goods were received from an intermediate bailee as qualifying or otherwise affecting responsibility to the owner if the owner consented. As explained by their Lordships, it is the latter approach that has been adopted by English law and, in turn, the law of Hong Kong.[109]

**7.76** The decision in *The Mahkutai* has received criticism from scholars. Commenting on the judgement, Nossal felt that:

> The majority of the Court of Appeal (Litton J.A. and Mayo J., Bokhary J.A. dissenting) squandered an opportunity to harmonise the correlation between the legitimate commercial expectations of the parties and the law relating to carriage of goods by sea.[110]

105 Ibid., 335.

106 A P Bell, 'Sub-Bailment on Terms' in N E Palmer and E McKendrick (eds.), *Interests in Goods* (Ch 6, LLP 1993) 88–89.

107 N Palmer, 'Sub-Bailment on Terms' (1989) Lloyd's Maritime and Commercial Law Quarterly 31 et seq.

108 Alice Erh-Soon Tay, 'The Essence of Bailment: Contract, Agreement or Possession?' (1966) Sydney Law Review 239.

109 The Pioneer Container (n. 86) 341, 342.

110 S Nossal, *Bailment on Terms and the Carriage of Goods by Sea: The 'Mahkutai'* (Sweet & Maxwell, 1994) n. 1, 19–28.

**7.77** The rationale of the decision in *The Mahkutai*[111] and the interpretation that the judges gave to the bailment on terms are neatly summarised by the words of Lord Goff of Chieveley:

> In the light of the principle stated by Lord Sumner in the Elder Dempster case as interpreted by Fullagar J. of Darling Island, the next question for consideration is whether the shipowners can establish that they received the goods into their possession on the terms of the bill of lading, including the exclusive jurisdiction clause (clause 19), i.e., whether the shipowners' obligations as bailees were effectively subjected to the clause as a term upon which the shipowners implicitly received the goods into their possession. This was the ground upon which Bokhary J.A. expressed the opinion, in his dissenting judgment that the shipowners were entitled to succeed.[112]

**7.78** The Court in *The Mahkutai* found what they called 'an insuperable objection' to the argument of the shipowners. The bill of lading under which the goods were shipped on board contained a Himalaya clause under which the shipowners, as sub-contractors, were to be entitled to the benefit of certain terms in the bill of lading. However, as their Lordships held, those terms did not include the exclusive jurisdiction clause. The Court held that by receiving the goods pursuant to the bill of lading, the shipowners' obligations as bailees were effectively subjected to the exclusive jurisdiction clause as a term upon which they implicitly received the goods into their possession.[113]

**7.79** Another question in *The Pioneer Container* was whether the sub-bailees could invoke any of the terms on which the goods were sub-bailed to them, and in particular the exclusive jurisdiction clause. Lord Denning contended that 'the answer to the problem lies, I think, in this: the owner is bound by the conditions if he has expressly or impliedly consented to the bailee making a sub-bailment containing those conditions, but not otherwise'.[114]

**7.80** The cargo owners also argued that the shipowners' bill of lading contained a Himalaya clause which, following *The Eurymedon* case, would allow a third party the same protection of the carrier under the bill of lading, if the four rules laid out by Lord Reid are respected.[115] As reported in *The Pioneer Container* case, the Himalaya clause alone is not sufficient to exclude a sub-bailee from relying on the terms of his own contract with the bailee. Contrary to the statements of the cargo representatives, this is necessary in cases where Himalaya clauses are not mentioned in the contract, for instance, where a third party in need can rely on the terms of bailment and sub-bailment. In the judges' words:

> If it should transpire that there are consequently two alternative regimes which the sub-bailee may invoke, it does not necessarily follow that they will be inconsistent;

111 Referring to *The Pioneer Container* (n. 86) case.
112 The Mahkutai *(n. 33).*
113 Ibid.
114 In *Morris* (n. 34) 729.
115 *The Eurymedon* (n. 1).

> nor does it follow, if they are inconsistent, that the sub-bailee should not be entitled to choose to rely upon one or other of them as against the owner of the goods.[116]

**7.81** The judges went on to say that, even if a Himalaya clause is applicable and is satisfied, it does not defeat the shipowners' reliance on bailment.[117]

**7.82** In case of *The Mahkutai*, the shipowner argument was unsuccessful both in bailment and in tort. Since the Himalaya clause does not include a jurisdiction clause in the bill of lading, the Court decided that bailment should not succeed on the bill of lading terms. In this case, the application of judgements from the *Elder Dempster* case were precluded by special circumstances.[118] As in *Scrutton*, *The Mahkutai* – although failing to grant protection to third parties – improved the mechanism of the protection in reality:

> So long as the principle continues to be understood to rest upon an enforceable contract as between cargo owners and the stevedores entered into through the agency of the shipowners, it is inevitable that technical points of contract and agency law will continue to be invoked by cargo owners seeking to enforce tortious remedies against the stevedores and others uninhibited by the exceptions and limitations in the relevant bill of lading contract.[119]

**7.83** Lord Goff's criticisms of *The Eurymedon* do not run counter to the principle of protection of a third party. Nonetheless, he expresses concern that the mechanism used to extend such protection is wrong. For Goff, the importance lies in discovering the factual basis from which the rendering of the bailment subject to such provision can be properly influenced.[120]

**7.84** *The Mahkutai* re-established the orthodox view on third party protection in English law. In contrast to the Court in *The Mahkutai*, the Court in *The Pioneer Container* emphasise the importance of commerce in deciding whether to rule in favour of the third party asking for legal protection.[121] The same commercial sense and commercial unreasonableness of the contrary seems to be also the foundation behind the Contract (Right of Third Parties) Act 1999.

## The Contract (Right of Third Parties) Act 1999: protection clauses on a statutory footing

**7.85** The shipping industry has tried to circumvent privity and consideration and allow protection to those who are not part of the contract. Because English law has always had theoretical difficulties with this, the industry has

116 See Bell (n. 106).
117 The Pioneer Container (n. 86) 344.
118 Liang (n. 80).
119 Tetley (n. 26).
120 *The Mahkutai* (n. 33).
121 Ibid. (Lord Goff). The submission of the plaintiffs in the present case was that the 'Himalaya' clause gives sufficient effect to the commercial expectations of the parties.

not hesitated in its attempts to circumvent it. It is evident, however, that privity and consideration have been an uncomfortable obstacle for the pragmatism of English law. Relating this to shipping, this is also apparent in a debate that forms part of the preparatory work to the Hague and Hague-Visby Rules, regarding the insertion of Article 4 bis. The discussion focussed on whether or not carrier protection should be extended to third parties and whether there had to be a difference between servant and agent on the one hand and independent contractors on the other hand. The delegation from the Netherlands criticised the United Kingdom's delegation, who were on that occasion happy to allow a broader protection to third parties (but only servant and agents and not independent contractors). The delegation from Netherland stated: 'We should be very glad if you make that amendment in your own domestic law, but we pray you humbly leave the Hague Rules alone'.[122] The United Kingdom delegation answered that, as a matter of fact:

> A problem arises because of the fundamental problem of the English law of contract which is that a person who is not a party to a contract can derive no benefit from it.

**7.86** The delegation continued:

> [I]t would be impossible to put the matter right by proposing this to the Parliament because an amendment of this general principle of law of contract would require an Act of Parliament asking them to provide by statute that a person who is not a party to a contract can derive benefit from it because the answer would be that the only people hampered by that principle would only be a very small section, though a very important class of people, an important class of traders, those who carry goods by sea.[123]

**7.87** At the time, the English delegation rationalised that a state should not alter a fundamental principle of its own law just because a somewhat narrow domestic difficulty arises. Instead, they argued, it is better to alter the international law of convention. At this point, it is worth noting the following:

1. Although English law had a problem 'at home' lawmakers were willing to open the door to a broader protection in an international environment.
2. At that time, the reluctance to propose an action of that nature to the British Parliament was based on the assessment that it would represent a major upheaval and administrative undertaking that was not proportionate to the very small number of people who demanded it or who would benefit from it.
3. It was considered an unalterable fundamental principle of English Law.

122 Delegation of the United Kingdom, Hague-Visby Rules, *Travaux Préparatoires*, 603. In favour, amongst others, were Sweden, Italy, and Canada.
123 Ibid.

**7.88** Despite all of this, in 1999 the United Kingdom adopted the Contract (Right of third parties) Act 1999.[124] The judgement in *Dunlop Pneumatic* has now been reversed:

> My Lords, in the law of England certain principles are fundamental. One is that only a person who is a party to a contract can sue on it. Our law knows nothing of a *jus* quaesitum tertio arising by way of contract.[125]

**7.89** As previously stated, there has always been a battle against the privity and consideration rule. They were seen as a barrier and, in response, the Contract (Right of Third Parties) Act 1999 was enacted.[126]

**7.90** The Act essentially allows a third party to benefit from the contract. Section 1(1) grants a third party the right to enforce a term of the agreement if either the contract expressly provides he may or, under Section 1(1)(b) 'the term purports to confer a benefit upon him'. In relation to a clause excluding or limiting liability, Section 1(6) provides: 'Where a term of a contract excludes or limits liability in relation to any matter references in this Act to the third party enforcing the term shall be construed as references to availing himself of the exclusion or limitation'.

**7.91** Section 6 of the statute addresses exceptions to the right of a third party under Section 1 to enforce a benefiting contractual term. In particular, under Section 6(5)(a), a third party has no right to enforce such a term for his benefit, in the case of a contract for the carriage of goods by sea. A contract for the carriage of goods by sea is defined as a contract either: (i) 'contained in or evidenced by a bill of lading, sea waybill or a corresponding electronic transaction' according to Section 6(6)(a)(i), or; (ii) 'under or for the purposes of which there is given an undertaking which is contained in a ship's delivery order or a corresponding electronic transaction', according to Section 6(6)(b).

**7.92** There is, however, one fundamental exception, which permits the third party beneficiary, in reliance on Section 1, to 'avail himself of an exclusion or limitation of liability in such a contract' (Section 6(5)(a)). It is this exception to an exception in the Contracts (Rights of Third Parties) Act 1999 that places the

124 Law Commission, 'Privity of Contract: Contracts for the Benefit of Third Parties: The Legal Systems of Most Member States of the European Union Allow Third Parties to Enforce Contracts' (1996) Law Commission 242 para 8. A further factor in support of reforming the third party rule in English law is the fact that the legal systems of most of the member states of the European Union recognise and enforce the rights of third party beneficiaries under contracts.

125 *Dunlop* (n. 10).

126 Its full title which states, 'An Act to make provision for the enforcement of contractual terms by third parties'. This reform started long before 1999, in 1937. In the Recommendation (The Editorial Committee of the Modern Law Review, 'The Law Revision Committee's Sixth Interim Report' (1937) 1 The Modern Law Review 2) it says:

> The rule that a stranger to a contract cannot maintain an action upon it has been one of the most unsatisfactory features of the law relating to consideration. It has been tenaciously adhered to in all but a few cases, which were of minor importance. The rule is completely out of harmony with the conditions of modern commerce and industry.

Himalaya clause on a statutory footing in the United Kingdom. As the Explanatory Note to Section 6(5) states:

> Subsection (5), which excludes certain contracts relating to the carriage of goods, nevertheless does not prevent a third party from taking advantage of a term excluding or limiting liability. In particular, this enables clauses which seek to extend an exclusion or limitation of liability of a carrier of goods by the sea to servants, agents and independent contractors engaged in the loading and unloading process to be enforced by those servants, agents or independent contractors (so called 'Himalaya' clauses).

**7.93** Analysing the Contracts (Rights of Third Parties) Act 1999, it appears first that the Act expressly provides that the contract has to explicitly confer a benefit to a third party. As Stevens states, it seems that the third party must be expressly identified in the contract by name, as a member of a class or as answering a particular description but need not be in existence when the contract is entered. This is substantially the equivalent of the Himalaya clause but in a statutory guise. Rather than abolishing the need to satisfy privity and consideration, the Contracts (Rights of Third Parties) Act 1999 has created another exception to each of them.[127] Had it been utilised in *Scrutton*, the Act would have had limited application. In his article, 'A Birthday Present for Lord Denning', Macmillan explains the following:

> Here, the relevant contract was the bill of lading which contained a limitation of liability clause. The contract was initially between the shipper and the carrier; after the sale of the goods it was between the shipper and the consignee. In order for the new Act to have allowed the stevedores to avail themselves of the limitation clause in this contract, the contract would have needed to contain a term which purported to benefit them (s 1(1)(b), (2) & (6)). It is by no means clear that it did. The Law Lords, including Lord Denning, did not believe that the bill of lading was intended to protect the stevedores. However, the Law Lords were considering a different issue: whether the carriers had acted as agents of the stevedores and not whether the contract extended an enforceable benefit to the stevedores. The bill of lading did seek to allow a bailee of the goods to avail himself of the limitation of liability and on this basis it is at least arguable that the new Act would have allowed the stevedores to raise the limitation of liability in their defence. This last example serves to illustrate that difficult cases are bound to arise even after the new Act.[128]

**7.94** Smith outlines the rationale behind the Act: 'If the contracting parties intend to benefit a third party then the law should support this intention by allowing the third party to enforce the contract'.[129] However, although the Act confers rights to third parties and a Himalaya clause has a statutory footing,

127 R Stevens, 'The Contracts (Rights of Third Parties) Act 1999' (2004) Law Quarterly Review 120.

128 Catharine MacMillan, 'A Birthday Present for Lord Denning: The Contracts (Rights of Third Parties) Act 1999' (2000) 63 The Modern Law Review 5, 721–738.

129 Stephen A Smith, 'Contracts for the Benefit of Third Parties: In Defence of the Third-Party Rule' (1997) 17 Oxford Journal of Legal Studies 643.

it still needs a juridical justification. It requires consideration for an implied contract. This consideration – as in *The Eurymedon*, for example – could be performing one of the carrier activities. It is difficult, however, to accurately define the activities of modern carriers. In the past such definitions were easier; the activities were related only to the sea-side of operations (see Hague-Visby Rules and Hamburg Rules). But, with the Rotterdam Rules, and with the carrier taking responsibilities for the whole carriage, it would be very difficult to differentiate categories of third parties.[130]

**7.95** An article by Clifford Chance's International Maritime Trade & Insurance Group states:

> One of the clear benefits of the Act is to render virtually obsolete Himalaya-type provisions. The new Act effectively dispenses with all but one of the four conditions that were set out in Scruttons Ltd v Midlands Silicones Ltd The remaining condition is the two-fold test in Section 1(1) of the Act. For this reason, while the new Act greatly alleviates the previous problem and largely replaces the need for Himalaya clauses, it does not automatically follow that Himalaya provisions are completely obsolete or no longer necessary.[131]

**7.96** Lord noted that Section 7(1) of the Contract (Right of Third Parties) Act 1999 maintains any right or remedy of a third party that exists outside the Act. Article IV bis (2) of the Hague-Visby Rules allows servants and agents of the carriers to rely on the protection to which the carrier is entitled under the rules. This is unaffected by the Contract (Right of Third Parties) Act 1999. The protection granted by the rules does not extend to independent contractors, whose position is therefore greatly improved by the Contract (Right of Third Parties) Act 1999.[132]

**7.97** Under the Contract (Right of Third Parties) Act 1999, tools such as protection clauses and agency might in general terms no longer be needed; the consent of the parties could be adequate to extend the protection.[133]

**7.98** Tetley contends that the 1999 statute provides a less complex foundation for applying a standard limitation of liability clause. The statute requires merely that the third party beneficiaries be identified with sufficient clarity; expressly (Section 1(1)(a)), or by class, name or description (Section 1(1)(b) and 1(3)). The carrier's permission from the third party to stipulate the clause, the third party's ratification of the benefit conferred by the clause, and the passing of consideration are no longer a concern.[134]

**7.99** This undeniably confirms that third parties in the carriage of goods by sea cannot be left stranded without proper protection. However, introducing a

130 Ibid.

131 Tony Vlasto and Julian Clark, 'The Effect of the Contracts (Rights of Third Parties) Act 1999 on Voyage and Time Charter Parties' (2000–2001) 25 Tulane Maritime Law Journal 519.

132 David Lord, 'Insurable Interest: Is There a Rule?' (*3 Stone Buildings*, 2005), 159 <http://clients.squareeye.net/uploads/3sb/events/121005_lord.pdf>. Accessed 5 May 2013.

133 In case the carriage of goods by sea contract in question is under English law.

134 Tetley (n. 26).

Himalaya clause on a statutory footing does not equate to provision of the clause with full effect. It simply states that in some circumstances, under the Act, a third party can rely on an exclusion clause of a contract of which they are not part. It is clear from the explanatory notes that the activities of the third parties are related to the loading and unloading process. Since 1999, when the Act was drafted, commerce has changed a great deal. Convincing arguments have been made that, as a result of these changes, the Act has been rendered almost obsolete. Restricting reliance on this clause to only third parties involved in the loading and unloading processes means leaving outside the law all the others involved in the multilateral common enterprise.

## Conclusion

**7.100** In summary, English law and third party protection do not sit comfortably with one another. Consideration may indeed be 'too firmly fixed to be overthrown by a side-wind', but it has nonetheless been circumvented.

**7.101** Bailment, agency, protection clauses, and the Contract (Right of Third Parties) Act 1999 are all geared towards attaining the same objective, but none of them provide third parties with adequate, up-to-date, and juridically justified protection.

**7.102** These concepts have created various difficulties in the aforementioned cases: *Elder Dempster*, *Scrutton*, *The Eurymedon* and, more recently, *The Pioneer Container* and *The Mahkutai*.[135]

**7.103** *The Eurymedon* warrants particular mention here. In it, the House of Lords accepted that a promise by A could enforce separate contracts with B and with C.[136] The Privy Council's view on *The Eurymedon* elucidated the unnecessary complexities which emerge in the event of a digression from the doctrine and giving effect to the parties' intention. Since the Privy Council's decision in *The Eurymedon*, the extension of rights to third parties by virtue of the Himalaya clause has been acknowledged in the United Kingdom. This was further developed by case of *The Pioneer Container*, in which:

1. The Privy Council was attracted to a solution which accorded with commercial convenience and practical good sense.
2. The Himalaya clause route and the doctrine of bailment on terms were deemed cumulative rather than alternative solutions.[137]

**7.104** The difference between the cases of *The Pioneer Container* and *The Mahkutai* is that the former has been decided in a very commercial way, whilst the latter involved a very conservative approach to third party protection.

135 Merkin (n. 1) 18.
136 Ibid.
137 *The Pioneer Container* (n. 86).

**7.105** Finally, although the Contract (Right of Third Parties) Act 1999 improves the situation of third party protection, it still relies on the presence of an implied contract to function. Moreover, the Act substantially only moves the third party protection on a statutory level. As the full title of the Act implies, it is concerned with the rights of third parties. However, the situation of third party protection in the carriage of goods by sea differs from the one envisaged by the Act. Not only that, but it is twenty years since the Act was passed, and its drafting began many years earlier. The Act seems to have placed the Himalaya clause on a statutory footing but the four criteria outlined Lord Reid must still be satisfied.

**7.106** Taking into account Nossal's criticisms of *The Mahkutai* case – and considering that carriage has evolved into a multilateral sector – it is believed that strict application of legal concepts such as privity and consideration fails to do justice to a fundamental commercial principle: namely, that if a party performing the carriage enterprise is sued by the cargo owner (who aims to circumvent the limitation of liability in the contract) the party sued in tort has to rely on that clause.[138] Denying it is fundamentally wrong because it fails to respect not only the parties' wishes, but also the reliance that the third party has on that principle. Once established, bailment, agency and protection clauses become mere instruments in applying that principle.

138 Nossal (n. 110).

CHAPTER 8

# Third party protection under United States law

**8.1** The political role of transportation in the United States differs substantially from its political role in England, courtesy of its deep involvement with multimodalism.[1] The 'intermodal system' of the United States is a transport network that links the transfer of cargo from one side of the country to the other.[2] Its aim is to reduce costs as much as possible, and to do this, it requires economies of scale (for terminal operators) and economies of scope (for carriers and port workers).[3] All of which gives different context to third party protection in the United States.

**8.2** United States law understands third parties rather differently to English law, and its willingness to grant them protection correspondingly different.[4] The United States has a completely different historical background to England in the carriage of goods by sea. Curiously, Sturley notes that 'England is a leading carrier nation, but the House of Lords' initial response to the Himalaya clause problem was strongly pro-cargo. The United States is a cargo nation, but its Himalaya clause jurisprudence favours the carrier'.[5] With the exception of Himalaya clauses, Courts in the United States are generally more open to third party protection.[6]

1 The geographical extension of the United States and its geographical position as a link between East and West is another main difference between the two countries and is one of the main reasons why the multimodality has been developed in this country.

2 The terms 'multimodal' and 'intermodal' are variously defined. They are sometimes considered different from each other and some other time considered as a synonym. It is safe to say that both are linked with the involvement of different modes of transport. Martin Stopford for instance, in the book Maritime Economics refer to intermodalism and define it as: 'system concerned with the transfer of cargo from one mode to another'. Bes defines 'chartering' as: '*intermodalism (or multimodalism) which is carriage of goods by a mixture of modes of transport*'. This book recognises that they can be essentially used interchangeably but prefer to use the term 'multimodalism'. However, in United States literature is frequent to find the term 'intermodalism' and the system that this chapter refers to is formally called 'United States Intermodal System'.

3 Delmy L Salin, *Impact of Panama Canal Expansion on the U.S. Intermodal System*. United States Department of Agriculture, Marketing and Regulatory Programs, Agricultural Marketing Service, January 2010 <www.ams.usda.gov/sites/default/files/media/Impact%20of%20Panama%20Canal%20Expansion%20on%20the%20U.S.%20Intermodal%20System.pdf>. Accessed 7 October 2015.

4 Michael F Sturley, 'International Uniform Laws in National Courts: The Influence of Domestic Law in Conflicts of Interpretation' (1986–1987) 27 Virginia Journal of International Law 729.

5 Ibid., 742.

6 The modern third party beneficiary rule in the United States has started with the case of *Lawrence v Fox* (1859) 20 NY 268 (NYCA).

**8.3** United States law has two unique features that impact on the carriage of goods by sea:

1. The conflicts between COGSA and state law, and the enactment of the Harter Act.
2. United States law is federal in nature; thus third party protection varies from state to state. According to Zawitosky, the laws of some states provide that an agent of the carrier acting within the scope of its authority is entitled to the benefit of any contractual limit upon the liability of its principal, including any limitation under COGSA or the bill of lading.[7]

**8.4** Zawitosky also reports that there exist two other sources of authority under state law for the extension to stevedores and terminal operators of limitation provisions in the carrier's bill of lading: Sections 7-20429 and 7-3093 of the Uniform Commercial Code (UCC), which together allow contractual limitation of liability under specific conditions for warehousemen and carriers.[8]

**8.5** Under Section 7-204(2) of the UCC, a warehouseman may validly contract to limit their liability to a specific amount per package. This section states:

> Damages may be limited by a term in the warehouse receipt or storage agreement limiting the amount of liability in case of loss or damage, and setting forth a specific liability per article or item, or value per unit of weight beyond which the warehouseman shall not be liable; provided, however, that such liability may on written request of the bailor at the time of signing such storage agreement or within a reasonable time after receipt of the warehouse receipt be increased on part or all of the goods thereunder, in which event increased rates may be charged based on such increased valuation, but that no such increase shall be permitted contrary to the lawful limitation of liability contained in the warehouseman's tariff, if any. No such limitation is effective with respect to the warehouseman's liability for conversion to his own use.[9]

**8.6** In general terms, it is clear that multilateral transport in the United States faces a problem of jurisdiction (i.e., Admiralty and federal regulation of railroads).[10]

7 Joanne Zawitoski, 'Limitation of Liability for Stevedores and Terminal Operators under the Carrier's Bill of Lading and COGSA' (1985) 16 Journal of Maritime Law and Commerce 3, 337.

8 Ibid.

9 Thomas R Denniston, Carter T Gunn and Alfred E Yudes, 'Liabilities of Multimodal Operators and Parties Other than Carriers and Shippers' (1989–1990) 64 Tulane Law Review 517.

10 The issue of the conflict between Admiralty law and federal law in the United States is outside the scope of this book. However, it is worth specifying that, as reported by J C Sweeney – 'Crossing the Himalayas: Exculpatory Clauses in Global Transport – *Norfolk Southern Railway Co. v James N. Kirby*' (2005) 36 Journal of Maritime Law and Commerce, 155 – the approach of admiralty jurisdiction has most probably been adapted after the Kirby decision. In Kirby, Justice O'Connor defined the case as a 'maritime case about a train wreck' therefore under Admiralty jurisdiction. Sweeney aptly point it out that this definition is shocking 'only' for those who are not familiar with modern transport. For who is part of modern transport instead it should be a natural consequence of the current factual context.

## Agency and bailment in United States law

**8.7** Agency and bailment held great importance under United States law up to a certain point. After the case of *Herd*, however, the Courts' approach changed.[11]

**8.8** According to American Restatement,[12] an agency is the fiduciary relationship that arises when one person (a 'principal') manifests assent to another person (an 'agent') that the agent shall act on the principal's behalf and subject to the principal's control, and the agent manifests or otherwise consents so to act.[13]

**8.9** Also under United States law, agency is strictly connected with bailment. A treatise from 1914 on the law of bailment and carrier reports that most contracts could be entered into by an agent of the contractor[14]; the principles of agency apply to bailment. In the same treatise, Elliot refers to his statement as especially true in reference to the law of carriers, since today most carriers are great corporations, which can contract only by and via their agent.[15]

**8.10** Bailment in the United States is dealt with by the UCC,[16] which defines a bailee as 'a person that by a warehouse receipt, bill of lading, or other document of title acknowledges possession of goods and contracts to deliver them'.[17] As explained by the Uniform Law Commission:

> The storage and shipment of tangible goods for commercial purposes has been going on for centuries. The physical side of the business is carried on by entities that provide warehouses (warehousemen) and entities that carry the goods from place of origin to destination (common carriers). These are tangible, visible businesses. What is not tangible and visible is the transfer of rights in the goods while they are stored and/or shipped. The common law provided the rules of bailment.[18]

**8.11** Writing in 1992, Helmholz said that the preceding 60 years had seen no systematic treatise devoted to the law of bailment in the United States.[19] Nearly three decades later, little has changed.

11 *Herd & Co. v Krawill Machinery Corp.* 359 US 297, 1959 AMC 879 (1959).

12 American Law Institute, *Restatement of the Law of Agency* (3rd edn, American Law Institute 2006) para 1.01.

13 Ibid. Agency under United States law also affects the relationship between employer and employee which is dealt with the concept of the *respondeat* that states that an employer is subject to liability for torts committed by employees while acting within the scope of their employment.

14 William F Elliot, *A Treatise on the Law of Bailment and Carriers* (Bobbs-Merrill Company 1914) 266.

15 Ibid.

16 The Uniform Commercial Code (UCC or 'the Code'), first published in 1952, is one of a number of Uniform Acts that have been promulgated in conjunction with efforts to harmonise the Law of Sales and other commercial transactions in all 50 American states. The goal of harmonising State Law is important because of the prevalence of commercial transactions that extend beyond one state.

17 Section 7-102(1). Therefore, it is acknowledged that according to the UCC it has to be under a document and not just possession.

18 Uniform Law Commission, 'UCC Article 7, Documents of Title (2003) Summary' (Uniform Law Commission, 2015) <www.uniformlaws.org/ActSummary.aspx?title=UCC%20Article%207,%20Documents%20of%20Title%20(2003)>. Accessed 9 February 2014.

19 Richard H Helmholz, 'Bailment Theories and the Liability of Bailees: The Elusive Uniform Standard of Reasonable Care' (1992) 41 University of Kansas Law Review 97.

**8.12** Street stresses that possession is severed from ownership.[20] Decisions under United States regarding bailment have tended to swing, pendulum-like, between possession and contract. In his article 'The definition of a bailment', Cullen actually specifies that although it is usually created by a contract, this is not always the case.[21]

**8.13** Laidlaw explained in 1932 that nineteenth-century Courts gave a great deal of attention to contract, frequently stipulating its requirement where – in Laidlaw's opinion – none should have been needed.[22] In a variety of American cases, bailment was not found because no contract existed.[23] Other Courts have nonetheless contradicted this approach, suggesting, for example, that bailment does not always depend upon a contractual relation. It is an element of lawful possession no matter how it is created and duty to account for it as the property of another that creates bailment, regardless of whether such possession is based upon contract in the ordinary sense.[24] According to Laidlaw,[25] if there is a bailment whenever there is possession of the chattel, every possessor who is not an owner is a bailee.

In the United States, as in England, third parties have historically sought legal protection under agency and bailment law.

### Third parties in United States case law prior to *Herd & Co.*

**8.14** The willingness of the United States to allow protection to third parties seems to have waxed and waned over time. In the middle of the last century, according to Zawitosky, a United States Court would have held a third party employed by the carrier to receive a benefit from the contract by virtue of that employment relationship alone, under the principles of agency law.[26] In contrast to English law, the United States has not had problems with the concepts of privity and consideration.[27]

**8.15** Early judgements in the United States extended bill of lading exceptions even where the bill of lading clauses in question were far from specific. Until the middle of the twentieth century, in fact, a terminal operator or a stevedore could rely on the protection from the bill of lading even without specific clauses in the bill of lading.[28]

20 Thomas Atkin Street, 2 Foundations of Legal Liability (1906) New York at 232

21 (1926) 11 St. Louis Law Review 257, 264.

22 William King Laidlaw, 'Principles of Bailment' (1932) 37 Commercial Law Journal 134.

23 *Berting v Norman* 101 Ark 75, 141 SW 201 (1911); *Bohannon v Springfield* Ala 789 (1846); *Cowen v Pressprich* 202 App Div 796, 196 NY Supp 921.

24 *Foulke v New York Consolidated R.R.* 228 NY 269, 127 NE 237 (1920).

25 Laidlaw (n. 22).

26 Joanne Zawitoski, 'Limitation of Liability for Stevedores and Terminal Operators under the Carrier's Bill of Lading and COGSA' (1985) 16 Journal of Maritime Law and Commerce 3, 337.

27 The Restatement (Second) Contracts 1981, Section 304, which provides, 'A promise in a contract creates a duty in the promisor to any intended beneficiary to perform the promise, and the intended beneficiary may enforce the duty'. Comment (b) to Section 304 states, 'This Section reflects the basic principle that the parties to a contract have the power, if they so intend, to create a right in a third person'.

28 *National Federation of Coffee Growers of Colombia v Isbrandtsen Co.* (1957) AMC 1571 (Sup Ct NY). *United States v The South Star* 210 F 2d 44 (2d Cir *1954*).

**8.16** Citing *Reid v Fargo*, Healy argues that the extraordinary lack of litigation on this question in the years between 1913 and 1952 is responsible for the denial of extension of liability limitation to the stevedore; a time when the case of *Collins & Co. v Panama Railway Co.* was appealed to the Court of Appeal for the Fifth Circuit.[29]

**8.17** The concepts of bailment and agency have been cornerstones of the protection afforded during this period, giving the effect of limitation clauses (such as the Himalaya clause) and the concept of vicarious liability. During this period, the case of *Collins* emerged as a leading authority on the issue of whether or not a stevedore might vicariously have the benefit of a contractual limitation of liability as an agent of the named carrier in the bill of lading.[30] In it, the Court of Appeals for the Fifth Circuit had held that where the provisions of the Carriage of Goods by Sea Act was expressly incorporated into the bill of lading, the stevedore had equal benefit with the carrier of Section 4(5) of the Act, which states that:

> Neither the carrier nor the ship shall in any event be or become liable for any loss or damage to or in connection with the transportation of goods in an amount exceeding $500 per package lawful money of the United States, or in case of goods not shipped in packages, per customary freight unit, or the equivalent of that sum in other currency, unless the nature and value of such goods have been declared by the shipper before shipment and inserted in the bill of lading. This declaration, if embodied in the bill of lading, shall be prima facie evidence, but shall not be conclusive on the carrier.[31]

**8.18** The Court provided a staunchly commercial rationale, summarised below:

- Ships are usually unloaded by stevedores.
- Carriage of goods by sea covers the period from the time of loading to discharging.
- The stevedore was contracted by the carrier to carry out the carrier's obligations to discharge cargo.
- The goods went damaged during this period.

**8.19** The stevedores were therefore entitled to the same limitation of liability of the carrier. The Court in *Collins* applied the principle of the Restatement of agency (Paragraph 347), which states that 'an agent who is acting in pursuance of his authority has such immunities of the principal as are not personal to the principal'.[32]

29 Marie Healy, *'Carriage of Goods by Sea: Application of the Himalaya Clause to Subdelegees of the Carrier' (1977)* 2 The Maritime Lawyer 91.
30 *A.M. Collins & Co v Panama R. Co* (1952) 197 F 2d.
31 Ibid.
32 Ibid.

**8.20** Almost a decade later, the legal landscape in the United States changed again with the Supreme Court's ruling in *Herd*. This case disregarded the nature of the relationship between the third party and the main party of the contract and therefore the concepts of bailment and agency. On the contrary, the discussions in *Herd* focussed on how Courts would have construed the clauses. The Court passed over bailment and agency, taking the protection of third parties to a purely contractual level and, in doing so, highlighting the autonomy of the parties of a contract. *Herd* defines the modern way in which clauses have to be construed in order to do justice to the intention of the parties. *Herd* was something of a watershed for the United States' approach to third party protection and has greatly influenced cases in the carriage of goods by sea. The situation changed again, though, with *Kirby*: a case in which it is stated that the intent of a maritime contract goes beyond any barrier.

### The case of *Herd & Co.*

**8.21** *Herd* involved stevedores, contracted verbally by the carrier, who, while loading the cargo, dropped it into the water. The stevedore attempted to rely on the bill of lading and to take advantage of the $500 per package limitation. The district Court refused to extend the package limitation to the stevedores holding that:

> Contracts purporting to grant immunity from, or limitation of, liability must be strictly construed and limited to intended beneficiaries, for they 'are not to be applied to alter familiar rules visiting liability upon a tortfeasor for the consequences of his negligence, unless the clarity of the language used expresses such to be the understanding of the contracting parties'.[33]

**8.22** The case reached the Supreme Court of the United States which also refused to extend the $500 per package limitation to stevedores who had been contracted orally by the carrier. The Court in *Herd* changed its approach towards third party protection, stating that:

1. The language of the Himalaya clause must be very specific as to whom it protects.
2. Courts will not interpret bills of lading to benefit third parties not mentioned in any way whatsoever.

**8.23** In deciding *Herd*, the United States Supreme Court made it difficult for third parties to benefit from exculpatory clauses in bills of lading to which they were not a party. The result was that, in order to be viewed as protected by an exculpatory clause in a contract for carriage, a third-party contractor would have to be named with some degree of specificity. However, in the case, the Court did not establish a rule regarding how specific the identification of a party must be.

33 *Herd* (n. 11)

**8.24** It became apparent that, after *Herd*, a simple agency relationship between stevedore and carrier would be insufficient to extend the carrier's bill of lading protections to the stevedore. To facilitate the application of the protection, the clause must reflect the intention of the parties to protect the third party. In the period following *Herd*, the Supreme Court's request for precision in the wording of clauses to be extended to third parties was reiterated by other Courts.[34]

**8.25** In *Herd*, the Court commented in detail on the text of the Hague Rules and their adoption by the United States Congress:

> The debates and Committee Reports in the Senate and the House upon the bill that became the Carriage of Goods by Sea Act likewise do not mention stevedores or agents. There is, thus, nothing in the language, the legislative history or environment of the Act that expressly or impliedly indicates any intention of Congress to regulate stevedores or other agents of a carrier, or to limit the amount of their liability for damages caused by their negligence.[35]

**8.26** The Supreme Court stated in *Herd* that 'no statute has limited its liability, and it was not a party to nor a beneficiary of the contract of carriage between the shipper and the carrier, and hence its liability was not limited by that contract'.[36]

**8.27** After *Herd*, the shipping industry started to comply with the Supreme Court's requirement in order to allow protection to parties outside the contract. As a matter of fact, the Himalaya clause benefiting the stevedore and the terminal operator is valid in the United States as a result of *Herd*, but certain conditions must be met:

> There must be a contractual relationship between the contracting party and anyone who purports to claim the benefit of any clause in that contract. Furthermore, the party claiming the benefits bestowed by a Himalaya clause must be performing part of the contract that actually contains the clause. As said before, in case of independent contractors, some courts have required that the operation being performed be of a 'maritime nature'.[37]

**8.28** As Tetley points out, *Herd* also impacted upon the relationship between independent contractor and employer. Generally speaking, the employer of an independent contractor is not held liable vicariously for any tortious acts and omissions of the contractor; the control and supervision existing in an employer-employee or principal-agent relationship is absent. However, vicarious liability will be imposed only if the clause is sufficiently clear and drafted narrowly enough to cover only the intended beneficiaries.[38]

34 Zawitoski (n. 26).
35 *Herd* (n. 11) 358.
36 Ibid., 359.
37 *Taisho Marine & Fire Insurance Co. v The Vessel Gladiolus* 762 F 2d 1364 (2d Cir 1985).
38 William Tetley, 'Case Comment: The House of Lords Decision in *The Starsin*' (2004) 35 JMLC 121–139.

**8.29** *Herd* achieved in the United States what the case of *Scrutton* had achieved in England. By denying third parties the ability to benefit from a limitation of liability, these two cases opened the door for third party protection.

## From *Herd & Co.* to *Kirby*

**8.30** In the period between *Herd* and *Kirby*, United States case law established various limits for third party protection, such as the maritime nature of the service, the clarity of the language of the protection clause, and the relationship that the third party has to have with the main party.

**8.31** There are several cases demonstrating this, but one in particular summarises the criteria quite well; the 1998 case known as *Akiyama Corporation of America*. The Court in allowing the stevedores and terminal operators to receive protection under the bill of lading, formally summarised that there are three factors to consider in determining the intent of the contracting parties:

1. Nature of the service performed
2. Clarity of language to extend to third party
3. Contractual relation between third party and main party[39]

**8.32** There are a substantial number of cases from that period. The analysis below does not attempt to cover all of them but instead refers to the most relevant cases to support the arguments made in this book.

**8.33** An example of limiting the nature of the service to geographical boundary is the case of *Virgin Island Corp. v Merwin Lighterage Co., Inc.* As Healey reports, this was the first case to rely on the *Herd* mandate. The Court stated that the carrier's $500 per package limitation of liability was not intended to be extended to the carrier's negligent lighterman, where the bill of lading expressly included protection for the carrier or bailee only before the goods left the ship's tackle, and where it expressly provided that lighterage was at the 'risk of the goods'.[40]

**8.34** In a case known as *The Vessel Gladiolus*, a trucking company was not allowed to benefit from a Himalaya clause because it was not performing a 'maritime function'.[41]

**8.35** In 1991, the case of *Caterpillar Overseas* reinstated the concept that the operation being performed should be of a maritime nature. In the words of the Court:

> In determining the meaning of the term independent contractor in the application of the Himalaya clause the court is to take into consideration the nature of the

39 *Akiyama Corporation of America v M.V Hanjin Marseilles* (1998) 162 F.3d 571.
40 Healy (n. 29).
41 *The Vessels Gladiolus* (n. 37).

services performed compared to the carrier's responsibilities under the carriage contract and that if the independent contractor is performing a non-maritime service, that is another factor to be given weight in ascertaining whether the third party qualifies for the Himalaya limitation.[42]

**8.36** In the same period, the Court of Maryland in the *Herr-Voss Corporation* case allowed a Himalaya clause to a cover a trucking services company because it was judged that 'while in truth non-maritime, the trucking company was performing a service crucial for the maritime services'.[43]

**8.37** A similar case is *Acciai Speciali*, in which the Court stated that the Himalaya clause could be extended to third parties only 'while acting in the course of or in connection with their employment'.[44] Such clauses, following *Herd*, must be strictly construed and limited to intended beneficiaries.

**8.38** It is noted that maritime boundaries also seem to have been adopted a few years later, in the preparation of the Rotterdam Rules, where the United States delegation insisted on putting forward a geographic approach.[45]

**8.39** However, an opposing and more conceptual view (even though strictly related to the specificity of the clause) is given by the Court in *Carle & Montanari*:

> It is understood and agreed that, other than said shipowner or demise charterer, no person, firm or corporation or other legal entity whatsoever (including the Master, officers and crew of the vessel, all agents and all stevedores and other independent contractors whatsoever) is, or shall be deemed to be liable with respect to the goods as carrier, bailee or otherwise howsoever, in contract or in tort. If, however, it shall be adjudged that any other than said shipowner or demise charterer is carrier or

42 *Caterpillar Overseas, S.A. v Marine Transports, Inc.* 900 F 2d 714, 724, 1991 AMC 75, 92–93 (4 Cir 1990); *Herr-Voss Corporation v Columbus Line (Herr-Voss)* 1994 AMC 77, 81 (D Md 1992).

43 *Herr-Voss*, ibid.

44 *Acciai Speciali Terni v M/V Berance, et al., Defendants* (181 F.Supp.2d 458).

45 As set out in the 'Transport Law Draft Convention on the Carriage of Goods (Wholly or Partly) (by Sea) Note by the Secretariat' (United Nations Commission on International Trade Law Working Group III (Transport Law) Nineteenth Session (New York, 16–27 April 2007 A/CN.9/WG.III/WP.81)), the definition of 'maritime performing party' (Draft Article 1(7) of the Draft Convention) should be edited to clarify that a rail carrier, even if it performs services that might be considered the carrier's responsibilities after the arrival of the goods at the port of loading or prior to the departure of the goods from the port of discharge, should be considered a non-maritime performing party. 2. The Convention applies to actions against the carrier or a maritime performing party (Draft Art 4) but not to actions against a non-maritime performing party. The suggestion outlined in para 1 was made at the behest of the Association of American Railroads (AAR) (representing the United States, Canadian, and Mexican railroads). The AAR made it known to the United States from the beginning of the negotiation that it is concerned it might inadvertently be deemed to be a maritime performing party when it performs services within a port area, even though the ultimate purpose of those services will virtually always be to move goods into or out of a port and not to move goods from one place to another within a port. Therefore, the United States supports the suggestion reflected in para 1. 3. The United States proposes the following sentence be added at the end of Draft Art 1(7) of A/CN.9/WG.III/WP.81 (the definition of 'maritime performing party'), 'A rail carrier, even if it performs services that are the carrier's responsibilities after arrival of the goods at the port of loading or prior to the departure of the goods from the port of discharge, is a non-maritime performing party'.

> bailee of the goods or under any responsibility with respect thereto, all limitations of and exonerations from liability provided by law or by the terms hereof shall be available to such other.[46]

**8.40** The Court here acknowledges the authority of *Herd* and the fact that a bill of lading can extend the legal protection to a third party, but only if there is a clear and expressed intention to do so. In this case the Court held that there was such intention and duly extended the $500 liability to the stevedores. In *Middle East Export Co. v Concordia Line* – where the $500 per package limitation was extended by the bill of lading to 'any other legal entity whatsoever', including 'all agents and independent contractors' – the Court were of the same opinion.[47]

**8.41** In the case of *Cabot Corp. v S. S. Mormacsan*, by contrast, the language in the bill of lading was found to be insufficiently precise to meet the standards of clarity demanded by *Herd*.[48] The judges in *Cabot Corporation* laid particular stress on the idea that the parties have to be expressly mentioned:

> The failure to include similar language here would lead one to believe that the protection of stevedores against liability was not intended. In any case such an intention was not expressed with sufficient clarity of language. We will not stretch the language when the party drafting such a form contract has not included a provision it easily might have.[49]

**8.42** During this period, clarity of language was essential in order to extend the carrier's COGSA benefits to 'independent contractors'. Zawitoski reports that the mere presence of the term 'independent contractor' in the Himalaya clause was sufficient to encompass stevedores, terminal operators, and other non-enumerated third parties.[50] However, in determining the scope of protection offered by the simple term 'independent contractor' in the carrier's Himalaya clause, federal Courts in the United States started to distinguish between an independent contractor employed by the carrier and one employed by a party other than the carrier. In *Toyomenka, Inc. v S.S. Tosaharu Maru*,[51] the Second Circuit held that a security service company hired by the carrier's stevedore was not entitled to limit its liability under a Himalaya clause covering 'all servants, agents and independent contractors ... used or employed by the carrier', since the security service company had not been employed by the carrier.[52]

**8.43** In the aforementioned case of *Carle & Montanari*, the bill of lading extended 'all limitations of and exonerations from liability' to 'all agents

46 *Carle & Montanari, Inc. v American Export Isbrandtsen Lines*, Inc., 275 F Supp 76, 1967 A M C 1637 (S D N Y), aff'd 386 F 2d 839, 1967 A M C 2529 (2d Cir 1967).

47 64 Misc 2d 270, 314 NYS 2d 390 (NYC Civ Ct 1970) aff'd 71 Misc 2d 365, 336 NYS 2d 217 (Sup Ct App Term 1st Dept 1972).

48 441 F 2d 476 (2 Cir 1971).

49 Ibid.

50 Zawitoski (n. 26).

51 *Toyomenka Inc. v Tosaharu Maru (Tosaharu Maru)* 523 F2d 518, 1975 AMC 1820 (2 Cir 1975).

52 Zawitoski (n. 26).

and all stevedores and other independent contractors whatsoever'.[53] In this period the Courts allowed protection only in cases where the third party for whom protection was sought was precisely mentioned and as an independent contractor was considered not sufficient to protect a specific category of third party. Conversely, the Court held that the term 'agent' was adequate to protect stevedores.[54] As well as describing third parties merely as 'bailees' or as 'all persons rendering services in connection with the performance of this contract' did not meet the test of specificity in the past.[55] In 1990, however, it was stated that the term 'bailee' as used in a bill of lading is sufficiently clear in expressing intent to extend limitation benefits to stevedores or other non-carriers.[56]

**8.44** Other cases, in this period recognise that the description 'independent contractors' was considered sufficiently specific until the 1970s, around which time it came to be viewed as imprecise.[57]

**8.45** The importance of the relationship with the carrier is highlighted in *Assicurazioni Generali v D'Amico*, in which the Himalaya clause had been extended to a bailee. The judges interpreted the situation in favour of the bailee, explaining that it was the clear intention of the carrier, 'to extend limitation of liability benefits to those who may be engaged by, and on behalf of the carrier to handle the subject cargo during the time in which the carrier was responsible for that cargo'.[58]

**8.46** In the aforementioned case *Toyomenka, Inc. v S.S. Tosaharu Maru,* for instance, the security company hired by the stevedores was not allowed the benefit of the clause.[59] In *Mikinberg v Baltic Steamship Co.*, the United States Court of Appeals for the Second Circuit explained its rationale:

> There must be a contractual relationship between [the stevedore] and [the carrier] in order for the provisions in the 'Himalaya clause' to apply. It is not enough that [the stevedore] merely handled the cargo shipped by [the carrier]. Otherwise, any transporter in the flow of commerce would be automatically protected by a single bill of lading regardless of its contractual privity with the shipper or carrier. We decline to extend COGSA protections through the 'Himalaya clause' to indefinite and unforeseeable defendants who may have only an attenuated connection to the 'carriage of goods by sea'.[60]

53 *Carle & Montanari* (n. 46).

54 Michael F Sturley, 'An Overview of the Considerations Involved in Handling the Cargo Case' (1996–1997) 21 Tulane Maritime Law Journal 263.

55 *De Laval Turbine v West India Industries* 502 F.2d 259 (3d Cir. 1974); *Rupp v I.T.O. Co.* 479 F 2d 674, 1973 AMC 1093 (2 Cir. 1973); *Cabot Corp v Mormacscan* 441 F2d 476, 1971 AMC 1130 (2 Cir 1971), cert. denied 404 United States. 855, 1971 AMC 565 (1971); *Royal Embassy v Ioannis Martinos* 1986 AMC 790, 801 (ED NC 1984).

56 *Barretto Peat, Inc. v Luis Ayala Colon Sucrs. Inc.* (1990) 896 F.2d 656.

57 *Tosaharu Maru* (n. 51); *Schiess-Froriep Corp. v Finnsailor* 574 F2d 123, 127, 1978 AMC 1101, 1107 (2 Cir 1975), See also *LaSalle Machine Tool v Maker Terminals* 611 F2d 56, 60, 1978 AMC 1374, 1380 (4 Cir 1979).

58 766, F 2d 485 (11th Cir 1985).

59 *Tosaharu Maru* (n. 51).

60 (1993) 988 F 2d 327 246.

**8.47** In a similar vein, the *Vessel Gladiolus* Court ruled that a trucker was not an independent contractor 'used or employed' by the ocean carrier as required by the Himalaya clause because he contracted with the consignee. Consequently, he was not entitled to the COGSA protection.[61] In the case of *Taisho Marine v Maersk Line*, the defendant trucker contracted directly with the ocean carrier, and a separate bill of lading was not issued. Analysing the 'nature' of the services provided by trucker, the Court held that his portion of the trip was within the scope of the carrier through bill of lading that required land transportation. The Court held, therefore, that the trucker was an intended beneficiary of the bill of lading.[62]

**8.48** In the case of *Bellmer v Terminal Service Houston* it was argued by Bellmer (the shipper) that stevedores could not claim the benefit of the clause because that clause is limited to independent contractors 'engaged by the carrier'. In this case the stevedores were hired by the carrier's agents. The Court's explanation is helpful in understanding the concept of a multilateral common enterprise.

**8.49** The District Court in *Bellmer* explained that the carrier's agent had indeed hired the stevedores. However, the stevedores and the agents have ownership in common, occupying the same office and telephone number. The personnel conducting the unloading operation were a mixture of the stevedores and the agent. The orders to the stevedores' drivers were usually given by the agent's employees. The evidence also revealed that the owners represented various steamship lines and stevedoring companies in the Houston Ship Channel area.[63] Therefore the Court allowed the limitation of liability concluding that a contrary conclusion would be unrealistic under the facts of the case. This proves a very specific point; factual context is incredibly relevant for deciding the law.

**8.50** In summary, in the period between *Herd* and *Kirby*, the Courts were in accord that a bill of lading may extend its benefits to third parties through a Himalaya clause if the bill's language clearly expresses the intent to do so. Other cases, however, have yielded inconsistent results. Generally, the more specific the language designating the third party as entitled to the bill's benefits, the better the chance that the Courts would, in this period at least, allow the third party's protection.

## The case of *Kirby*: 'a maritime case about a train wreck'

**8.51** *Norfolk Southern Railway Company v James N. Kirby* raised the question of whether or not a train company can rely on a Himalaya clause

61 Sturley (n. 54).

62 Charles S Donovan and Jill M Haley, 'Who Done It and Who's Gonna Pay? Rights of Shippers and Consignees against Non-Ocean Carriers Performing Part of a Contract of Carriage Covered by a Through Bill of Lading' (1998) 7 Journal of International Law and Practice 415.

63 *Gebr. Bellmer KG v Terminal Services Houston Inc.* (1983) 711 F.2d 622.

if participating in a multimodal carriage of goods? In *Kirby*, there were two bills of lading issued and both contained a Himalaya clause. The train company was not a party to both bills of lading. The Court allowed the train company to benefit from the exclusion in the bill of lading. The facts are as follows:

- The parties were Kirby, a manufacturer from Australia and ICC, a freight-forwarder.
- The scope of the contract was transporting ten packages of machinery.
- The port of loading was Sydney, Australia.
- The port of unloading was Savannah, GA, United States.
- The place of delivery was an inland city in Alabama.
- Two bills of lading were issued: one by the freight forwarder, ICC, to the shipper, Kirby; and one by the carrier, Hamburg Sud, to ICC. Both bills extended 'beyond the tackles', and included both sea and land leg. The two bills included provisions limiting the liability of the freight forwarder and carrier, respectively, as well as other parties assisting in the performance of the contract of carriage.
- The train involved in the land leg derailed causing $1.5 million of damages. Consequently, Kirby sued the Railway (Norfolk), who claimed coverage under the limitations of liability in both the ICC and Hamburg Sud bills of lading.

**8.52** The Eleventh Circuit held that Norfolk could not claim protection under the Himalaya clause in the first contract, the ICC bill. They excluded from the protection parties such as Norfolk that had not been in privity with ICC. The Court confirmed that 'a special degree of linguistic specificity is required to extend the benefits of a Himalaya clause to an inland carrier'.[64] The eleventh circuit strictly followed the route set by the *Herd* case.

**8.53** The case went to the Supreme Court, who held that contracts for the carriage of goods by sea must be construed like any other contracts: by their terms and consistent with the intent of the parties.[65] The Court had to address two different problems: admiralty jurisdiction and the attribution of liability. The second problem is of immediate relevance for this book.

**8.54** The Court's reasoning rested on three grounds. First, the need for the parties involved in the carriage contracts to be able to rely on their contracts. Second, the need to retain a structure of interaction in this area that is consistent with the statutory and decisional law promoting non-discrimination in common carriage. Third, for equitable reasons, the shipper should be allowed, in cases

64 *Norfolk Southern Ry. v James N. Kirby, Pty Ltd. (Kirby)* (2004) 543 US 14.

65 William T J de la Mare, 'Jurisprudential Problems of Attribution of Liability in the Area of Admiralty Contracts for Carriage Following *Norfolk Southern Railway v Kirby*' (2007) 22 Connecticut Journal of International Law 203.

such as *Kirby*, to sue the forwarder for any loss that exceeds the liability limitation they agreed upon.[66] As Costabel states:

> Answering in the positive, the Kirby Court announced three rules. First, the land segments of multimodal transports fall under admiralty jurisdiction unless the ocean segment is 'insubstantial' (the 'Jurisdiction Rule') Second, Himalaya clauses, properly drafted, extend downstream to all sub-carriers, because the contemplation of various modes of transport means that the parties must have anticipated that a land carrier's services would be necessary in performing the contract (the 'Beneficiary Rule'). Third, Himalaya clauses extend upstream to the shipper (not party to a sub-carrier's bill of lading) only as far as limitations of liability are concerned'. For anything else, there is no relation of agency between the shipper and the carrier (the 'Agency Rule').[67]

**8.55** Before *Kirby*, the law considered an intermodal contract to be a mixed contract: part was maritime and therefore governed by maritime law; part was land (involving inland carriers) and therefore governed by land law. *Kirby*, however, changed the legal approach towards intermodal contracts in cases where a bill of lading issued by the carriers is involved. The case holds that, if there is a bill of lading governing a maritime leg, the contract also requires a land leg so the contract has to be considered maritime as a whole. As stated by the Court regarding the case:

> The conceptual approach vindicates that interest by focusing the Court's inquiry on whether the principal objective of a contract is maritime commerce. While it may once have seemed natural to think that only contracts embodying commercial obligations between the 'tackles' (i.e., from port to port) have maritime objectives, the shore is now an artificial place to draw a line. Maritime commerce has evolved along with the nature of transportation and is often inseparable from some land-based obligations. The international transportation industry has moved into a new era, in which cargo owners can contract for transportation across oceans and to inland destinations in a single transaction. The popularity of an efficient choice, to assimilate land legs into international ocean bills of lading, should not render bills for ocean carriage non-maritime contracts. Lower court cases that appear to have depended solely on geography in fashioning a rule for identifying maritime contracts are inconsistent with the conceptual approach required by this Court's precedent.[68]

**8.56** In this case, the United States Supreme Court took a significant step forward in third party protection making clear that the maritime nature of the bill of lading cannot be altered by multimodal element:

> The maritime character of an ocean bill of lading is not altered by multimodal components ... The maritime 'nature and character' of the bill of lading contract was a

66 Ibid.

67 Attilio M Costabel, 'Himalaya Strain?: A Forensic Examination of *Norfolk Southern Railway Co. v James N Kirby, Pty Ltd* and *Doe v Celebrity Cruises, Inc.*' (2004–2005) 29 Tulane Maritime Law Journal 217.

68 *Kirby* (n. 64). As shown by Carl R Neil, 'Maritime Contract Law Moves Inland: The *Kirby* Decision' (*Lindsay, Hart, Neil & Weigler LLP*, 2011) <http://lindsayhart.com/wp-content/uploads/2010/10/Neil_Martime-Contract-Law.pdf>. Accessed 3 September 2014.

> preeminent consideration in Kirby ... The lesson of Kirby is that geography has no place in the maritime contract analysis, because that analysis must be conceptual, not spatial.[69]

**8.57** The conceptual approach articulated by the Court in this case focusses upon the purpose of the contract and mandates that if its 'purpose' is to 'effectuate maritime commerce', it is a maritime contract.[70] In *Kirby*, the judges stated:

> We recognise that our decision does no more than provide a legal backdrop against which future bills of lading will be negotiated. It is not, of course, this court's task to structure the international shipping industry. Future parties remain free to adapt their contracts to the rules set forth here, only now with the benefit of greater predictability concerning the rules for which their contracts might compensate.[71]

**8.58** It is believed that the authority of *Kirby* will go much further than the Court had anticipated. In the end, the case did create a new, modern structure for the international shipping future. It also changed evaluations of third party protection and introduced the idea of *substantial* carriage of goods by sea.[72]

**8.59** Gurley contends that prior to *Kirby*, the general principle was that 'parties may benefit when properly described, even when not specifically listed in the clause, provided that they at least belong to a readily identifiable class of beneficiaries'.[73] *Kirby* expanded Himalaya clause coverage for pragmatic reasons. If the language of the Himalaya clause is plain, and if it extends to anyone whose services contribute to the performance of the contract, and the contract clearly contemplates more than ocean carriage, the terms of the bill of lading may be extended.[74]

**8.60** Justice O'Connor shrewdly noted that, after *Kirby*, drawing a line at the shore is essentially artificial. If this is true, then the legal implications and protection that follow must take it into account.

## *Mazda Motors*: the vessel as a third party

**8.61** One case following *Kirby* that deserves particular mention in this context is the case of *Mazda Motors*.[75]

69 Marva Jo Wyatt, 'Contract Terms in Intermodal Transport: COGSA Comes Ashore' (1991–1992) 16 Tulane Maritime Law Journal 177.

70 Ibid.

71 Sweeney (n. 10).

72 Ibid.

73 G Gurley, 'The Ninth Circuit Breathes Life into a Vessel as a Himalaya Beneficiary: *Mazda Motors of America, Inc. v MV Cougar Ace*' (2009–2010) 34 Tulane Maritime Law Journal 619.

74 Ibid.

75 *Mazda Motors of America, Inc. v M//V Cougar Ace (Mazda Motors)* (2009) 565 E3d 573; 2009 AMC 1220 (9th Cir. 2009). Another case from 2010 that was, to a certain extent, similar to *Kirby* and therefore worth mentioning was *Kawasaki Kisen Kaisha Ltd. v Regal-Beloit Corp.* (2010) 561 U.S.

**8.62** In this case, the United States Court of Appeals for the Ninth Circuit had to decide whether the defendant ocean vessel could invoke a forum selection clause in the bills of lading governing the contract. The action was brought by Mazda's subrogated insurer against the vessel *in rem*. There was a Himalaya clause in the bill of lading. The clause stated:

> The Merchant undertakes that no claim or allegation shall be made against any servant, agent or Sub-Contractor of the Carrier which imposes or attempts to impose upon any of them, or upon any vessel owned or operated by any of them, any liability whatsoever in connection with the Goods, and, if any such claim or allegation should nevertheless be made, to indemnify the Carrier against all consequences thereof. Without prejudice to the foregoing, every such servant, agent and Sub-Contractor shall have the benefit of all provisions herein benefiting the Carrier as if such provisions were expressly for their benefit; and in entering into this contract, the Carrier, to the extent of those provisions, does so not only on its own behalf, but also as agent and trustee for such servants, agents and Sub-Contractors.[76]

**8.63** *Mazda Motors* is particularly relevant, not only because the Court found that a Himalaya clause covered a defendant vessel *in rem*, but also because of the Court's reasoning. Until *Mazda Motors*, the action *in rem* was not so strictly related to the concept of third party protection. When Mazda's counsel stressed the lack of case law supporting the thesis that the vessel sued *in rem* was a Himalaya beneficiary, the Court drew the counsel's attention to *Kirby*. The Court pointed out that 'refusing to apply the Himalaya clause to the defendant vessel because the otherwise unambiguous clause does not specifically name the vessel would contravene *Kirby*'s rule that Himalaya clauses need not be drafted with 'linguistic specificity''.[77]

**8.64** In *Mazda Motors*, the Court held that, because the vessel assisted in the performance of the contract of carriage, it was a Himalaya clause beneficiary and was thus entitled to rely on the forum selection clause.[78] Like a terminal operator falling under the umbrella of the Himalaya clause as a subcontractor (because his services are the same services of the carrier), the Court held that the term 'subcontractor' in *Mazda Motors* was broad enough to include the vessel.[79]

**8.65** The Court applied general principles of contract interpretation to decide whether or not the vessel was covered by the Himalaya clause, and defined the bill of lading as 'a contract like any other'. The Court also took a broad interpretation of the term 'subcontractor', extending coverage to: 'anyone assisting the performance of the carriage'. Since the vessel assisted the performance of the carriage, the Court found her to be a sub-contractor within the meaning of the Himalaya clause.[80]

76 Ibid

77 Ibid.

78 Ibid. In *Mazda Motors* the Judges stated that in order to decide whether an entity benefits from a Himalaya clause 'the proper test is to consider the nature of the service performed compared to the carrier's responsibility under the carriage contract'.

79 Ibid.

80 Ibid; see also Gurley (n. 73).

**8.66** The cases of *Mazda* and *Kirby* were decided several years apart, highlighting the new modern perspective that Courts in the United States adopt a broader approach regarding third party protection.

## Conclusion

**8.67** As Chuah stated: 'The law, for better or worse, in many jurisdictions continues to maintain a distinction between carrier and terminal operator though the reality is that the dividing line between actual carrier and terminal operator has become blurred'.[81]

**8.68** The decision in *Kirby* – although referring to a train company and not a terminal operator – has given credence to the idea that the line between the ocean carrier and other parties is now blurred.[82]

**8.69** United States law has generally been more willing to allow protection to third parties outside the contract. Cases against it, however (such as *Herd*), have been useful for future construction of clauses and relationship, showing that the industry, regardless of what the law says, will always attempt to find a way to circumvent it. Furthermore, the industry uses Court decisions and suggestions to improve their protection clause – as happened in the United States after *Herd* – until *Kirby* moved the concept of protection to a new era (i.e., the conceptual era).

81 Jason Chuah, 'Impact of the Rotterdam Rules on the Himalaya Clause: The Port Terminal Operators' Case' in D Rhidian Thomas (ed.), *The Carriage of Goods by Sea under the Rotterdam Rules* (Informa 2010).

82 The following cases on the same matter have partially followed the ratio in Kirby. *Delphi-Delco Electronics Syst. v M/V Nedlloyd Europa*, 324 F Supp 2d 403, 419–420, 2004 AMC 1217 (SDNY 2004); *Green Fire & Marine Insurance, Co. v M/V Hyundai Liberty* 125 S.Ct. 494 (2004), *Littlefield v Acadia Ins. Co.*, 392. F.3d 1 (1st Cir. 2004). *American Home Assurance Co. v TGL Container Lines*, 347 F. Supp. 2d 749 (N.D. Cal. 2004).

# CHAPTER 9

# Remarks and afterthoughts

> The law is developed by the application of old principles to new circumstances. Therein lies its genius.[1]

## Remarks

**9.1** The late Professor Tetley was once asked whether a person without entering into a contract could benefit from its terms (in particular a third party from a bill of lading). He replied that, under common law, it is not possible unless the third party carries out one of the carriers' duties. He then explained that carriers' duties are to carry, discharge, and deliver the goods. Only then can the third party benefit from the protection and only if cargo is damaged during the carrier's stage of operation.[2]

**9.2** The fact that the carrier cannot carry out the whole job alone and needs a network of other parties at hand is undebated. The issue is that, in the past, the meaning of carriage was clearly defined; now it is more broader and more nebulous. As Chuah explains, the distinction between sea and land is, at present and in a commercial sense, artificial.[3] In the context of a supply chain, the difference between what is and is not considered carriage no longer exists, rendering each party's role very complicated.

**9.3** Third parties should be regarded as part of the multilateral common enterprise, and it should be ascertained whether or not they should still receive protection based on the bilateral relationship between carrier and shipper, a question currently decided by contractual autonomy of the party and geographically limited by the international community.

**9.4** Since third parties constitute a link between the carriage of goods by sea and the supply chain, any attempts to geographically draw a line would not be prudent. On the contrary, the protection should be understood and conceptualised regarding the involvement of third parties and their role in the chain in order to create a sturdy foundation for their future protection.

1 *Scruttons Ltd. v Midland Silicones Ltd. (Scruttons)* (1961) 2 Lloyd's Rep 365.

2 William Tetley, 'The Himalaya Clause – Revisited' (2003) 9 Journal of International Maritime Law 40.

3 Jason Chuah, 'Impact of the Rotterdam Rules on the Himalaya clause: The Port Terminal Operators' Case' in D Rhidian Thomas (ed.), *The Carriage of Goods by Sea Under the Rotterdam Rules* (Informa 2010).

**9.5** This book stresses, therefore, that third parties are an integral part of the enterprise and that only on this assumption it is possible to build new protections for them. It proposes that third parties have become an integral part of the new carriage structure, therefore becoming 'primary parties', instead of 'third parties' existing outside of the enterprise and thus the contract as in accordance with the Contract (Right of Third Parties) Act 1999.

**9.6** If third party protection continues to be analysed from a traditional perspective, the whole sector runs the risk of not finding a proper or satisfactory solution. If, however, third party protection is conceptualised and analysed from the roots up, and rendered with the modern industry in mind, future legislations become easier to conceive of and to implement.

**9.7** The shipping industry currently takes an inappropriate view of the role of third parties; it considers them an appendix to the enterprise, rather than an essential part of it. This misinterpretation creates obstacles along the route to a solution. Consequently, it is necessary to transform the perception of third parties from appendices to central parts of the enterprise.

**9.8** The economic factual context of the shipping industry has indisputably changed, moving the industry to a wider framework. Consequently, this structure should be taken into account when addressing third party issues. A lack of uniform and consistent solutions to the problem brings further complexity. The result is an arbitrary protection, left to the will of the parties via contract clauses. Uniformity has to be a prime consideration, especially in a field such as maritime law, which transcends national barriers. According to the United States Supreme Court in the 1874 case of *Lottowanna*:

> The maritime law is part of the law of nations, one of the great beauties of which is its universality. Uniformity has been declared to be its essence. The worst maritime code would be one which should be dictated by the separate interest and influenced by the peculiar manner of only one people.[4]

**9.9** With this in mind, this work has examined the uniformity of third party protection in order to create a stable default approach for the legal defence of these parties. In a leading case regarding exclusion clauses,[5] Lord Diplock provided a somewhat more practical and commercially orientated approach:

> In commercial contracts negotiated between business men capable of looking after their own interests and of deciding how risks inherent in the performance of various kinds of contract can be most economically borne (generally by insurance), it is, in my view, wrong to place a strained construction upon words in an exclusion clauses.[6]

4 N J Margetson, 'The System of Liability of Articles III and IV of the Hague (Visby) Rules' (PhD thesis, University of Amsterdam, 2008).

5 *Photo Production Ltd. v Securicor Transport Ltd.* (1980) AC 827, 851.

6 Ibid., 851.

**9.10** He then followed on to say:

> In commercial matters generally, when the parties are not of unequal bargaining power, and when risks are normally borne by insurance, not only is the case for judicial intervention undemonstrated, but there is everything to be said … for leaving the parties free to apportion the risks as they think fit and for respecting their decision.[7]

**9.11** This book acknowledges Diplock's view, but argues that it is now time to expand the apportionment of risk in the carriage of goods by sea to a multilateral common enterprise and not only to the two included parties.

**9.12** The freedom of contract that Sir Norman Hill mentions in the preparatory work of the Hague Rules should be extended to numerous categories: 'Now surely the only possible basis of freedom in international commerce is freedom to the individual to make such contracts as he thinks will best help him in the conduct of his trade'.[8]

**9.13** This is supported further by an old proposal made by a delegation from the Netherlands:

> The difficulty is this. Here in paragraph 3 it is clearly shown that an amount up to the maximum provided for in the Convention may be claimed against the carrier, his servants, agents and independent contractors, in all against three or four classes of persons and it may be ten, fifteen or twenty persons. Now the only question I want to put before this Committee is would it not be equitable to have provisions allowing a man who under these provisions has to pay the full maximum to ask for contributions from the other people who are liable to the same maximum? Would it not be a good thing if either in this meeting or in the Maritime Committee something was said on that question?[9]

**9.14** Although it was presented in the twentieth century, it gives an idea that the apportionment of risk had already begun to be considered multilaterally. Today, this concept is a reality. Furthermore, the Institute of Unification of Private Law (UNIDROIT) in its body of principle in 2010, restating the importance of freedom of contract in today's international trade,[10] extended it (although with certain limitations and specifying that the main parties are conferring the right) to third parties.[11]

7 Ibid., 843.

8 Hague-Visby Rules, *Travaux Préparatoires*, 32 (in 1921 at a Conference attended by representatives of the shipowning industry of 14 maritime countries, its main purpose being to consider the adoption of the Hague Rules).

9 *Travaux Préparatoires* (n. 8) 618.

10 In fact at Art 1 (ibid.) they state,

> Freedom of contract is a basic and paramount principle in the context of international trade. The possibility for parties freely to agree on the terms of individual transactions, are the cornerstone of an open, market orientated and competitive international economic order If the parties to a contract wish to extend benefit to a third party they can. The conferment of rights in the beneficiary includes the right to invoke a clause in the contract which excludes or limits the liability of the beneficiary.

11 Even more specifically at section 2 called 'Third parties rights' they state:

> ARTICLE 5.2.1 (Contracts in favour of third parties) (1) The parties (the 'promisor' and the 'promisee') may confer by express or implied agreement a right on a third party (the

So far the protection has been mainly regulated by autonomy of parties through contract clauses. In the case that elaborated the agency theory and as a result of which the Himalaya clause now has effect in the United Kingdom, Viscount Simonds commented:

> For to me heterodoxy, or, as some might say, heresy, is not the more attractive because it is dignified by the name of reform. Nor will I easily be led by an undiscerning zeal for some abstract kind of justice to ignore our first duty, which is to administer justice according to law, the law which is established for us by Act of Parliament or the binding authority of precedent. The law is developed by the application of old principles to new circumstances. Therein lies its genius.[12]

**9.15** Tetley commented that the Himalaya clause is 'an ingenious, short-term solution to a difficult problem, but is a solution which raises infinitely more problems than it solves'.[13]

**9.16** Had these sentiments been put forth in 1961, around which time *Scrutton* and *Herd* were decided – and when one could view the context around such case – they would no doubt have been considered as heterodoxy and heresy.

**9.17** In today's shipping context, it appears to be the only practical solution on offer. Nevertheless, it remains unsatisfactory because it leaves third party protection to the unmethodical will of the parties to the contract.

**9.18** Moving from the micro-level of autonomy of party to the macro-level of the international legislation, UNCITRAL has made a substantial effort in order to find a more adequate solution and, as this book has argued, the approach of the Rotterdam Rules is not completely wrong. The Rotterdam Rules are bold and ambitious, as Thomas has defined them,[14] but their shortcomings stem from the fact that they rely on the drawing of a geographical line. If the concern is whether or not they are appropriate for the current shipping industry, this book states they are a reasonable but unworkable compromise. The shipping industry is evolving very fast, and the Rotterdam Rules arise from the failure of the multimodal conventions of the 1980s; something that gave birth to the Rules' main rationale of the 'maritime plus' compromise.

---

'beneficiary'). (2) The existence and content of the beneficiary's right against the promisor are determined by the agreement of the parties and are subject to any conditions or other limitations under the agreement.

ARTICLE 5.2.2 (Third party identifiable) The beneficiary must be identifiable with adequate certainty by the contract but need not be in existence at the time the contract is made.

ARTICLE 5.2.3 (Exclusion and limitation clauses) The conferment of rights in the beneficiary includes the right to invoke a clause in the contract which excludes or limits the liability of the beneficiary.

ARTICLE 5.2.4 (Defences) The promisor may assert against the beneficiary all defences which the promisor could assert against the promisee.

12 *Midland Silicones* (n. 1).

13 Tetley (n. 2).

14 D Rhidian Thomas 'And Then there were the Rotterdam Rules' (2008) 14 Editorial of the Journal of International Maritime Law (JIML) 189–190.

**9.19** In favour of the Rotterdam Rules, Berlingieri states that, in many jurisdictions, the freedom of contract for third parties is restricted, thus affording them a high level of protection from the Rules, which also ensure uniformity.[15] However, overwhelming evidence shows that many third parties are against this convention for many reasons, including the fact that it confuses their area of operation.

**9.20** As previously mentioned, the Rotterdam Rules have rightly addressed part of the issue. Viewing the carriage of goods by sea as being part of something broader is considered as the correct approach. It will inevitably be hard for an international convention to deal with such matters; a convention that deals with supply chains is not easy to create. Therefore, the Rotterdam Rules had to draw a line somewhere, and in general terms it was probably wise (especially after the failure of the multimodal convention) to produce a door-to-door convention with port-to-port geographic protection. In order to do this, however, the Rotterdam Rules wrongly decided to extend the Himalaya protection only to maritime-related third parties. Furthermore, the swiftness with which the Rotterdam Rules were ratified suggests they may not be suitable as the legislative future of the carriage of goods by sea. This book suggests, therefore, that the international community should focus on a new regime with different approaches or amend the existing regime to incorporate a protocol that approaches third party protection in a less geographic but more commercial way.[16]

**9.21** The international conventions on the carriage of goods by sea effectively regulate the particular contract that incorporates them. They are themselves a contract, in essence. The difference is that, while in a contract, autonomy lies between the parties; in this case the freedom to negotiate has moved to a macro-level, i.e., the international community, with all its restrictions and all the parties that have an interest in it.

**9.22** At beginning of the nineteenth century – when for the first time the transport industry felt the need to allocate loss and protect parties involved in the carriage of goods by sea – there were only two parties involved and all the efforts were focussed on them.

**9.23** This is the rationale behind the Harter Act and the Hague Rules, and the reason why little reference is made in either to third parties. When the Harter Act and Hague Rules were written there was no representative of third parties at the negotiating table. In the intervening years, the industry and the world more broadly have changed dramatically.

**9.24** Third parties, who at the beginning of this period were protected under the auspices of the carrier or shipper, are becoming bigger and more powerful; their role is no longer marginal. During the *travaux préparatoires* of the Rotterdam Rules, the participants included different third party associations on the one side but also international intergovernmental organisations on the other.

15 Francesco Berlingieri, 'A Comparative Analysis of The Hague-Visby Rules, The Hamburg Rules and the Rotterdam Rules' (Paper delivered at the General Assembly of the AMD, Marrakesh, 5–6 November 2009).

16 Perhaps resuming the not travelled by functional approach mentioned in the *travaux préparatoires*.

**9.25** For some, the Hamburg Rules function satisfactorily. According to Tetley Article 4 solves the problem of the Himalaya clause by extending the responsibility of the carrier from port-to-port, while Article 10 holds the carrier responsible for the acts of the actual carrier, who, by the definition in Article 1(2), would include the stevedore and the terminal agent.[17]

**9.26** The Rotterdam Rules do not assess the trade in a proper way because they still look at it only from the maritime-geographic perspective and not from the maritime-commercial perspective.

Some corners of the academic community believe that the Rotterdam Rules do not represent a retrograde move, primarily because they were never intended to replace the United Nations Convention on International Multimodal Transport of Goods, nor the UNCTAD/ICC Rules for Multimodal Transport Documents. Instead, they were created to replace the Hague and Hague-Visby or the Hamburg Rules. Thus, they feel it is inappropriate to view the Rotterdam Rules as an 'imperfect' multimodal transport law convention.[18]

**9.27** Although international conventions can make new provisions on third parties, nothing prevents the industry from adding provisions contractually. As shown already, parties (under the Rotterdam Rules) can in some cases agree on a Himalaya clause for the benefit of non-maritime performing parties or other persons who are not covered by Article 4(1).[19]

**9.28** Adding a contractual provision is also significant because the Rotterdam Rules confer responsibility and protection to only the narrow category of maritime performing parties and not all the performing parties; the convention seeks to avoid interference with the other conventions in cases of multimodal transport.[20] Although this approach is highly respectable, it seems to exclude certain categories of third parties (for example, the inland carrier) who can be sued in tort by the shipper, and confusion can thus arise.

**9.29** The difference between the bilateral approach of the Hague, Hague-Visby, Hamburg Rules, and Rotterdam Rules lies in the rationale for extending carrier protection to third parties. In the bilateral approach, the rationale was to avoid cargo owners circumventing the bill of lading and to protect the carrier because the third parties were related to him. In the Rotterdam Rules, the primary motivation is protection of the performing parties. Thus, the idea of protection is changing. The Rotterdam Rules acknowledge that shipping has become a network and many parties are now involved. As a solution, however, the Rotterdam Rules pose too much of a compromise, and room for improvement certainly

17 William Tetley, 'Case Comment: The House of Lords Decision in *The Starsin*' (2004) 35 JMLC 121–139.

18 Manuel Alba, Francesco Berlingieri, Philippe Delebecque, Tomotaka Fujita, Hannu Honka, Rafael Illescas, Anders Moellmann, Michael Sturley and Alexander Von Ziegler, 'Montevideo Declaration The Facts' (2010) <https://asadip.files.wordpress.com/2010/10/rr-answer-to-montevideo-declaration-eng.pdf>. Accessed 1 January 2013.

19 United Nations Commission on International Trade Law 'Report of the Working Group on Transport Law'.

20 Ibid.

exists.[21] In this respect, the exchange between CLECAT and CMI is particularly pertinent. CLECAT argues that the Rotterdam Rules are not appropriate for the evolution of modern logistics. CLECAT states, in fact, that the evolution of modern logistics 'would have been better served by a convention that focussed on the intermodal nature of containerisation'.[22] The CMI responded by saying that this has been precisely what the Rotterdam Rules have done, by providing door-to-door application if the parties choose so to do.[23]

**9.30** The International Multimodal Transport Association (IMMTA) holds a similar view, believing that existing transport liability regimes are not adequate, fragmented, and expensive, and also that a more efficient system is needed. The IMMTA calls for a new, comprehensive approach to cover all modes of transport in a uniform manner.[24]

**9.31** The same association recognises, however, that this proposal could be too forward-thinking for the transportation industry. They propose, therefore, an alternative: working towards achieving coherence at least in the movement of goods from door-to-door, regardless of the individual modes being used. This should not, however, simply be a maritime convention extended beyond the port, but rather a truly multimodal instrument.[25]

**9.32** The UNECE Secretariat believes that if and when a clear mandate is acquired on the elaboration of a multimodal convention, it is right – given the procession towards a global logistic chain – that the new regime should apply to all possible combinations of transport; it must not be restricted to the presence of a maritime leg. It is also crucial that representatives from all modes involved in multimodal transport – as well as from shippers and from other interested parties – be consulted and participate in the drafting process.[26]

21 United Nations Commission on International Trade Law, 'Report of the Working Group on Transport Law on the Work of Its Ninth Session' (New York, 15–26 April 2002, A/CN.9/510).

> The current definition of performing party was a compromise as shown by below: 'Some favoured including any party that performs any of the carrier's responsibilities under a contract of carriage if that party is working, directly or indirectly, for the carrier. Others advocated excluding the "performing party" definition entirely. The relatively restrictive definition in the current text was presented as a compromise.'

22 CLECAT, position paper 'RE: 2008 – United Nations Convention on Contracts for the International Carriage of Goods Wholly or Partly by Sea – the 'Rotterdam Rules'' Brussels, 11 May 2009.

23 CMI, 'The Rotterdam Rules: An Attempt to Clarify Certain Concerns that have Emerged' (2009) <http://comitemaritime.org/Uploads/Rotterdam%20Rules/5RRULES.pdf>. Accessed 13 December 2013.

24 United Nations Commission on International Trade Law, 'Preparation of a Draft Instrument on the Carriage of Goods (by Sea) Addendum to Compilation of Replies to a Questionnaire on Door-to-door Transport and Additional Comments by States and International Organisations on the Scope of the Draft Instrument' (Working Group III (Transport Law) 12th Session Vienna, 6–17 October 2003, A/CN.9/WG.III/WP.28/Add.1).

25 Ibid. The association states that in a contrary case, it would surely fail.

26 United Nations Commission on International Trade Law, 'Transport Law Preliminary Draft Instrument on the Carriage of Goods by Sea' (Working Group III (Transport Law) Ninth Session New York, 15–26 April 2002, A/CN.9/WG.III/WP.21/Add.1).

**9.33** As far as the analysis of the difference between maritime and non-maritime performing parties is concerned, Berlingieri believes there is a marginal doubt as to whether the maritime performing party is an innovation with respect to the Hamburg Rules.[27] It is argued here that this could be considered more as an extension than a proper conceptual improvement.

**9.34** Debattista has said that the Rotterdam Rules are not perfect, but nevertheless better than the alternatives against which they are updated.[28] Although this might be correct, it is not a sufficient argument for the international maritime community to rest on its laurels in the future. The Rotterdam Rules are surely the best effort that can be made in a 'maritime plus' scenario. However, trade requires a more modern and pragmatic solution, and in this sense the commercial approach proposed by *Kirby* is superior.

**9.35** As Sturley states, the Rotterdam Rules are deliberately evolutionary and not revolutionary.[29] It is not unreasonable to argue, however, that the shipping industry in recent times has undergone a revolution; therefore a revolutionary convention would be more appropriate than an evolutionary convention.

**9.36** Moving to the common law domestic tradition analysed, England and the United States present considerable issues. First, they hold a considerable sway over shipping law. Second, there are provisions in their respective domestic laws that make the potential protection hard to achieve. The shipping industry relies on these jurisdictions, and third party protection has become an important issue to tackle. Law does not always operate in harmony with trade. Consequently, some authorities in these jurisdictions have been considering the evolution of the role of third parties and the need for the shipping industry to have its third party protection progressively expanded.

**9.37** England and the United States are both countries with common law traditions.[30] They have the flexibility of the common law jurisdiction, which perhaps explains why so many major commercial contracts – especially shipping contracts – are drawn up under these jurisdictions. English law in particular, however, has had problems in accepting the principle that someone outside a contract should benefit from it. This has not always been the case. Before 1900, in fact, the situation was different. It has changed as a result of the context and consequently the law has altered in step. Nevertheless, change is now required again.

**9.38** England and the United States might share the same legal system, but they do not approach third party protection in a similar way. After a century of

27 Berlingieri (n. 15).

28 Charles Debattista, 'UNCITRAL Colloquium on Rotterdam Rules: The Goods Carried – Who Gets Them and Who Controls Them?' (*Stone Chambers*, 2009) <www.rotterdamrules2009.com/cms/uploads/Def%20%20tekst%20Charles%20Debattista%2031%20OKT29.pdf>. Accessed 18 September 2013.

29 Michael F Sturley, 'Modernising and Reforming United States Maritime Law: The Impact of the Rotterdam Rules in the United States' (2008–2009) 44 Texas International Law Journal 427.

30 With one major difference: in the US maritime law is a matter of federal law.

problems, England has now put third party protection on a statutory footing with the Contract (Right of Third Parties) Act 1999.[31]

**9.39** In the case of the carriage of goods by sea, however, the Act alone might not be enough. Of further interest is how the Courts have responded to the need for multilateral protection. English Courts have established (through a series of decisions) a path for third party protection through the potential pitfalls of Himalaya clauses, Lord Reid's agency theory, and so on. With the case of *Kirby*, the United States Courts have probably fully recognised the commercial, practical approach that has to be given to this protection; an encouraging first step towards the future. The *Kirby* decision is substantially different from the geographic protection that the international community proposes with the Rotterdam Rules. However references to the multilateral protection resulting are very limited.

**9.40** The industry's legal needs derive from the context of the moment. Factual context influences the development of an instrument such as third party protection due to the interest in that protection. The concept of third party protection is not an absolute and unchangeable concept and the protection changes according to the interest of the moment.

**9.41** For example, third party protection in the United States is influenced by the country's multilateral factual context. The legal protection of categories such as third parties cannot be separated from the economic factual context. Doing so would be to underestimate the potential benefit that good protection could bring to the industry as a whole. Each jurisdiction is influenced in a different way by its own factual context, and tends to address third party protection and define the legal route to achieve it differently as well.

**9.42** Third party protection in the law of England and the United States has been challenged on the grounds that autonomy of parties is very much considered to be the easiest way to solve the problem; in certain circumstances the will of the contracted parties is normally achieved. However, in the context of third party protection in the carriage of goods by sea, it is dangerous to leave the regulation of the topic solely to the will of the contracted parties; by the very nature of the contract, they are the first and second party and the third party is thus not represented. On the contrary, sovereignty law should interfere and make sure that the problem is tackled in a correct manner.

**9.43** The protection of third parties has been encouraged by several different aspects of law. Specifically:

- From case law, there is a line of authority starting with the *Elder Dempster* case[32] and running through to the notable *Himalaya* case.[33] Further

31 Merkin reports that the majority of members of the European Union are favourable to the recognition of the rights of third-party beneficiaries under contracts (Robert Merkin, *Privity of Contract, Privity of Contract: The Impact of the Contracts (Right of Third Parties) Act 1999* (Oxford, Taylor & Francis 2013) 67).

32 *Elder, Dempster & Co. Ltd. v Paterson, Zochonis & Co. Ltd. (Elder Demspter)* (1924) AC 522 (HL).

33 *Adler v Dickson (The Himalaya)* (1954) 2 Lloyd's Rep 267; (1955) 1 QB 158.

influence came from *Scrutton*[34] where the problem of consideration was formally declared, and the *Eurymedon* case,[35] which explained how to deal with consideration for third parties. A similar development of authority exists in the United States, starting with *Herd* and *Kirby* and implemented by subsequent cases. However, there is still a great a dependence upon precisely written clauses detailing both the intention of the parties as well as who can be protected; nothing can be left open to interpretation.[36]

- Within statutory law[37] the Contract (Right of Third Parties) Act 1999 represents a significant example, changing the attitude towards third party protection and presenting another route around the conceptual obstacles of privity and consideration. It is arguable that the Act completely removed these, but its significance is well expressed by Vlasto and Clark in their article 'The Effect of the Contracts (Rights of Third Parties) Act 1999 on Voyage and Time Charter Parties'.[38]

**9.44** In a final analysis, it is believed that third party protection can indeed be approached from a multilateral perspective. This, of course, requires a different framework.[39] At the time of writing, and from a purely contractual perspective, third parties receive an almost random level of protection governed by the extent to which the two main parties are willing to extend the protection. Contractually, Himalaya clauses and similar clauses could provide protection for a broader category of third parties. When the parties to a contract wish to extend their contractual protection to a non-contractual claim brought against a third party by the owner of goods, the mechanism provided by a Himalaya clause gives

34 In *Midland Silicones* (n. 1), Lord Reid raised the problem of consideration in order to permit protection of third parties.

35 The answer was supplied in *The Eurymedon* (1975) AC 154, 169. The Privy Council held that the consideration was the discharging of the goods by the stevedore for the benefit of the shipper.

36 Amongst them even *Norfolk Southern Ry. v James N. Kirby, Pty Ltd. (Kirby)* (2004) 543 US 14.

37 It might be worth restating that Civil Law has always had fewer problems with third party protection. Reference has to be made to, amongst others, Ralph De Wit, *Multimodal Transport Carrier Liability and Documentation* (Lloyds of London Press Ltd 1995); Catharine MacMillan, 'A Birthday Present for Lord Denning: The Contracts (Rights of Third Parties) Act 1999' (2000) 63 The Modern Law Review 5, 721–738; Tetley (n. 17) and William Tetley, 'The Himalaya Clause, *'stipulation pour autrui'* Non-Responsibility Clauses and Gross Negligence under the Civil Code' (1979) 20 Le Cahiers de Droit 3, 449–483.

38 Tony Vlasto and Julian Clark, 'The Effect of the Contracts (Rights of Third Parties) Act 1999 on Voyage and Time Charter Parties' (2000–2001) 25 Tulane Maritime Law Journal 519: 'It is rare that a single piece of legislation removes a principle of English law hitherto considered an essential foundation. The Contracts (Rights of Third Parties) Act 1999' (Act) did just that by removing the English law principle of privity of contract which had been established law since the early nineteenth century, albeit a concept which had attracted criticism from the judiciary on a number of occasions'.

39 Alternatively, following the example of other industries that already work as a network, a multilateral approach could be adopted where the party with the greatest interest at stake shoulders the risk for its chain of contractors, channelling full liabilities towards itself. Or with a multilateral insurance framework.

adequate effect to the commercial expectation of the parties. International conventions instead should follow a commercial rather than geographic approach. Among these conventions and their drafters, there has been a growing interest in protecting third party interests, from the first attempt in the Harter Act that merely considers anyone outside the relationship, to the Rotterdam Rules that (arguably) dedicate an extensive part of the convention to third parties.[40] The relevant international community should focus on a new approach that takes into account the above or amending the Hague/Hague-Visby Rules.

**9.45** Regarding domestic law, substantive law still plays an important role in third party protection, despite the increasing dependence on private remedies and international solutions. The pragmatism of case law in common law countries could surely match the reality of the multilateral common enterprise.

**9.46** Returning to the first 'contemporary' decision regarding the topic – that of *Elder Dempster* – Hallebeek and Dundorp argue that the decision to allow a shipowner to be protected by a bill of lading to which he was not part reflected the general belief in the commercial world at the time; it was right to protect him for commercial reasons.[41] Digging a little deeper, Hallebeek and Dundorp explain that the reasoning was more likely to have been dictated by the commercial absurdity of the contrary than by any doctrinal nicety.

**9.47** Today, almost 100 years later, the position has not yet fully solidified. Many decisions regarding the field have been influenced more by practical reasons (and still from the absurdity of the contrary) than by a desire for clarification.

**9.48** It seems inarguable that, in order to achieve any changes, parties such as carriers, shippers, third parties, and insurers, must acknowledge and allocate their risks accordingly.

**9.49** The shipping industry has a seemingly irrational resistance to change but the established 'balance of interests' should be revised and adapted to the current climate.

**9.50** In a final consideration, Maitland argues that legal history should enable every age to be the master of its own law and not the slave of its past.[42] The shipping industry should accordingly focus on an alternative, innovative solution, rather than doggedly persevering with existing measures.

40 The latest attempt, the Rotterdam Rules are far from being ratified and have been criticised extensively. See generally Stefano Zunarelli, 'Elementi Di Novita' E Di Continuita' Della Regolamentazione Della Responsabilita' Del Vettore Marittimo Di Cose Nell'attivita' Del Gruppo Di Lavoro Dell' UNCITRAL' (UNCITRAL 2008) <www.aidim.org/pdf/rel_zunarelli.pdf>. Accessed 7 September 2013; Chuah (n. 3); Carlo Corcione, 'The Evolution of Third Party Protection in Carriage of Goods by Sea: From the Himalaya Clause to the Himalaya Protection' (2014) 49 European Transport Law Journal 3, 271.

41 Jan Hallebeek and Harry Dondorp, *Contracts for a Third-Party Beneficiary: A Historical and Comparative Account* (Martinus Nijhoff Publishers 2008) 121.

42 Quoted in K O Shatwell, 'The Doctrine of Consideration in the Modern Law' (1953–1955) 1 Sydney Law Review 289.

## Afterthoughts – solutions or new issues?

### *Risk control: channelling of liability*

**9.51** Multilateral common enterprises are, in essence, informal networks of parties who share a common aim. Furthermore, it is argued that, when issues of protection arise amongst participants in this multilateral common enterprise, perspectives should be adjusted to encompass and give consideration to networked aspects of the enterprise rather than focussing solely on single, individual relationships.

**9.52** Adams and Brownsword define a network of contracts as a set of contracts where there is a principal contract giving the set an overall objective, and secondary contracts that contribute – directly or indirectly – to the attainment of the overall objective. They go on to explain that the network of contractors expands until a sufficiency of contractors are obligated, whether to the parties to the principal contract or to other contractors within the set, in order to attain the overall objective.[43]

**9.53** Following such assertions, it seems reasonable to consider how this could work in practice. This notion is already at work in many other sectors, and these offer an indication of the effect that such a definition could have on the carriage of goods by sea. The most similar is the offshore oil and gas industry. This market is closely aligned with shipping and can almost be considered two parts of the same industry; offshore being the upstream, shipping being the downstream. For instance, they share similar features as the role of the shipowner, the insurance (P&I Clubs) and the Baltic International Maritime Council (BIMCO).

**9.54** In the offshore oil and gas industry, the legal protection schemes in place operate under a rationale that assumes the party in the best position should bear the risk. Offshore systems should be considered as models for the implementation of third party protection in the carriage of goods by sea. While doing this, consideration should be given to the channelling protection and its efficiency in the new carriage of goods by sea scenario should be tested.[44]

**9.55** Offshore protection uses a scheme called 'knock-for-knock' that has previously been defined as a 'crude and workable' structure.[45] The Pooling Agreement of P&I Clubs explains and endorses knock-for-knock with a provision that stipulates:

> Each party to a contract shall be similarly responsible for loss of or damage to, and/or death of or injury to any of its own property or personnel and/or the property or personnel of its contractors and/or of its and their sub-contractors and/or of other third parties; and that (ii) such responsibility shall be without recourse to the other

43 John Adams and Roger Brownsword, 'Privity and the Concept of a Network Contract' (1990) 10 Legal Studies 12.

44 For example, channelling of liability was proposed by ICS, IG of P&I during the Rotterdam Rules, *Travaux Préparatoires*. In any case, it must be said that there are other systems working as such for example construction system/construction Law. Most recently the Knock-for-Knock has been applied also to charters servicing wind farms (WINDTIME).

45 Chidi Egbochue, 'Reviewing 'Knock for Knock' Indemnities Following the Macondo Well Blowout' (2013) 7 Construction Law International 4.

> party, and arise notwithstanding any fault or neglect of any party; and that (iii) each party shall, in respect of those losses, damages or other liabilities for which It has assumed responsibility, correspondingly indemnify the other against any liability that that party shall incur in relation thereto.[46]

**9.56** Slater, Ballew and Sartain aptly describe the offshore industry as a highly risky and complex field involving multiple parties, each with their own risk profile and capacity for assumption of risks (bargaining power, market power, financial possibility, and so on).[47]

**9.57** The fine detail present in the drafting and managing of contracts between its parties bears witness to the complexity of the sector.[48] Typically, offshore projects rely on complex networks of contracts to govern the relationship between the many parties involved.[49]

**9.58** The same complexity led to the industry's use of the knock-for-knock; an almost unique[50] system of allocating liabilities.[51]

**9.59** In the House of Lords, Lord Bingham has given his approval to the basis of the knock-for-knock system. Apart from cases where negligence or breach of statutory duty of the party seeking indemnity is the sole cause of death or injury, he concurs that no limits should exist to the rule that, regardless of fault, each primary party[52] assumes responsibility for compensating its own employees.[53]

**9.60** The notion of the 'group' warrants special attention here. For the purpose of liability allocation, both primary party to the knock-for-knock agreement and all their contractors and sub-contractors represent a specific group. The loss, damage, or injury suffered by a primary party – or by any member of that primary party's group – is to be shouldered by that primary party alone. This still holds even if the negligence of the other primary party or any member of that party's group has caused the loss, damage, or injury.[54]

46 Pooling Agreement at page 4. The pooling agreement has the only definition of K4K according to Fabien Lerede (Chapter 9: Knock-For-Knock: The P&I Perspective) in Bariş Soyer and Andrew Tettenborn, *Offshore Contracts and Liabilities* (Informa Law from Routledge 2014).

47 Robert Slater, J Wayne Ballew and Charles W Sartain, *Our Fault, My Fault, Their Fault ... Does It Even Matter? Indemnification and Exculpatory Agreements in the Oil Patch* (AAPL Southwest Land Institute – Dallas 30 April 2013).

48 Standard P&I Club Bulletin, November 2008.

49 Operators, joint ventures, contractors, sub-contractors, and service providers. Ibid.

50 Save for other fields such as construction law, even though they are not exactly the same. Under the traditional construction contracting system, the person who carries out this work is the main contractor. The contractor sub-contracts or sub-lets parts of his work to one or more sub-contractors. Uff reports that most of the larger contracting companies now see their role as being managers of the sub-contractors who will perform the physical work (see generally J Uff, *Construction Law*, 11th edn, 138).

51 Tim Taylor, 'Offshore Energy Construction Insurance: Allocation of Risk Issues' (2013) 87 Tulane Law Review 1165.

52 For example, the operator of an oil rig and the contractors.

53 In *Caledonia North Sea Ltd. v London Bridge Engineering Ltd.* [2002] UKHL 4. As also detailed by Soyer and Tettenborn (n. 787).

54 Soyer and Tettenborn, ibid.

**9.61** Offshore projects will tend to involve one or more main contracts, such as the contract between an oil-rig operator and a contractor (e.g., the shipowner of a platform supply vessel). Their group will identify all the other parties that are involved in that project but do not have a contractual relationship with the other primary party.[55] In the aforementioned example, the contract regulating the relationship between the owner of the supply vessel and the oil-rig operator is a BIMCO Supply Time contract. This contractual template defines an owner's group as:

> Owners, their contractors and sub-contractors, and employees of any of the foregoing and charterers group as charterers, their contractors, sub-contractors, co-ventures and customers (having a contractual relationship with the Charterers, always with respect to the job or project on which the Vessel is employed) and employees of the foregoing.[56]

**9.62** As explained by Taylor, one effect of adopting the group approach is that, in practice, there may be relatively few true 'third parties' for the purpose of indemnity between the operator and the contractor.[57] For example, according to a similar agreement drawn up by British Petroleum: 'A third party shall mean any person not included in the charterers group or owners group'.[58]

**9.63** Usually, the scope of the group definition is very broad and, consequently, it is unlikely that a party will be excluded. As a result, the instances in which it is necessary to determine actual fault – in the sense of negligence or breach of contract – are very rare.[59]

**9.64** Knock-for-knock agreements in some ways translate the concept of multilateral common enterprise into the concept of a group with the difference that the concept of 'group' is already formally accepted.

**9.65** Contracting under terms of the knock-for-knock agreement is, in the offshore market, vital for securing insurance coverage from the P&I Clubs.[60]

**9.66** An obvious advantage of this is the ability to channel claims to one sole party. This party will be obliged, therefore, to ensure adequate insurance is taken out to protect the interests of the various parties to the knock-for-knock agreement. The advantages of such a scheme are varied and much debated. Amongst others, such a scheme reduces the cost of inquiry and litigation, strips away layers of insurance, minimises disruption of the primary activity, facilitates settlements, and encourages co-operation in the establishment of good and safe work practices.[61]

55 Specifically, this group might include the contractor's employees, affiliates, agents, and sub-contractors. In the case of the company, its group would normally include the company's employees, affiliates, co-venturers, and other contractors engaged by the company to provide related services.

56 BIMCO SUPPLYTIME 2005 Time charter for Offshore Service Vessels clause 14, Liabilities and Indemnities. In many cases, oil-rig operators will propose their own contract with its own terms.

57 Taylor (n. 51).

58 Clause 48.12 definition BP charterparty.

59 Taylor (n. 57).

60 Soyer and Tettenborn (n. 46).

61 Ibid.

**9.67** That entities such as BIMCO and insurance P&I clubs play common roles in both fields (i.e., shipping and offshore) offers an encouraging starting point for the implementation of such a scheme in the sphere of the carriage of goods by sea.

**9.68** Nonetheless, in some respects the two businesses differ substantially in nature, and this brings its own ramifications. In the shipping sector, the cargo is sold continuously and the parties involved enter and exit the business continuously. Offshore projects are, on the other hand, much more stable and the relevant knock-for-knock group is fairly easy to identify. Furthermore, it is clear in most offshore agreements that the oil-rig operator is the party assuming the most risk. This is in stark contrast with agreements covering the carriage of goods by sea, in which the risk and commercial balance is much more evenly distributed, making it harder to establish which party would bear the risk in a knock-for-knock agreement.

*Risk transfer: multilateral marine insurance*

**9.69** Risk transfer is the other side of the risk management coin. Within a multilateral common enterprise, the allocation of risk can be complicated. There are many different aspects to consider, including which party should insure the risk and the idea that the risk to insure must surely extend beyond maritime boundaries. As reported by Lemon, it is not only marine-related parties such as shipowners, ship operators, charterers, terminal operators, wharfingers, and stevedores that require insurance to protect them against such risks; parties involved at any point in the cargo chain need insurance, regardless of their position or sphere of operation.[62]

**9.70** Support for multilateral insurance has also been given by the International Union of Marine Insurance (IUMI).[63] IUMI that represents insurers of both carriers and cargo interests, supports the creation of a modern uniform, treaty for the carriage of goods by sea that would be fair, balanced, and reasonable for all parties involved.[64]

**9.71** At the moment, the general scheme that could give coverage to a multilateral common enterprise offers the following framework.

62 Robert T Lemon II, 'Allocation of Marine Risks: An Overview of the Marine Insurance Package' (2006–2007) 81 Tulane Law Review 1467.

63 IUMI was founded in 1874 and represents 53 national marine insurance associations from markets all over the world. IUMI members cover 80% of the world premium in marine insurance, totalling approximately USD 10.5 billion (2001).

64 United Nations Commission on International Trade Law, 'Preparation of a Draft Instrument on the Carriage of Goods (by Sea) Addendum to Compilation of Replies to a Questionnaire on Door-to-door Transport and Additional Comments by States and International Organisations on the Scope of the Draft Instrument' (Working Group III (Transport Law) 12th Session Vienna, 6–17 October 2003, A/CN.9/WG.III/WP.28/Add.1).

P&I cover

**9.72** P&I clubs currently insure shipowners beyond their liability under international conventions. The P&I clubs' standard terms, however, do not always cover the specialised needs of shipowners engaged in multimodal transportation. Liability for cargo ought to be limited to the period during which the carrier has responsibility for the cargo. In any contract governed by the Hague and Hague-Visby rules, for instance, it should be limited to tackle-to-tackle.[65] However, extending on a door to door basis the operation of a containership, the clubs cover shipowners liabilities for cargo arising in connection with the operation of the ship. If, on the other hand, the claims are brought directly by the third party in tort, there is no cover for them.[66]

Through transport insurances

**9.73** That which the P&I clubs do not cover has traditionally been supplemented by insurers such as the TT Club. 'TT' stands for 'through transport', reflecting the door-to-door nature of this approach. They are a club in the sense of mutuality (like the P&I clubs), and the TT Club aims and claims to be an insurer for all the operators involved in a specific supply chain process.[67] The TT club insures risks for NVOCCs, freight forwarders, port terminals, and so on.

**9.74** The TT Club was created to fill the gap left by the P&I clubs when multimodalism became prevalent throughout the industry, i.e., when the P&I clubs wanted to remain 'water-borne' insurers. TT insurance covers five main areas:

1. Container risks for ship operators and others
2. Transport and logistics operator liabilities
3. Cargo handling facility liabilities and assets
4. Port authority liabilities and assets
5. Forwarders' cargo all risks

**9.75** The aim of P&I and TT clubs is to operate in concert to minimise the likelihood of gaps between covers, or overlapping covers.[68] However, attempts to remedy the situation with the 'insurance cost' might be considered overly simple.

65 Amongst others: E Gold, *Gard Handbook on P&I Insurance* (5th edn, Arendal: Gard Assuranceforeningen 2002); Steven J Hazelwood, *P&I Clubs: Law and Practice* (3rd edn, London: Lloyd's of London Press 2000); The London P&I Club 2016–2017 Rules <www.londonpandi.com/_common/updateable/downloads/documents/5rules2016.pdf>. Accessed 20 February 2016; Understanding P&I Club, A Presentation by Gillian Musgrave – Regional Claims Director, Standard Asia & David Heaselden – Loss Prevention Director, Shipowners' Mutual <www.gia.org.sg/pdfs/Industry/Marine/MKSS/SS18_Presentation.pdf>. Accessed 14 March 2015.

66 Ibid.

67 Anon., 'Supply Chain Claims – The Same Old Story' (*TT Club*, 16 September 2015) <www.ttclub.com/news-events/articles/article/supply-chain-claims-the-same-old-story-133454/>. Accessed 9 January 2016.

68 Anon., 'Ship Operator Cover Liability, Equipment and Property Insurance for Ship Operators' (*TT Club Bulletin*, 2015) <www.ttclub.com/fileadmin/uploads/tt-club/Publications___Resources/New_Document_Store_2015/Ship_Operator_Cover.pdf>. Accessed 11 February 2015.

**9.76** First, a club should ensure, so far as possible, that the insured owner preserves his rights of recourse against others involved in the performance of the contract of carriage. This will be of particular importance in the case of a combined transport bill of lading, where the insured owner issuing the bill of lading must preserve his rights of recourse against his sub-carriers, even if the sub-carrier is a subsidiary or associated company of the insured owner. This, however, runs counter to the concept of multilateral common enterprise.

**9.77** Other problems include: that this extension is not poolable and therefore the insurance costs are increased; that a similar coverage is not available for breaking bulk cargo; that in this case parties are not protected from tort claims; and that, although the TT Club claims to cover the whole supply chain, it is not an easily identifiable branch and, in reality, it seems they are more focussed on a classic multimodal/door-to-door journey.

**9.78** The key issue is that, if a network of parties – such as the multilateral common enterprise – is not formally recognised as such, and companies still work on their own risks, each party will be accountable for its own insurance and therefore the general cost and level of insurance would certainly increase.

**9.79** Thus, motivation and scope exist to explore the concept of multilateral insurance. Consider Lemon's suggestion for insurance that could integrate commercial general liability, marine P&I policy, stevedores, terminal operators' liability, and contractual liability. This would be insurance covering all categories of participant (including those performing both sea- and land-based activities), focussing mainly on the commercial rather than geographical aspect of the job, and could be taken out by a single party.[69]

**9.80** A maritime insurance that takes into consideration not only different phases of the carriage but also ancillary services and the network of parties as a whole is, at the time of writing, currently unexplored. In this respect, the outcome of the *Feseay* case, which reviewed the concept of insurable interest, might be of use.[70] In it, the Court of Appeal stressed two things relevant for this work. First, in modern insurance, particular attention must be paid to commercial relations. Second that the concept of insurable interest probably ought to be abolished or at least reviewed.[71] The idea of an insurable interest has changed dramatically over the years – in line with a changing market – and the Court of Appeal has considerably reconsidered the definition.[72]

69 Robert T Lemon II (n. 62).

70 *Feasey v Sun Life Assurance Company of Canada and Another*; *Steamship Mutual Underwriting Association (Bermuda) Ltd. v Feasey* (2003) EWCA Civ 885.

71 David Lord, 'Insurable Interest: Is There a Rule?' (*3 Stone Buildings*, 12 October 2005) 159 <http://clients.squareeye.net/uploads/3sb/events/121005_lord.pdf>. Accessed 5 May 2013.

72 Robert Merkin, *Reforming Insurance Law: Is there a Case for Reverse Transportation? A Report for the English and Scottish Law Commissions on the Australian Experience of Insurance Law Reform* (London, Edinburgh, Scotland, Law Commission/Scottish Law Commission 2006).

**9.81** Once again, the offshore sector – particularly the construction phases[73] – could provide valuable input here. Oil and gas companies (known as principals) often maintain in contractual negotiations that any Contractors' All Risks (CAR) cover provided will adequately protect the majority of contractors' and sub-contractors' insurable risks, based on the main policy outlined in WELCAR 2001. However, as many offshore contractors and service providers will have experienced, the coverage provided by the principal is often not able or adequate to protect these risks to the extent desired by the contractor.[74]

**9.82** In a general coverage (such as that provided by WELCAR 2001), the principal assured is defined as:

1. Company and/or joint venturers as they may now or subsequently exist
2. Parent and/or subsidiary and/or affiliated and/or associated and/or inter-related companies of the above as they are now or may hereafter be constituted and their directors, officers, and employees, while acting in their capacities as such

**9.83** While other assureds are defined as:

> Project managers and any other company, firm, person or party (including contractors and/or sub-contractors and/or manufacturers and/or suppliers) with whom the Assured(s) named in i, ii, iii and iv have entered into written contract(s) directly in connection with the Project.[75]

**9.84** Taking these problems into consideration, a framework covering all of the transportation means, as well as all the accompanying activities with a single insurance policy could lead to fruitful suggestions for a new insurance model for the multimodal common enterprise.

*The civil law perspective*

**9.85** Civil law traditions do not have specific issues with recognising that a third party can be protected by a contract.[76] They can be put forward as an

73 Standard Bulletin, February 2013, reports that: From the club's perspective, offshore construction operations typically fall into three categories: A. Fixed platform construction and associated sub-sea field development (including float-over, lift-on, pipe- or cable-lay operations, sub-sea installation and windfarm construction). B. FPSO navigation from yard to field (whether under own steam, wet tow, or dry tow), including hook-up, installation, and pre-production testing up to point of delivery to the ultimate client. C. Maintenance or servicing of oil field infrastructure (including maintenance, sub-sea and ROV operations).

74 Gayner Warner, 'Suitability of CAR Cover for Offshore Contractors' (*Marine and Offshore Contractors Group*, October 2012) <http://standard-club.com/media/1557668/suitability-of-car-cover-for-offshore-contractors.pdf>. Accessed 2 March 2016.

75 WELCAR 2001 OFFSHORE CONSTRUCTION PROJECT POLICY.

76 Canada represents a relevant jurisdiction in this respect. In Canada, under Common Law there is a problem of linking a limitation clause to someone who is not part of the contract. Conversely, under the Civil Law tradition of the state of Quebec, contracts in favour of a third party, and Himalaya clauses are accepted.

example for implementation of the protection of third parties in the carriage of goods by sea.[77]

**9.86** As Tetley states, not only common jurisdictions but also civil one held that only the parties to a contract are to be affected by it.[78] The same Tetley however details their exceptions.[79]

**9.87** Some legal systems grant servants and independent contractors of the carrier immunity from liability towards third parties – including cargo interests – except in case of wilful misconduct.[80]

**9.88** Under Belgian law, servants and 'performance agents' of the carrier (e.g., stevedores) benefit from such immunity from liability.[81] As De Wit says, Belgian law recognises that carriage by sea involves complex contract networks, and the Belgian provision avoids the difficulties with identity of carrier clauses, which attempt to single out one particular party in the network as carrier against whom an action should be brought, to the exclusion of all others.[82] A rule to the effect that all persons for whom the carrier is vicariously liable can invoke the same protection allowed to the carrier has been adopted by Scandinavian countries.[83] In French law, contracts only have effect between the parties to them. Parties may, however, expressly or impliedly confer rights in contracts for the benefit of a third party in such a way that the third party may enforce those rights by suing the promisor under the contract.[84]

**9.89** The most relevant positions are those of Germany and the Netherlands. Under German law, the protection for third parties derives from economic and risk efficiency, applying what is called the 'material factor'. Germany recognises contracts for the benefit of third parties and applies more liberal rules of contract construction. Due to these differences in domestic law, the German Courts have inferred enforceable Himalaya clauses even when the bills of lading did not contain them.

77 One must acknowledge that the essence of this book is not comparative law.

78 Tetley (n. 2) mentions the following article for each jurisdiction: Article 1440 cc (Québec 1994); Article 1165 cc (France); Article 1165 cc (Belgium); Articles 1983 and 1985 cc (Louisiana); Article 1372 cc (Italy) and Article 1257 cc (Spain).

79 Articles 1444–1452 cc (Québec 1994); Articles 1119–1122 cc (France); Articles 1119–1122 cc (Belgium); Articles 1985 and 1978–1982 cc (Louisiana); Articles 1411–1413 cc (Italy); Articles 1257 cc (Spain) and Article 328 BGB (Germany).

80 Massimo Piras, La clausola Himalaya, trattato breve di diritto marittimo (capitol xiii) Giuffrè 2008, 281–292. Under Italian law, for instance, there is no a specific rule for this kind of contract apart from the general rule that states wilful misconduct is not allowed. For clauses such as the Himalaya clause, these have to be approved by the shipper in writing according to what is called *clausole vessatorie*, Articles 1341 and 1342 cc.

81 Cécile Legros, 'Relations between the Rotterdam Rules and the Convention on the Carriage of Goods by Road' (2011–2012) 36 Tulane Maritime Law Journal 725. As Vasto and Clark report (n. 631) in Belgium stevedores have a full immunity under National Law.

82 De Wit (n. 37).

83 Ibid.

84 Vlasto and Clark (n. 38). This is made possible by operation of the concept *of stipulation pour autrui* (stipulation for another). See generally Article 1444 cc (Québec 1994); Article 1121 cc (France); Article 1121 cc (Belgium); Article 1978 cc (Louisiana); Article 1411 cc (Italy); Article 1257 cc (Spain); Article 328 BGB (Germany); Article 6:253–256 cc (Netherlands 1991).

**9.90** Under German statutory law, therefore, the logic of a protection clause is not at issue. Stevedores can rely on a protection clause that extends the carrier's legal protection to third parties. Contracts for the benefit of a third party are expressly permitted by the German Civil Code. Carrier and shipper can extend to stevedores the benefits of the contract. Even when there is no protection clause, German law also allows for a third party to claim the benefit of the carrier's limitations on liability.

**9.91** The rationale behind third party protection under German case law, according to Sturley, includes:

1. The shipper's knowledge that people such as the master would perform the contract.
2. The fact that the shipper's interest is the same no matter who performed the contract.
3. The purpose of the exclusionary clause is to establish the carrier's risk, which was a factor in setting the freight rate. A risk of higher liability would result in a higher freight rate. Since the purpose of the clause rather than its wording is the material factor, the Court would not allow the shipper to evade the exclusion after paying the lower rate.[85]

**9.92** Furthermore, Sturley reports, more recent decisions have extended the principle beyond the carrier's employees. In a case from 40 years ago – in which the shipper tried to sue a carrier contractor – the Court allowed the protection stating that it was implicitly in the carrier's interests to limit its liability and implicit in the fact that the carrier offered lower rates to the shipper in return.[86]

Hallebeek and Dondorp point out that, under German law, future persons can be named as beneficiaries of a third party benefit contract. Definitions can also be constructed generically for members of a class of persons; that the third party is ascertainable, for example, is sufficient. Third party rights come into existence as and when the third party is determined.

**9.93** The Netherlands adopt a similar approach. Third parties do not have to be designated specifically, nor is it necessary that they exist at the time of contracting. Dutch law goes a step further – following the contract's acceptance – as part of the contract. In situations with only one third party, a three-party contract comes into existence. This contract is governed by the rules of multiparty contracts.[87]

**9.94** According to De Wit, a sub-contractor under Dutch law can rely on the terms and conditions of his contract with his principal in order to defend himself against a claimant with whom he had no contract and who had sued him in tort.

85 Michael F Sturley, 'International Uniform Laws in National Courts: The Influence of Domestic Law in Conflicts of Interpretation' (1986–1987) 27 Virginia Journal of International Law 729.

86 Ibid.

87 Hallebeek and Dondorp (n. 41) 132, 156.

In other words, a protection provision in the subcontractor defendant's contract provides the defence against an action in tort.[88] A claimant who has accepted that his contracting party may rely on certain protection clauses must be prepared to let these clauses operate to the benefit of other parties to the contract network.

**9.95** Following this concept, in any contract network for the carriage of goods, parties who are member of the contract network (De Wit says created by the multimodal transport operator – this book says by the multilateral common enterprise) would be protected by the rule. The same system applies to all servants of third parties. They might rely on the contract on which their principal would rely.[89]

**9.96** As already demonstrated, civil law traditions do not take issue with the extension of protection to a party who is not part of a contract. Some countries (such as Belgium) narrow this provision to cover only some categories of third parties. Scandinavian countries still rely on the carrier's vicarious liability. *Stipulation pur autri* is a pillar of the French system and in civil law traditions more generally. The most relevant approach seems to be that of the German system, which relies on the fact that, in reality, it is not the carrier who performs the job but third parties, and they should be protected as such. The Dutch approach also recognises the network of interests.

**9.97** There is scope for applying the civil law concepts of third party protection and evaluating the extent to which it could implement the multilateral common enterprise.

88 De Wit (n. 37).
89 Ibid.

# INDEX

Note: page numbers followed by 'n' denote to footnotes.

For Product Safety Concerns and Information please contact our EU
representative GPSR@taylorandfrancis.com
Taylor & Francis Verlag GmbH, Kaufingerstraße 24, 80331 München, Germany

www.ingramcontent.com/pod-product-compliance
Ingram Content Group UK Ltd.
Pitfield, Milton Keynes, MK11 3LW, UK
UKHW011016180926
475701UK00004B/773

* 9 7 8 0 3 6 7 7 7 8 0 2 6 *